DogLife ❧ Lifelong Care for Your Dog™

AMERICAN
PIT BULL TERRIER

tfh

Amy Shojai

AMERICAN PIT BULL TERRIER

Project Team
Editor: Heather Russell-Revesz
Copy Editor: Ellen Bingham
Indexer: Dianne L. Schneider
Series Design: Mary Ann Kahn
Book Design: Angela Stanford

T.F.H. Publications
President/CEO: Glen S. Axelrod
Executive Vice President: Mark E. Johnson
Publisher: Christopher T. Reggio
Production Manager: Kathy Bontz

T.F.H. Publications, Inc.
One TFH Plaza
Third and Union Avenues
Neptune City, NJ 07753

Printed and bound in China
11 12 13 14 15   3 5 7 9 8 6 4

Library of Congress Cataloging-in-Publication Data

Shojai, Amy, 1956-
  American pit bull terrier / Amy Shojai.
    p. cm. -- (Dog life. Lifelong care for your dog)
  Includes bibliographical references and index.
  ISBN 978-0-7938-3600-0 (alk. paper)
  1. American pit bull terrier. I. Title.
  SF429.A72S46 2010
  636.755'9--dc22
                              2010001867

This book has been published with the intent to provide accurate and authoritative information in regard to the subject matter within. While every reasonable precaution has been taken in preparation of this book, the author and publisher expressly disclaim responsibility for any errors, omissions, or adverse effects arising from the use or application of the information contained herein. The techniques and suggestions are used at the reader's discretion and are not to be considered a substitute for veterinary care. If you suspect a medical problem, consult your veterinarian.

Note: In the interest of concise writing, "he" is used when referring to puppies and dogs unless the text is specifically referring to females or males. "She" is used when referring to people. However, the information contained herein is equally applicable to both sexes.

The Leader In Responsible Animal Care for Over 50 Years!®
www.tfh.com

CONTENTS

INTRODUCTION

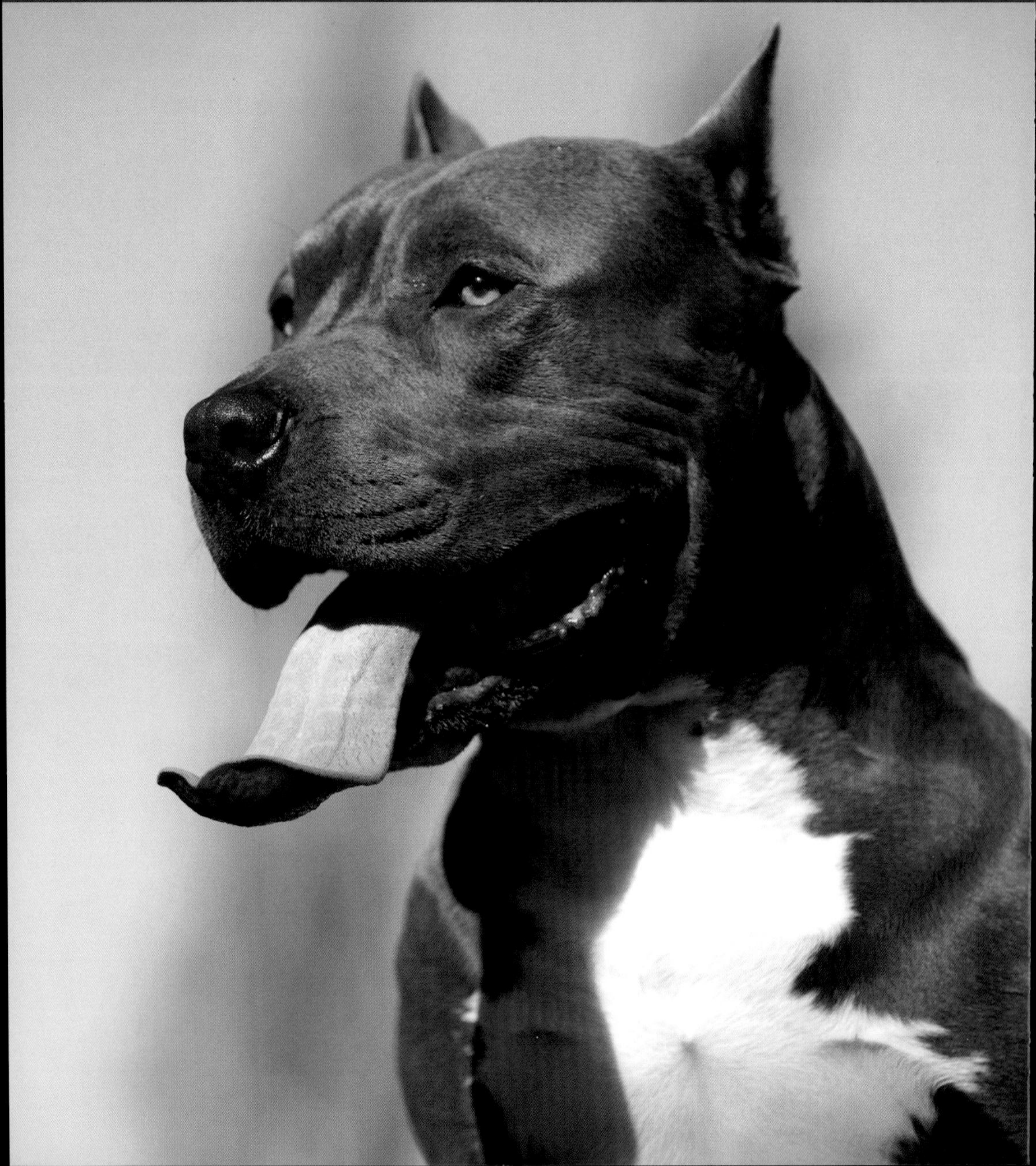

INTRODUCING THE AMERICAN PIT BULL TERRIER

The American Pit Bull Terrier (APBT) is admired and cherished by those familiar with his gregarious attitude and courageous nature. The breed routinely serves society in a variety of roles, such as police dog, search and rescue dog, therapy animal, and utility farm dog. He excels in competitions of strength and intelligence, and as a companion dog has no rival. But due to his heritage, strength, and tenacity, the APBT has been singled out by the media as the poster dog for dog fighting and aggression, leading many cities to condemn the breed as a community problem.

This strong-minded dog may not be the best choice for first-time dog owners. APBTs require owners who understand the challenges of the breed, understand society's attitudes and legal issues about them, and are dedicated to properly training and socializing their dogs. Owners must be willing to work toward countering negative perceptions in order to allow the APBT to become the loyal and loving family member he's meant to be.

HISTORY OF DOG DOMESTICATION

In prehistoric times, humans hunted woolly mammoths and rhinoceroses. As long as they had access to this plentiful smorgasbord, humans didn't directly compete with the dog ancestor—the wolf. But once the large, slow-moving food animals became extinct, people and wolves competed for the same prey.

The wolves—as well as the humans—couldn't have helped but notice the advantages of an interactive relationship. People admired the animals' incredible scenting ability, which easily found prey invisible to humans. Some wolves could even identify and cut weaker animals out of the herd. Early people must have watched these creatures in awe and probably even followed them to find the animals they all preyed upon.

Archeological evidence shows that Stone Age people often hunted by stampeding herds with fire until they were driven over cliffs to their death. Not all the slaughtered beasts could be eaten, and the bounty drew other predators to the feast. It benefited wolves to be camp followers, let others do all the hard work of hunting, and then scavenge the rich remains. The clueless humans did everything but fill up the doggy bowl.

From Forest to Firelight

How did wolves make that final leap from

Wolves are dogs' ancestors.

Wolf packs living near people would have been desirable additions to a human community because of their territorial natures. The bark or howl that alerted other wolves to danger also gave warning to humans—and the watchdog, er, watchwolf was born. If hunters happened to kill a mother wolf, they may have brought the cubs home and raised them.

The social structure of wolves paralleled that of people. Baby wolves raised by humans fit in, transferring their allegiance to the human pack. And as human youngsters grew up alongside the wolf cubs, the affection between the two must have grown strong. Unlike other wild animals, wolf cubs that are handled and played with don't outgrow their fondness and respect for people but retain certain tame behaviors as adults.

People selected the best herders from among the wolves. Wolves with allegiance to people picked out the prey, separated it from the others, then herded it toward waiting human hunters. This teamwork, often used in wolf packs, simply added humans to the equation. As time passed and generations of these wolves lived with people, the tamest and most responsive were bred, further strengthening the qualities people liked. A strain of tame hunting wolves probably developed very quickly.

When prey was scarce, combining forces offered both parties a better chance of success. Rather than competing, everybody won. People were no longer left in the dust chasing a herd animal they had no hope of catching. Wolves found the prey and chased it, perhaps caught and held onto the nose (catch dog) until the human could make the kill.

Over time, camp wolves changed, reflecting their relationship to humans as well as the conditions of the time. From a very large animal, the wolf size decreased. The long, narrow muzzle so important to capturing prey

the forest and fields into the human ring of firelight? Archeological and DNA evidence supports a number of theories, but experts can only speculate what are the direct ancestors of modern dogs.

The term domesticate means "to alter or change a once-wild creature to one that can live harmoniously with, and for the benefit of, people." But it's likely that wolves entered the domestication process as willing participants. Instinct for survival would have caused early wolves to select the safest and most productive manner to secure food and shelter. A relationship with people offered that and more.

shortened, since killing food was no longer required for survival. This foreshortening of the muzzle caused a crowding of the teeth rows and a reduction in tooth size.

At the same time, human societies continued to hunt game but also gathered wild grain. Eventually, these nomadic hunters traded the restless life for more permanent settlements. Tame wolves followed people throughout the world, tracking game, pointing it out, catch-and-holding it for the kill, carrying/pulling burdens, or retrieving prey when killed. Some served as bed-warmers or were eaten when other food was scarce. These short-faced wolves were the precursors of true dogs and took the first tentative steps over the threshold into domestication.

Archeological and DNA Evidence

It may be that wolves became domesticated at different times throughout the world and then fell out of favor and disappeared without a trace. That could explain why archeological and DNA evidence doesn't always agree. In 2008, it was reported that an international team of scientists excavating at Goyet Cave in Belgium identified the earliest known dog, who lived 31,700 years ago. They believe that the Aurignacian people of Europe, from the Upper Paleolithic period, first domesticated dogs. The second oldest known dog, found in Russia, dates to 14,000 years ago.

However, the first study comparing dog and wolf DNA in 1997 by Robert Wayne's team at the University of California, Los Angeles, initially suggested that wolves and dogs split

In prehistoric times, wolves found the prey and chased it until the human could make the kill.

into different species much earlier, around 135,000 years ago. That conclusion has been somewhat tempered since the canine genome has been mapped, with Wayne guesstimating a more accurate timeframe might be 50,000 years. In 2009, an extensive genetic study on the ancestry of African village dogs points to a Eurasian—possibly North African or Egypt—origin for the domestication of dogs, rather than East Asian, as previously thought.

A Siberian study by Russian geneticist Dmitry K. Belyaev began an effort in the 1950s to breed a population of tame foxes. The tamest silver foxes (those not fearful or aggressive) were chosen from a fur farm to breed. With each subsequent generation, only the tamest were allowed to breed. Within only three generations, aggression went away. In the eighth generation, the foxes solicited human affection with wagging tails. The silver color and pattern of the fox also changed dramatically; tails became curly, some youngsters kept floppy ears longer than normal, and limbs and tails became shorter. It follows that when you select against aggression, the same types of changes become apparent as when you compare wolves to modern dogs. Geneticists have located several genetic regions responsible for tameness.

Domesticated Dogs

More than 400 distinct canine breeds are recognized around the world, and along with random bred combinations, all domestic dogs are designated *Canis familiaris*. Although some behaviors are "hotwired" into the brains of every puppy born, domestication has rendered pet dogs unsuited for life on the wild side. Today's dog remains 99.8 percent genetically identical to the wolf, and there may be an ancestral wolf buried deep beneath the fur, but dogs are no longer wild animals. Today's pets live with people because they must; they can't survive on their own.

The American Pit Bull Terrier may have ties to ancient Mastiff-type dogs.

EARLY DEVELOPMENT OF THE APBT

We can't be certain of the American Pit Bull Terrier's origin, but many believe it to have ties to the ancient Molossian family of dogs. These were large, muscular hounds known for their fierceness. They were used as war dogs and guardians by people of the Molossi tribe of ancient Greece.

First the Greeks and later the Romans began writing descriptions of the various types of dogs, and in 350 B.C.E. Aristotle listed the "most useful" known breeds, which included the rough-coated, stocky Molossian, who came in two sizes. The flock guardians were huge, ferocious longer-muzzled dogs who protected livestock from wolves and leopards, and would have preferentially been light-colored to not startle the sheep. The dark-coated, smaller hounds had wider, boxier muzzles, often undershot jaws, and were used to hunt boar (pigs) and guard homes.

It is believed that boxier-muzzled Molossian dogs were forbears of the Mastiff group of dogs employed by the ancient Britons for protection and as fighting dogs. History tells us that in 50 C.E., the Roman emperor Claudius began exporting fighting Mastiff-type dogs to perform in the arenas and coliseums of Rome. The sport of dog fighting was born.

Once in Rome, the British and Roman dogs were bred to create and refine dog types for specific functions. Records indicate that the fighting dogs spread throughout the Roman Empire up to and including 400 C.E. and were crossbred with other breeds throughout Europe during this period. This conglomeration of fighting, hunting, and guardian heritage dogs are the many times great-grandfather dogs of the American Pit Bull Terrier we know today.

APBT HISTORY IN EUROPE

When the Normans invaded England in 1066, they introduced a new sport. Baiting originated with butchers who kept dogs to handle unruly bulls herded to the market for slaughter. The dogs would clamp down on the out-of-line bull's nose and hang on until the handler could regain control. If a dog let go, the bull could maim or kill, and soon only the surviving bulldogs (those able to tenaciously bite and not let go) passed on their genes. The butchers celebrated their dogs' prowess in public displays of "bull baiting," which became popular entertainment of the day.

By the 16th century, nearly every town in England had its own baiting ring, horrendous

displays in which one or two dogs tormented a bull for three or four hours at a time until it collapsed. The torture was thought to help tenderize the meat. When the public became bored with bulls, they baited the dogs with bears, boars, and even monkeys.

The British parliament made baiting illegal in 1835. But the public remained hungry for fighting spectacles. Instead, people turned to ratting, in which a dog thrown into a pit with rats raced the clock and other dogs to see which one could kill the most rats in the shortest time. The "pit" in the breed name comes from the pits used to keep the vermin from escaping. Eventually, even ratting wasn't enough, and dogs were pitted against each other. Dog fighting was more exciting than ratting, and it was certainly easier to hide two 40-pound (18 kg) dogs than a 5,000-pound (2,268 kg) bull.

Since dog fighting required smaller, more agile competitors than dogs used for baiting bulls, dog fanciers in England and Ireland began to

In earlier times, the APBT was used to drove cattle and sheep.

breed fighting bulldogs with feisty, tenacious terriers. They wanted a dog with the gameness of the terrier and strength and athleticism of the Bulldog. The result was the bull-and-terrier, more commonly known as the first pit bull terrier. Rather than terrier in nature (which is an "earth dog"), the breed is a "gripping" dog, like the butcher's helper, that catches hold and hangs on to prey. This muscular canine gladiator's sole purpose was to fight other dogs. Written pedigrees of these earliest pit bull fighting dogs exist from the late 1700s, and it is one of the oldest line of pedigreed dogs in existence. However, the most successful breeders of these dogs rarely committed pedigree to paper. They didn't want their secrets stolen. Thus, much of the true heritage of how these dogs came about can only be speculated.

Grueling training included long workouts on treadmills running after a small animal kept just out of reach—the dog was rewarded with a kill at the end of the session. Fighting dogs were expected to ferociously attack other dogs without hesitation and never give ground. Turning away could be grounds for forfeit, and such dogs often were killed outright by handlers who viewed it as a sign of weakness. Dogs who showed aggression toward humans also were killed, because during a fight, the handlers needed to be able to handle the dogs without fear of injury themselves. The same heritage that kept dogs impervious to the blows of bulls, the fearless tenacity that said, "hang on, or die!" lived on in these original bulldog and terrier crosses.

The Cruelty to Animals Act of 1835 in the United Kingdom made dog fighting illegal, and forbade the keeping of any house, pit, or other place for baiting or fighting any bull, bear, dog, or other animal. The horrendous spectacle of dog fighting is now illegal in all first world countries and many third world countries—and rightly so!

APBT HISTORY IN THE UNITED STATES

When English and Irish immigrants came to America, their "bulldogs" came with them. Dog fighting was common in America throughout the 19th century. But as immigrants traveled west, the dog's talents were redirected and expanded.

The American Pit Bull Terrier, no longer a one-dimensional bruiser, became an all-purpose dog who drove cattle and sheep, protected against thieves and wild animals, hauled wood, hunted hogs, and once again served as "catch dogs" for those pesky bulls. During the day, the dogs played with settlers' children. And at night, the dogs controlled vermin in the barn.

RECOGNITION BY MAJOR CLUBS

The breed faced major challenges in gaining official recognition.

American Kennel Club

The American Kennel Club (AKC) was formed in 1884 to promote the interests of purebred dogs and their owners. This included sponsored events designed to test various breeds in the areas of performance and conformation.

Conformation events that judged the dogs according to the breed standard weren't a problem. But performance trials test dogs on

the function for which they were bred, such as herding or hunting. The "pit bulldog," bred specifically for fighting, couldn't be tested in trials, since dog fighting was illegal and the AKC didn't want any association with the activity.

United Kennel Club

Frustrated dog fanciers founded the United Kennel Club (UKC) in 1898 to register breeds that were not eligible for certification by the AKC, and to emphasize working utility. Initially the word *American* was added and *pit* was dropped from the name, but after public outcry, the official name became American Pit Bull Terrier. Originally, to be accepted into the UKC for registration, the APBT had to have won three fights. Thankfully, that requirement was later dropped.

Today, the APBT is registered with the United Kennnel Club (UKC) and the American Dog Breeders Association (ADBA).

American Dog Breeders Association, Inc.

The American Dog Breeders Association, Inc. (ADBA) was formed in 1909 as a multiple breed association by fanciers of the APBT who wanted to promote the dogs as the great athletes and companions they were. The idea was to test performance quality of the APBT without actual pit fighting. Instead, the focus was on weight-pulling competitions. By 1951, the organization had become much smaller

Many APBTs make wonderful family pets.

and eventually focused only on APBTs. But in 1976, the ADBA Conformation Standard was adopted, which allowed conformation shows and weight-pulling events sponsored by the American Dog Breeders Show, Inc. In 2006, the ADBA opened its stud book and again became an all-breed registry.

Name Changes

It wasn't until 1936 that the AKC finally recognized the breed. However, the AKC wanted no association with the breed's dog-fighting history and sought distance by creating a new name. Although identical to the UKC dog, the AKC breed was named the Staffordshire Terrier as a nod to the region of England where the crossbreeding of terriers and bulldogs took place. But when pit bulls of a different look began arriving from England under the name "Staffordshire Bull Terrier" in the 1970s, the AKC sought to make their dogs distinct by adding the word American. The dogs actually were the same breed, and the UKC and AKC registered either one, but the English and American lines resulted in important physical differences. So the AKC divided the breed into the American Staffordshire Terrier and the Staffordshire Bull Terrier.

Today, the AKC recognizes the American Staffordshire Terrier, which is called the American Pit Bull Terrier when registered by the UKC and the ADBA. Depending on whom you talk to, they are identical dogs—or two very distinct breeds—with the American Staffordshire Terrier and UKC-registered dogs bred more with an eye toward conformation, and the ADBA-registered dogs bred for both conformation and working drive.

INFLUENTIAL PEOPLE

In the world of the American Pit Bull Terrier, nearly every road leads back to Colby dogs.

John P. Colby (1875–1941) began breeding fighting American Pit Bull Terriers in 1889, using the best dogs from England and Ireland brought to America by immigrants. His dog "Colby's Primo" was used to set the conformation standard of the AKC's American Staffordshire Terrier. The Colby dogs have been bred continuously, and his line of dogs is known throughout the world as tops in temperament, conformation, and "gameness."

The original president of the ADBA, Guy McCord, was a close friend of Colby. UKC founder Chauncey Z. Bennett also was a mover and shaker in APBT circles and is credited with adding the word American to the breed name. He assigned UKC registration #1 to his own dog, "Bennett's Ring."

Certainly there are other notable people in the world of the American Pit Bull Terrier breed. But these three men opened the door, in different ways, and made an extraordinary and positive impact on the preservation and promotion of the breed. Although all came from the world of dog fighting, these men recognized the negative impact that the horrors of dog fighting had on their beloved dogs and changed with the times to preserve their breed. Without John Colby, Guy McCord, and Chauncey Bennett, the APBT would not exist as it does today.

MEMORABLE DOGS

Before the APBT became the anti-hero of drug dealers and underground dog fights, the breed was the epitome of the dog-next-door faithful buddy. Many famous Americans have owned Pit Bulls. Mark Twain, Theodore Roosevelt, Laura Ingalls Wilder, Thomas Edison, Woodrow Wilson, and others enjoyed the affectionate, fun-filled American Pit Bull Terrier.

In World War I, Pit Bulls represented the US military on posters, as a testament to the country—and the dog's—strength and dignity. This became reality when a Pit Bull named Stubby was the unofficial mascot of the 102nd Infantry Division. Stubby fought for 18 months in the trenches for France during WWI for 17 battles. Stubby warned his fellow soldiers of gas attacks, located wounded soldiers, and listened for incoming artillery rounds. He was also responsible for the capture of a German spy at Argonne. After his time in the war, Stubby met Woodrow Wilson, Calvin Coolidge, and Warren G. Harding. He was also made a life member of the American Legion, the Red Cross, and the YMCA. Stubby won several medals and was even awarded the rank of sergeant! Sergeant Stubby came home from the war to a hero's welcome and went on to become the mascot for Georgetown University.

Nipper, owned by Thomas Edison, became part of the corporate logo for the RCA recording company—remember that dog tipping his head at the phonograph? Buster Brown Shoes also included a Pit Bull named Tige in their marketing advertisements.

One of the most famous Pit Bull ambassadors was named Petey, the ring-eyed pooch of the TV show Little Rascals. And two APBT dogs, Cheyenne and Dakota, are credited with being two of the first Search and Rescue (SAR) dogs as well as therapy dogs.

Truly, the APBT breed is so versatile that with the right owner, very little is beyond his ability.

PART I

PUPPYHOOD

CHAPTER 1

IS THE AMERICAN PIT BULL TERRIER RIGHT FOR YOU?

All puppies pull at your heartstrings. But each breed offers something unique and above the ordinary that appeals to different people. This goes beyond looks, and has as much to do with the dog's emotional and care requirements as the owner's. A good understanding of the breed allows you to make educated choices. It's not enough simply to love him. You must be prepared not only for today's puppy, but the adult dog he'll become.

Puppies look and act lovable. While they can be adopted as early as six weeks, they learn a great deal of important dog etiquette by staying with mom-dog and littermates until eight to ten weeks of age. The American Pit Bull Terrier matures slowly. While the United Kennel Club (UKC) categorizes them as an "adult" once the dog reaches a year of age, many retain puppy-like behaviors and rangy adolescent appearances until two years old.

Different lines of dogs also grow up at varying rates. Female pups seem to mature physically more quickly than the males. Some American Pit Bull Terrier puppies mature more evenly, and look like smaller versions of adult dogs when young. But the red nose line of dogs seem to grow "up" first with lots of leg length and a gangly appearance until they eventually mature into beautiful adults.

CHARACTERISTICS OF THE APBT

While every dog is an individual, American Pit Bull Terriers have a number of characteristics in common. Be sure to ask the breeder about any specifics notable in a particular line (family) of dogs as well.

The American Pit Bull Terrier is the "Quarter Horse" of the dog world, a canine athlete known for his incredible versatility. These high energy, confident and happy dogs love to work, and they want a job to do. Beware of allowing them to become bored because they are accomplished fence climbers and need an assertive and savvy owner to provide proper direction. The APBT is an intelligent dog who does well in most performance events. But he does not make a good guard dog since he'll make friends with the burglar.

While noted for eagerness to please, love of people, and trainability, the APBT is not a "starter dog" for a first-time dog owner. Some of these dogs love to cuddle and become couch-potatoes, but the majority of the breed are dogs-with-a-purpose and not cutesy

The APBT is known for his incredible versatility.

canines. Breeders refer to them as hard-drive dogs, and recommend that they not be left alone unsupervised as they can cause much property damage during goofy play. In a tug-of-war with a sofa, the APBT pup will win.

Often characterized as comedians, APBTs require owners with a firm but fair hand dedicated to proper socialization and training. Like any class clown, the breed can act like eternal two-year-old children and go through the "terrible twos" for life. The breed needs boundaries and rules, or will take advantage of any opening to do things their own way. Aggression toward people is not common, but they can be pushy.

PHYSICAL TRAITS

The APBT is a study in restrained power. This is not a massive dog. Nothing is overdone—he should look proportional from nose to tail. The ideal American Pit Bull Terrier is balanced and solid, yet agile. As a multi-purpose dog, the APBTs conformation reflects its ability to pull and push with great power, and also run well, exhibit stamina, and the ability to leap away from danger.

The United Kennel Club (UKC) and the American Dog Breeders Association (ADBA) are the two main registries for this breed and the standards for each of them do vary on the fine points. The following is a basic description of the breed. If looking to show an APBT you should refer to the standard that your dog is registered with for a more point by point description and list of faults both minor and serious.

Height and Weight

The breed standard has no height or weight limitations. The correct proportion of weight to height is more important, and so the breed can have quite a range in size. A medium size allows the dog the most flexibility in function. Most mature male APBTs range between 35 and 60 pounds (16 and 27 kg), with females between 30 to 50 pounds (14 to 23 kg). But dogs can weigh as much as 80 pounds (36 kg) and still compete in conformation, and are only penalized if rangy or disproportionate. Height ranges from 18 to 22 inches (46 to 56 cm) at the shoulders. Larger dogs may be preferred for some sports such as hunting, but an excessively large or massive dog is considered a serious fault in the show world.

Coat and Color

Any coat color, combination of colors or pattern is acceptable in the American Pit Bull Terrier except for merle. The dog has a very dense, short, close-fitting shiny coat without any fuzzy undercoat. A sparse, curly or wavy coat is considered a fault and a long coat is a disqualification.

Body

The APBT is medium size solid dog with well defined muscles. The body is a bit longer than tall, although females can be longer-bodied than males. The chest is deep, full and moderately wide but should never be wider than it is deep. The strong line of the back should be level after only a slight downward incline from the withers. Legs should be solid and well-muscled, and proportionate to the body, with the length of the front legs from the elbow to the ground equaling about half the dog's height at the tallest point above the shoulders (the withers).

The elbows are held close to the body with forelegs set moderately wide apart. The pasterns are short, powerful, straight, and flexible. The feet are round, pads tough and tight, and dewclaws may be removed. A relatively short tail is an extension of the topline, thick at the base and tapered to a point. A relaxed dog carries the tail low and when moving, he carries the tail level with his back. A gay tail (curled over the back) is a fault, as is a tail that's too long.

Head

The medium length head is flat or slightly rounded, and wide between the ears. From the front, the APBT head resembles a broad, blunt wedge. From the side, the skull and muzzle sit parallel to each other, until meeting a distinctive moderately deep stop. A deep furrow transverses the top of the dog's head.

This breed has a wide, deep muzzle with characteristic "grin" that accents the dog's prominent cheek muscles, making him look perpetually amused. His expressive face reveals wrinkles that form on the forehead when

By the Numbers

Dogs commonly eat their own or another animal's droppings (coprophagia). This is normal behavior for mom-dogs who must clean up after their babies, and some of the pups may end up mimicking this behavior. It first appears in pups age four to nine months of age. The frequency increases after one year of age, and while most pups outgrow the habit, it can persist throughout the dog's life. Dogs living with cats may treat the litter box as a snack bar because cat food contains more protein than dog food and so does the resulting feline waste.

Any coat color or combination of colors or pattern is acceptable in the APBT except for merle.

the dog concentrates. The muzzle is straight, broad, and deep with a very slight taper from the stop to the nose. Lips are clean and tight. The nose may be any color, and is large with wide, open nostrils.

The neck, also proportional, is well muscled and never deer-like, and smoothly fits into strong shoulders. The neck is of moderate length and muscular with a slight arch at the crest. The skin on the neck, as with the cheeks, is tight and without dewlap or wrinkles.

Round intelligent eyes are medium size, set low and wide apart. Dogs can have any color eyes as long as they match—but blue eyes are a serious fault in the UKC standard.

Ears can be either natural or cropped and are set high on the head.

Overall Look

This breed should never look muscle-bound, or the reverse—fine-boned or rangy—but should embody balance and harmony of work-purpose. Strength, athleticism, grace and agility must allow functional capability to be a catch dog who can hold, wrestle (push and pull) and breathe easily while doing its job.

SUITABILITY OF THE APBT

You may love the look of the American Pit Bull Terrier. The breed's temperament may be a perfect fit for your dream dog as well. But matchmaking the doggy love of your life goes beyond looks and personality. In order for you and your human family to be happy, and to be fair to your canine companion, honestly evaluate how the APBT fits into your life. While there are always exceptions to every rule, the following will help guide your decisions and help you create the best atmosphere for a successful, lifelong relationship with your dog.

Environment

The American Pit Bull Terrier thrives in many climates, but because of his short coat, keeping him warm in cold climates is required, and white dogs need more protection from the sun to prevent sunburn. The breed adjusts quite well to living in the suburbs and city because he loves being close to his people. However, the breed developed as a working farm dog, and must be provided with healthy exercise options whether living in a city apartment or on the hundred-acre ranch.

Before you adopt, research legal restrictions as well. Some cities have instituted laws prohibiting any "pit bull" type dog, or may require additional insurance for those who keep them. Owners renting their home or apartment may be restricted in the size or breed of pets they're allowed to keep. Some insurance companies may drop policies should they discover you have an American Pit Bull Terrier.

Exercise Requirements

In general, the APBT needs a lot of exercise. These smart dogs become easily bored and find something to do if not given direction. Young dogs need at least two hours a day of exercise, not necessarily all at once. Not giving your APBT the exercise he needs can lead to problem behaviors, so if you are looking for a low-energy companion, you should probably look elsewhere.

These dogs are tireless athletes. They move with a jaunty air, eager to discover something fun and exciting. Although he'll enjoy sharing your sofa and quiet time, the APBT is not a natural couch potato. Games of fetch and

tug-of-war are big hits with these dogs, and swimming appeals to many. Once trained, the dogs can enjoy running alongside a bike. Whenever outside of your yard, they should be on leash, which means you also should be athletic to keep up with them.

It's best to avoid dog parks. Even when your APBT has impeccable manners, the potential for other dogs getting in his face offers too much danger. He might not start a fight, but you can be certain he'll finish it. Don't set up your dog for failure by putting him in risky situations. Prevention means predicting the worst and taking steps to avoid it ever becoming a reality.

Therefore exercise can be a challenge if you have limited safe space, such as a fenced yard. One option could be a dog-powered treadmill, which professionals use to help condition dogs for showing and weight-pull competitions. The carpeted runner mounted in a hardwood frame simply spools around and around as the dog chooses his own pace—walk, jog, bursts of speed. He's not forced to run or

The APBT's body should embody balance and harmony of work purpose.

tethered in any way. Dogs enjoy exercising themselves, and typically push themselves more than owners otherwise would choose. Treadmills can fit in apartment living, to make exercise hassle free for even the worst weather or an owner's physical capabilities. Be aware, however, that while exercising your Greyhound or Schutzhund German Shepherd Dog on a treadmill won't raise eyebrows, it has sometimes been construed to be "dog fighting paraphernalia" when found in an APBT home.

Sociability—With Children

The American Pit Bull Terrier can be wonderful with children, if socialized and raised with kids. They are above all "people" dogs. But babies, toddlers, and young children talk

The APBT can be wonderful with children if they have been socialized to and raised with them.

in high-pitched voices, move, behave and even smell differently than adult humans. So to some pets, kids might as well be aliens. Children over the age of eight are the best match because these kids have matured enough to understand and respect the dog's sensibilities and follow parent's direction.

In addition, any dog—and especially terriers—can react in a predatory fashion toward smaller creatures (including infants) when not appropriately trained. Even kid-friendly dogs can be overpowering to small children because of their high energy and strength. Although most of these dogs pose no threat, they should always be supervised—as should dogs of any breed—when around youngsters.

An adult APBT who has never been around children would not be a good choice for a family with young children. A better choice would be to adopt a puppy. That way, he and the children can both be taught proper kid-dog manners as they grow up together.

Making Sure Your Puppy and Children Get Along

Make kids part of the pet's routine so the new pup recognizes children are an important part of his world. Children can fill the food and water bowl, for example. That also sends a signal to the APBT that the child controls important resources.

Chasing the pup or cornering and trying to pick him up could prompt puppy fear and nipping—something you never want to start. Instead, ask children to sit quietly on the floor and challenge them to see who can ignore the new puppy the longest. Ignoring sparks curiosity so the pup chooses to approach and interact with the children. They can toss a ball and that keeps the puppy's teeth at a distance, while all of them get to enjoy the interaction.

Children can also offer treats to the puppy for good behavior. Have the child direct the pup to "sit" first, and only after performing the action should the treat be offered, either in a flat open palm or tossed to the floor.

Your APBT puppy must learn from the very beginning that fun and games interacting with the children only continue as long as puppy behaves nicely.

Sociability—With Strangers

The APBT does not make a good guard or protection dog, despite media coverage to the contrary. They've been bred for generations to be people-pleasers. There are exceptions, particularly with dogs who have not received proper puppy socialization and training. But for the most part, the Pit Bull may simply bark at, or will be neutral or even friendly toward nonthreatening strangers.

Any dog who's provoked or can't escape from a chain or tether and feels cornered will defend himself and/or his territory. Create the proper environment for your dog to feel confident so he has no need to act defensively. Dogs who are left chained outside all day— neglected and not properly cared for—may be more aggressive if a stranger approaches. Aggression toward any human is abnormal for the breed and should be dealt with immediately, with help from an experienced trainer or behavior professional. The tendency for aggression can be inherited so find out about the temperament of the prospective pup's parents.

Sociability—With Other Dogs and Pets

As a general rule, the APBT should be an "only" dog unless the owner has experience and is prepared to properly manage the situation with training and supervision. Most APBTs

have some degree of aggression toward other dogs, from minor to very "hot." Dog-on-dog aggression is best prevented.

While basic obedience training and proper socialization can allow responsible owners to manage and control a dog-aggressive ABPT, this breed is not recommended to live with other pets. The terrier tendency to be driven, tenacious, and courageous can make them bad news for other pets.

Degrees of Dog-on-Dog Aggression

BadRap.org, a small nonprofit organization dedicated to educating people about the APBT, designates several degrees of dog-on-dog aggression.

• The "Social Dog" enjoys being around other dogs, and tolerates or even forgives rude

Temperament Testing

There are organizations such as the American Temperament Society that travel the country independently evaluating dogs of all breeds. This testing is usually indicated by a (TT) at the end of the parent dog's name and a certificate should be available to view when visiting a breeder who claims to have had their dog tested. Another all-breed temperament test is the American Kennel Club's Canine Good Citizen (CGC) test— again, the certificate should be made available by the breeder. These tests are independent from titles listed on registration papers given by the UKC and ADBA. Look for a breeder who uses these tests on their breeding stock when looking for your APBT puppy.

behavior from other canines. Most APBT puppies fall into this category, but this usually changes as they mature. Much depends on the pup's experiences with other dogs during this time, and positive experiences can influence the adult dog's perception of other canines. Only a small percentage of socially mature (about 14+ months of age) dogs will continue to be dog social. Some people call these "cold" pit bull terriers (as compared to "hot" dog-aggressive counterparts).

- "Dog Tolerant" canines include those properly socialized as puppies, and could be described as having a long fuse. While they don't necessarily seek out and enjoy the companionship of other dogs, they can learn to put up with the presence of other canines when out in public on a leash. A "dog tolerant" APBT may be able to coexist with other dogs in the house, when supervised appropriately.

- "Dog Selective" individuals may be tolerant of housemate dogs, but won't put up with strange dogs. These canines offend easily, and may act pushy and want to call the shots during dog interactions.

Multi-Dog Tip

The APBT is known to be dog aggressive, but puppies are the most forgiving. When you already have resident dogs, choose the newcomer with an eye toward keeping the peace. A puppy won't challenge the current pet's status. Choose a puppy of the opposite sex to reduce the chance of serious altercations once the baby matures.

With lots of obedience and proper management, these APBTs may learn to be more dog tolerant, but should never be left unsupervised with other dogs or pets. Most APBTs fall somewhere in the spectrum of tolerant-selective.

- "Dog Aggressive" animals have few or (more usually) no other dog friends, and are known as "hot." These canines require heavy supervision to keep them from lashing out toward other dogs, especially of the same sex. They often react quite strongly when on leash, and dog-play can quickly turn into aggression. Dog-aggressive dogs can become more tolerant with intensive training by experts.

Proper Introductions

When you already have dogs or other pets, an APBT puppy is the best choice. You can introduce the pets properly, and reinforce good behavior to help all involved be more dog-tolerant. However, even the best of APBT dog-friends should never be left out alone, unsupervised. Savvy professionals who show and compete in dog sports with APBTs admire their courage and ensure they're well trained, but still separate the dogs from each other and other pets when they can't supervise them, to prevent potential fights. If you have an American Pit Bull Terrier and other dogs, chances are very high that you will at some point have a fight on your hands. Separate crates keep the dogs safely confined and prevent possible altercations—this is the best way to prevent an accidental fight and save your dogs from injury. Always keep your dogs separated in their own crates when they can't be supervised.

If you already have resident pets, and have adopted an APBT puppy, take steps to introduce them properly. That will go a long way toward easing the stress that leads to fights. How would you feel if a stranger suddenly came into your house, ate from your plate, slept on your pillow and demanded attention from loved ones? Resident pets get their nose out of joint, too, and require time to accept newcomers. Humans must be referees.

- Dogs tend to follow your lead, so make it clear you welcome the newcomer.

- First meetings between dogs are best done on neutral territory through a safe barrier like a fence. The barrier gives you a safety net—literally—while the resident dog won't feel as defensive when he doesn't "own" the offsite property the way he would the back yard.

- When you don't have the fence option available, put both dogs on leash and take them for a walk in a large open area, parallel to each other about 10 feet (3 m) apart.

- If they show positive interest let them meet and sniff each other for only ten minutes to keep from tiring the dogs.

- A puppy should show deference to the adult dog, with face-licking, submissive wetting and/or showing its tummy to the older dog.

- Let them play for a few minutes, then break it up and end on a good note. Repeat the meeting later at the house in the yard, off leash if it's fenced.

- Monitor the dogs together until you are sure they are friendly and the new puppy is large enough not to be accidentally injured by the larger adult.

Cat-Proof Your Puppy

If you have a feline friend in residence, take these steps to help everyone get along.

- Ensure the cat's safety by keeping your puppy under leash control. Prevent any chase from taking place, because the activity feels so good to your dog he'll gladly ignore or give up any other type of reward. Even if the cat instigates the session (some cats tease dogs unmercifully), don't allow any chase or tag games.

- Have plenty of smelly, tasty treats handy, ready to reinforce your puppy at the presence of a cat. These special treats should only be used for cat-proofing lessons.

- Give the puppy a treat every time (and I mean every time) the cat makes an appearance. Say, "Cookie-Cat!" and give him the treat. Offer this payday whether he acts calm, excited, looks at the cat, barks, or anything else. The equation should be: Cat's Presence = Dog Treat.

The APBT is one of the most easily trained terriers.

- Use the leash only to keep him a safe distance from the kitty, not to force his attention or behavior into what you want him to do. Let his brain process the equation on its own time. Some dogs "get it" right away and others take longer. Within a few sessions, nearly every dog will start to look to you for a treat each time they hear "Cookie-Cat!" or the cat appears. Rather than lunging and chasing instinctively, he's learned to expect a reward.

- Reinforce this behavior for at least a week or two. Brush up with more training sessions as needed—for some dogs that might be every month. Make sure the dog stays leashed and the pets separated when not supervised, until you are confident the new canine response has become ingrained.

Want to Know More?

For more details about important health issues in the APBT, see Chapter 8: American Pit Bull Terrier Health and Wellness.

Grooming Needs

The APBT has few grooming requirements. His short, easy to care for coat benefits from regular brushing with a soft bristle brush. A rubber massage/curry brush works very well to keep shedding under control. Although the breed doesn't have poofs of undercoat, the tiny shed hairs can become aggravating. Bathing once a month can help keep your APBT smelling fresh and help cut down on dander. Like most dogs, nails should be trimmed as needed and ears should be wiped out with a clean tissue or ear cleaning pads as needed.

Health Issues

The American Pit Bull Terrier generally is a healthy dog.

Hip Dysplasia

Probably the most common concern is hip dysplasia. Like many other medium to large athletic dogs, hip and sometimes elbow problems can develop. Dogs diagnosed with hip dysplasia should not be bred, because some cases may have a genetic factor. Professional breeders should be able to tell you about health screening tests such as Orthopedic Foundation for Animals (OFA) or PennHIP (University of Pennsylvania Hip Improvement Program) that certify the puppy's parents free of hip dysplasia and/or elbow dysplasia. While that's no guarantee the offspring won't develop problems, it tips the scales in favor of healthy joints.

Skin Problems

Perhaps because of the close-fitting tight fur, bug bites and stings easily penetrate to the skin and the APBT can have somewhat sensitive skin. A more serious skin condition, demodectic mange, can affect some lines of dogs. The mite that causes the skin disease actually lives as a normal part of the skin and a healthy immune system keeps the bug in check. Most puppies, if affected, outgrow the condition, but some adult dogs develop devastating disease. Immune competency can be inherited, so if the puppy's parents or relatives have this skin issue, the pup may also be at risk.

Heart Defects

In addition, congenital heart defects that cause heart murmurs may be present. OFA also screens puppies for congenital cardiac disease. Legitimate breeders know the risks in their dogs and should screen puppies for heart issues before they are placed. Some murmurs may not affect the dog's quality of life. However, for puppies with a future in competition, a heart defect could impact performance.

Day Blindness

A newly recognized but uncommon condition, called "day blindness," has been found throughout the American Pit Bull Terrier breed. Affected dogs fail to develop a normal connection from the retina (back of the eye) to the brain. This causes an affect similar to what you experience when walking from a dark house outside into bright sunlight. While it takes a normal eye several seconds to adjust, affected dogs take many minutes—if at all—to adjust. Puppies suffer from the condition in varying degrees. The dogs otherwise can be completely normal, but just don't see as well. It can easily be missed and attributed to silly crazy puppy antics, when the dog bumps into walls or chairs, or steps off a curb and stumbles. Researchers studying the condition hope to develop a genetic test, to allow breeders to plan dog match-making and so prevent the disorder from being perpetuated. At this time, there's no treatment or testing available.

Trainability

The American Pit Bull Terrier may be one of the smartest and most easily trained of the terriers. While they can be knuckleheads and take persuading, these dogs can be trained to excel at nearly any dog sport—conformation, agility, rally, weight pull and more. Because of their high intelligence, owners need to out-think their dogs, and give them clear, fair rules to follow. The breed's poor reputation and the inherent tendency of dog-aggression mean that training must be at the top of the list for all APBT owners to counter this perception.

Training Tidbit

Puppies learn very quickly. Training should begin as soon as your puppy comes home to take advantage of his curiosity. Look for opportunities to reward good behavior. Rather than scolding him for barking too much, praise when he's quiet. That leads to puppies looking for more ways to please you, a win-win situation for the whole family.

A high level of competition obedience certainly is possible, but not required. More importantly, basic polite behavior should be taught on a daily basis, from the moment the puppy arrives. Trainers and behavior professionals often recommend a program referred to as "nothing-in-life-is-free." The puppy learns that good things such as treats, toys, and attention can be earned with good behavior. A polite "sit" prompts you to open the door, for instance. Even a six- or eight-week-old puppy understands the concept very quickly.

This does more than teach neat tricks. Basic training can be fun and rewarding to the dog because he earns praise and attention. APBTs, like most dogs, will be the equivalent of a two or three-year-old child all their life, and people would never think it acceptable to turn a toddler loose on the world without proper supervision and manners. Equally important, he learns to respect your direction, and follow it, without any confrontation being necessary. If you obedience train your dog you have the launch pad for anything else you want to do.

CHAPTER 2

FINDING AND PREPPING FOR YOUR AMERICAN PIT BULL TERRIER PUPPY

Nothing beats a puppy for fun. An American Pit Bull Terrier puppy brings high energy and zest for life into your home and reminds you to celebrate and embrace exciting new experiences. Beyond that, both humans and pets produce natural chemicals during bonding that make us feel happy, content, safe, and even loved. This natural high can't be discounted and will carry us through the challenging and frustrating days that puppies also bring. Choosing the right puppy and communicating appropriately creates this bond. Humans must learn to understand the silent body language of animal companions, and pets must learn to figure out what their human intends.

WHY GET A PUPPY?

The blank slate of a young puppy appeals to many owners. While knowing the baby's background and heritage offers some broad strokes for predictable behaviors and looks, much of what this dog will become arises from the unique input that owners bring to the equation. You'll have the great fun of watching the puppy physically mature from a clueless, clumsy baby and leggy, goofy adolescent into a handsome, athletic adult dog. But with a puppy, you'll also have hands-on input into how the puppy's personality develops and what relationship you create together. That can be a priceless experience.

Whatever your pup's heritage, you know he's a star. But if you plan to show competitively, look for a purebred puppy from an established breeder who actively shows her own dogs. Professional breeding kennels strive to produce puppies according to the breed's written standards defined by registering associations. Purebred registered animals cost more because of the expense involved in producing healthy animals of a particular type. You'll get more than your money's worth, though, from a reputable breeder able to offer predictable health (sometimes with guarantees) and

Want to Know More?

Puppies are adorable but lots of work. Perhaps adopting an adult APBT would be better for your lifestyle? Read Chapter 5: Finding Your American Pit Bull Terrier Adult for information on finding the adult dog of your dreams.

temperament of your new dog. In addition, acquiring your American Pit Bull Terrier puppy from a responsible breeder can provide you with a knowledgeable resource able to help you raise your puppy to be the best dog possible, because a responsible breeder will be interested in developing a true long-term relationship with you.

If you have no inclination to show in the conformation ring, a pet-quality American Pit Bull Terrier puppy can be a wonderful choice. Out of every litter bred, only a small percentage develops into the "ideal" breed specimen

in terms of looks, able to be competitive in the conformation ring. But the rest of these puppies share the same good health and terrific personality, making pet-quality puppies wonderful companions. Dogs who have slight imperfections (maybe the eyes are the wrong color) can still be eligible to compete—and win!—in other dog sports, such as weight pulling, agility, and obedience.

FINDING THE PUPPY OF YOUR DREAMS

A good place to start in your puppy search can be friends and relatives who have dogs you've admired. This kind of valuable personal connection helps on several levels. They not only have the experience of a puppy from a particular line but also can tell you about the kind of interaction and support the breeder provides. Owners who returned more than once to the same breeder to acquire subsequent pets provide a strong recommendation for working with that individual. For the same reason, some professional breeders prefer referrals and recommendations from people who have acquired dogs from them, because that offers a level of comfort that you will provide a good home and adequate training.

You can develop a personal relationship with other American Pit Bull Terrier owners and breeders by attending dog shows. Watch newspaper listings in local cities, and attend dog sporting exhibitions and conformation shows. People love to talk about their dogs, so strike up a conversation with the handler of an APBT you admire. Even if they don't have puppies available, they usually can connect you with someone who does.

Contact one of the APBT registering organizations such as the United Kennel Club (UKC), or contact a local or regional breed club near you. The National American Pit Bull Terrier

The blank slate of a young puppy appeals to many owners.

Association (NAPBTA) often can provide contact information for a breed club in your area, which in turn can refer you to member breeders they consider to be a good fit. (Contact the NAPBTA at www.NAPBTA.com.)

Breeders and What to Expect

Once you've found the breeder, be prepared to be quizzed about the reasons you want an American Pit Bull Terrier from them, and why they should place a puppy with you. Responsible breeders take very seriously the future of the dogs they've brought into the world. And APBT enthusiasts have learned to be vigilant because of the potential for abuses that can be detrimental to the puppy, themselves personally, and the breed as a whole. Don't take offense—welcome the questions! If there are no questions from the breeder, you should not walk away but *run* as fast as you can.

Good breeders want prospective puppy owners to interview them as much as they interview you. They'll want to know that you've done your homework and know the basics about the breed. People who take the time to study books or other resources about the APBT make the best owners. This shows you're committed from the beginning to educating yourself about what the dog needs, what to expect, and how to create a lifetime home for your special dog. You can never have too much information.

Questions for the Breeder

Prepare to interview the breeder.

- **Find out how the puppies are raised:** Are the puppies kept outside or inside? Depending on the time of year and geographic region, the climate may be fine for some outdoor time. But puppies who have been "raised underfoot" have the

By the Numbers

APBT puppies should not be allowed to leave the breeder until ten weeks old if possible but definitely never before eight weeks. Puppies weaned too soon may experience problem behaviors and socialization issues. A good breeder uses those weeks to work with the puppies before they go to their new home, including crate training, housetraining, and some basic training.

benefit of positive hands-on, close contact with people.

- **Ask for testimonials:** If the breeder doesn't offer them right away, ask her for testimonials from satisfied puppy owners.

- **Determine the breeder's experience:** How long has the breeder been involved with the breed? What type of events does she compete in, if any at all? What breed clubs does she belong to? How many dogs does she personally have? How many puppies has she produced this year and/or ever? How many times does she breed her females? What are the youngest and oldest ages they will breed a female?

- **Ask about the parents:** Ask about the temperament, health status, and titles of the parents—even if the breeder doesn't own the sire. Good breeders use the best sire they can find—even ones from across the country. If the breeder chose an APBT male from "down the street" because it was convenient, this is a giant red flag. Have screening tests for hip dysplasia been done? Are the parents

You can never have too much information when it comes to finding out about your potential puppy from his breeder.

The answers to these questions will help you determine if the breeder is reputable and looking to improve the breed or is just a backyard breeder pushing out puppies to make money.

Temperament Testing

Temperament testing strives to be a canine crystal ball to identify personality tendencies and predict potential problems. It measures aspects of temperament such as stability, shyness, aggressiveness, and friendliness, and the pup fails if he exhibits unprovoked aggression, panic without recovery, or strong avoidance. Once tested, puppies can be better matched with owners.

No test is entirely predictive of behavior in the new home, and few, if any, have been well validated. If you have children, take them along and see which puppy actively seeks out their company. Tests for puppies between seven and ten weeks of age typically include these basics:

successfully competing in dog sports or conformation trials? What successes in competition have other litters of their breeding enjoyed? You can get an idea about your future puppy's performance potential with this information.

- **Temperament:** Ask about the temperament of the individual puppies and whether the breeder considers some more laid back or "driven" than others. Has a temperament test been done? This can help you choose the best puppy for your lifestyle, whether you are looking for a potential competition canine or a pet. Someone who has spent time and effort with a carefully planned breeding and litter should have no trouble offering this information.

- Cradle pup on his back like a baby, place a hand gently on his chest and look directly in his eyes. Pups that accept this handling are considered biddable, while those who resist are more likely to be independent-minded.

- Hold pup suspended under his armpits with hind legs dangling. Again, those pups that submit are said to have a low score for willfulness, while those that struggle or that freeze and stare straight ahead may want to do things their own way.

- Drop keys or tin pan to test him for noise sensitivity.

- See how pup reacts to a stranger entering the room—or to being left alone in the room. Does he run and greet, or cower and cry?

Many behaviors of personality, such as resistance to handling, possessive aggression, territorial vocalization, excessive reactivity, and many forms of fear might not emerge until the pet matures and will have greater predictability after three months of age. The later the test, the more likely you are to get an accurate reading.

Considerations When Buying a Purebred Puppy

A registered puppy should have pedigree information and legitimate registration documents available. Depending on whether the puppy is a pet or a show prospect, the breeder may limit the registration or withhold papers until he or she has been spayed or neutered.

Ask if the purchase price includes any sort of health guarantee and what health clearances have been done. At a minimum, the parents (and at the proper age, the puppies) should have Orthopedic Foundation for Animals (OFA) or PennHIP (University of Pennsylvania Hip Improvement Program) testing for hip and/or elbow dysplasia, an OFA heart screening, and Canine Eye Registration Foundation (CERF) testing for the eyes. Your breeder should provide medical history on the puppy, including a to-date list of vaccinations and other care. In most cases, the puppy should have had at least two sets of "puppy shots" prior to going to a new home.

Before you commit to taking a puppy, if at all possible visit the facilities and see where the dogs live and how they're raised. Ask to see the mother dog as well. Even when she has puppies, the typical APBT mom-dog shouldn't growl and should be accepting of strangers. If she acts fearful, growls, or must be locked away—those are not the pups for you, as they can inherit these poor traits. Look for cleanliness and a modest number of dogs, and go elsewhere if the yard or house is filthy and they've got dozens of dogs with multiple litters. Use common sense.

Two final questions should seal the deal. First, ask if the breeder has ever turned down a sale. You want the answer to be *yes*, rather than learning that they'll let a puppy go to just anyone who asks. Second, ask if the breeder will be available to offer help and advice along the way. Some of the best APBT folks not only insist on staying in touch, they will take a dog back later in life should circumstances warrant.

The purpose of temperament testing is to try to identify personality tendencies and predict potential problems.

A registered puppy should have pedigree information and legitimate registration documents available.

A reasonably priced puppy from a reputable breeder with a good bloodline may cost $600 and up. Local newspapers may post advertisements for $200 or less. These backyard breeders and puppy mill establishments offer "pit bull" puppies dirt cheap but probably cannot pass the test questions listed above. You'll get what you pay for.

BEFORE PUPPY COMES HOME

If you've done your research correctly—and you have, because you're reading this book!—then you know that preparations must be made before the new kid steps a paw into your home. In some cases, the breeder of choice won't have a litter old enough, or you must be placed on a waiting list for the next breeding. That's terrific, because it gives you time to plan. When you have existing resident pets, you can take steps to ensure they don't get anxious over the puppy's arrival. Even if you've had dogs before and he's to be an only dog, adjustments must be made.

Puppy-Proofing 101

Most people are familiar with the concept of baby-proofing for safety when a human infant comes home. Toddlers poke fingers into every nook and cranny, put unmentionables in their mouth, and damage breakables simply because they're curious and want to handle Great Aunt Gretchen's punch bowl. A puppy won't have fingers to poke, but everything else remains the same.

Anything that your APBT puppy can taste or chew will go into his mouth. He's bred to be a gripper and will eagerly chomp down and play tug with tablecloths, bedspreads, and more. When teething, besides potentially damaging your property, he can injure or even die from chewing or swallowing dangerous objects. It's up to owners to "think like a puppy" to make the environment safe.

In the Home

Invest in knee pads and crawl around the house on hands and knees to get a puppy-eye-view of the area. Electrical cords must be bundled and kept out of reach. Home product stores offer products designed to do this. When you have window blinds, be sure the cords remain tied up out of reach, or an inquisitive pup peeking outside could be tempted to play tug or even get caught and strangled in the strings.

Get in the habit of shutting bathroom doors and closing the lids on commodes. Drinking out of toilets is unsanitary or even dangerous when chemical cleaners are added. Toilet paper can turn into a fun game of TP-ing the house.

Wastebaskets become terrific puppy toy-boxes for scrounging. So does the laundry basket, bottom of the closet that holds shoes, and purses or brief cases left on the floor. Throw pillows become doggy chew toys, and if your APBT puppy genius watches you open kitchen cupboards, he may figure out how to raid the pantry (or the poisonous cleaners)—childproof latches may be necessary. Consider anything left within reach of the little guy to be fair game. Houseplants should be hung, set on tables out of reach, or thrown away, particularly if they're of the toxic variety. If you don't want teeth marks on your cell phone or television remote, find a safe place to store them.

In the Yard

Don't neglect the yard. The American Pit Bull Terrier finds entertainment wherever he goes. Put up garden hoses unless you want them punctured by puppy teeth and turned into

Be Honest With Your Breeder

APBT puppies raised by the same breeder can have very different personalities, even when from the same litter. Some will be more outgoing and confident and need a stronger hand, while others might be less hard-headed and more easily trained. Be honest with the breeder about your expectations. While all puppies potentially can be wonderful companions, you'll both be happier if you match the pup's needs with your own.

sprinklers. Lock away fertilizer, insecticides, rodenticides, antifreeze, and anything else in bags, boxes, or puppy-intriguing containers.

Check the fence. What may contain an adult-size dog could allow a pup to escape or become caught and injured when he tries to wiggle through. As with indoor concerns, ensure that your new puppy remains safe.

SUPPLIES

A number of must-have supplies make life easy for living with your new puppy. Many of these apply to any puppy, but there are some specific to the American Pit Bull Terrier.

Collar

Puppies grow very quickly, and your dog will need two or three (or more) before fully grown. Choose one that fits him now. It does no good if he can wiggle out of it. Flat-buckle collars work well and can be purchased in a variety of colors and materials, from woven nylon to leather with silver studs. The ideal collar fits snugly around the pup's neck while allowing you to easily slip two fingers underneath. A size that initially fits him when snugged to the smallest fitting could be adjusted while he grows.

Crate

A number of crate styles are available, from solid hard plastic to wire cages. Dogs like the den-like feel of a crate, though, so if you choose wire, also provide a blanket or towel to cover the sides. The proper size of a crate should be just large enough for the puppy to stand up, turn around, and sleep inside—too large of a crate means your puppy may take to pottying on one side and sleeping on the other, which will interfere with housetraining. Since he'll grow much larger, and the crate will be useful during adulthood, invest in one that can be used once he's mature. Look for one that includes a partition to make the crate into a smaller puppy-size container that can be enlarged as he grows.

Dog Bed

The crate can double as your puppy's bed. There are commercial dog beds available for any size dog, puppy to adult. Don't be surprised, though, if your APBT puppy turns the expensive bed into a chew toy. Your dog won't care what the bed looks like, and a tattered blanket suits him just as well. Be sure to choose washable fabric, whether a blanket or commercial bed—puppies are not known for neatness. Don't use blankets with padding inside that can be pulled out and choked on.

Food and Water Bowls

For a puppy, anything can turn into a toy or chew target. For food and water, choose containers that are dishwasher safe, and avoid plastic that can be chewed up and swallowed. Stainless steel works extremely well, but only the heaviest nonskid bowls won't be pushed and chased all over the room when the dog tries to eat. They can be pricy, but the cheaper metal bowls can be chewed and turned into hockey-puck-style toys. The dog won't be likely to chew glass, but it can break when a rambunctious puppy runs amuck. Crockery gets my recommendation.

Grooming Supplies

The APBTs are fairly easily maintained dogs. They have short hair, but it sheds. A regular brushing every week keeps the shedding under control. A rubber-nubbed curry brush

removes loose hair and loosens dander, and a soft bristle removes dander and polishes the coat.

He also won't need bathing more than one a month unless he becomes quite grubby. A basic dog-grooming shampoo works well. Avoid dishwashing detergent or human shampoo, which can dry out the dog's skin by stripping natural oils. Canine skin isn't as oily as a human scalp.

Choose a nail trimmer style that you feel comfortable using. Scissor-action, guillotine-style trimmers or grinding nail trimmers all work well. Each will require practice on your part and teaching your puppy to accept the attention.

Identification

More than 8 million pets are lost each year. One out of three pets becomes lost during its lifetime. Without identification, experts estimate that up to 90 percent won't return home. There are several ways for your pet to have a fighting chance to be homeward bound, should he become lost.

Tattoos

Tattoos continue to be used for identification. Typically, the dog's registration number is

Stainless steel works well for a puppy's food and water bowls.

placed inside the ear, inner thigh, or abdomen. With the APBT, the inner thigh and abdomen are recommended for tattooing, because a thief can crop out a tattoo placed on the ear, since this breed's ears are often cropped. The problem with tattooing is that folks must know to look for it and figure out what the numbers mean. Plus, tattoos can be altered or fade over time or may be hidden by the pet's fur.

ID Tags

Tags are the easiest for a Good Samaritan to notice. Even the rabies tag number can trace your dog to the clinic and reconnect you to your pet. Some tag products bring high-tech to help, using a tiny USB that holds reams of information you can download directly from your own computer. There are many services that allow you to register collar tag, tattoo, or other information on their database. But some pets lose tags or collars, and should your dog be taken by a thief, tags can be thrown away.

Microchips

Microchips are the gold standard for identification. Microchips can't be lost, they never wear out, and they are engineered to last a lifetime. They're also easy to find and to trace. The microchip, embedded in surgical glass about the size of a grain of rice, is injected beneath the pet's skin in the shoulder region. Even tiny pups won't react any worse to this procedure than when they're vaccinated. Owners provide the information that goes into the microchip, and it's stored on a pet-recovery database.

The microchips are read using a hand-held scanner over the shoulder region. Microchips transmit specific frequencies like a small radio station, and the scanner must be "tuned" correctly to read the information. It's important that shelters and veterinary hospitals in your locale have scanners able to read the

> ## Multi-Dog Tip
>
> Every dog in your house needs a private place where he won't be bothered by the adult dog or pestered by the new puppy. Crates work very well to offer a safe retreat as well as to sequester an obnoxious youngster who doesn't know when to quit. Giving the resident dog a break from the clueless baby dog helps him keep his canine sense of humor about the invasion.

specific microchip implanted in your pet, so ask before you 'chip. Local veterinarians and shelters provide the microchipping service and the cost varies.

DNA Identification

Both the UKC and the ADBA offer DNA services for identification. DNA is the only identification that can not be tampered with or altered. It will not help you find your dog, but having a DNA profile registered in your name will go a long way toward proving ownership.

Use Multiple Methods

It is strongly recommended to use multiple methods of identification and keep current photos of your APBT. Should he become lost or stolen, clear photos will be invaluable in finding and proving ownership of your pet. It's essential that you take all the precautions you can, as the APBT is a *very high-theft breed*.

Leash

A leash offers a way to control your puppy from a short distance away. It can be a great training tool, but more than that, it could be considered a safety net for your dog. He should be on the leash anytime he's outside and not within a fenced area. In some locals, the law requires your dog to be on leash whenever he's off your property.

Leashes are made from flat nylon mesh, chains, leather, braided rope, or cable and come in designer colors as well as plain, practical models. You may not need a heavy leash for your 8-pound (4-kg) puppy, and a lightweight style can be fine for first obedience lessons. Heavier versions will be needed as he grows.

For control, your puppy needs to be near you. A 6-foot (2-m) leash offers more than enough ranging room. Avoid the retractable cable leashes for two reasons: First, they give your dog too much ranging room, and you'll not be able to intercede in time when the puppy is 25 feet (8 m) away. Second, these leashes teach your puppy to pull the leash, rather than follow your lead. If he learns to pull as a youngster, he'll tug you all over the world as an adult.

Nylon and chain leashes won't be particularly comfortable for your bare hands, should the adolescent pup decide to challenge your control. And while designer colors may be stylish, your dog won't care. A versatile, rugged, soft 6-foot (2-m) leather leash works well for general dog walking and obedience training.

Parting Stick

While you won't need it for your puppy, you may want to consider having a parting stick (also called a breaking stick) in multi-dog homes that include adult American Pit Bull Terriers. This wedge of wood or plastic opens the mouth of an APBT who has a jaw hold on another dog. Ask for help from an experienced APBT person to learn how to use it properly. This tool can be dangerous if you don't know how to use it properly.

Toys

The American Pit Bull Terrier loves to play, and toys can be a great outlet for your active puppy. You must be responsible for ensuring that the toys are safe for your pet, though. Even so-called indestructible dog toys may not be safe for some determined APBT dogs. They require very tough toys (like the ones Nylabone makes), and adult dogs have been known to chew toys in half, swallow rope toys, and dismantle knuckle bones.

Young pups probably won't be able to manage such things but certainly can remove the squeakers from stuffed toys if left unattended. It's good to make a habit of being vigilant from the very beginning. Baby-proof your dog's toys with an eye to what can be chewed off and eaten. Ears, eyes, noses, and tails of stuffed toys commonly get targeted. Supervise your puppy with all toys until you know what he can and cannot do with them. If there are multiple dogs in your home, use caution when it comes to toys. High excitement and energetic playtime with any type of toy can be a catalyst for a dog fight.

Balls and Interactive Toys

Balls of all sizes can be great fun. Smaller balls, flying disks, and tug toys can be interactive fun for you and the pup. Ten- or even 25-inch (25-

or 63-cm) balls provide great solo-play fun as well and can be more difficult for dogs to grab, chew, or eat. You may find these at specialty dog product stores or even horse supply outlets—horse trainers use similar toys to keep equine pets engaged.

Flirt Poles

Flirt poles, a popular toy specifically for terriers, resembles a fishing-pole-style kitty lure toy. With the APBT, of course, it must be much sturdier and, even so, may eventually be destroyed. You can make one inexpensively, and with care, it should last through most of puppyhood before you need to replace it. Visit the local farmer supply store or horse tack shop and ask for the least expensive longe whip, the longer the better. Tie a toy (think of this as bait) to the end of the whip. Something like a piece of burlap, an old sock, or even a floppy dog toy can work. Then play keep-away with the toy, teasing (flirting) the dog to get him to chase and keeping it just out of reach. Don't let him catch it—and if he does, do not play tug games or he'll destroy the toy. The object of the flirt pole is to wear out the dog with healthy exercise, running him around and around,

allowing some leaps as well. You can stand still, while wearing out your puppy.

Spring Poles

A *spring pole* could be described as the ultimate stationary tug toy. It provides APBTs with a legal outlet for the sort of holding and wrestling activity for which they were bred. It can be used to condition performance dogs, but even owners of noncompeting APBTs appreciate the spring pole because it's inexpensive, can fit into even a small backyard, and works well to keep the dog entertained. Basically, a spring pole consists of a biting target with a good grip surface, such as burlap or rope, attached to a springy tether (garage door spring or rubber inner tubes), which is attached to a solid overhead structure. A tree branch works. Dogs enjoy grabbing, pulling, and shaking the target. The elevation should allow the puppy to keep his feet on the ground, or he could become injured attempting leaps his body is not yet prepared to endure. Adult dogs may enjoy jumping and grabbing higher-placed targets, but these should also not be so high as to allow the dog to hang off the ground. Prevent injuries by playing it safe.

SETTING UP A SCHEDULE

Before your pup comes home, consider what kind of schedule to set up. Establishing a routine helps build trust. Puppies come from a familiar environment with their littermates and mother to a strange house with people they don't know. A known schedule gives the new baby something to count on, and that helps reduce the normal stress of the transition.

Daily routine should include touching and playing to create an emotional connection that builds into love. Use the pet's name often, so he learns that pleasant things like games or dinner happen when you speak to or about him.

Training Tidbit

Training rewards can be anything that your puppy likes. It doesn't have to be a food treat. Pay attention to which toy the puppy returns to time after time and begs you to throw. Reserve that particular toy or game to use as a powerful reward during training.

Make sure your whole family agrees about pet issues. Animals become easily confused without consistency, and it's not fair to change the rules midstream. Decide if he's allowed on the furniture or not. Will he sleep on his own bed, in a crate, in the garage, or on your pillow? There are benefits to each, and it's up to you to decide. Choose your battles wisely. Sleeping together may accelerate the bonding process.

Decide on a convenient, easily cleaned, and accessible potty location for your pet. Pets become confused if you move their bathroom and are most faithful when they know when to expect an outing. So don't move the potty place, and stick to a bathroom schedule, to keep everyone regular and on target. Figure in times to pick up the waste, too.

Choose a dining time and location. Healthy treats from the table aren't evil, but begging or swiping food isn't polite. And it's not fair to the puppy if you insist on sticking to kibble in the bowl, while others sneak him treats. A good compromise is to either put table treats into his bowl after you've finished dining, or reserve them for use during training sessions, so there aren't mixed signals.

Healthy pets benefit from exercise. Your puppy will need several playtimes throughout the day to wear him out. Playing is an ideal way to bond with your new pet. Don't forget to schedule daily obedience lessons. Even five minutes a day teaches important lessons, including how to learn, and helps keep his brain engaged so he stays out of trouble.

BRINGING PUPPY HOME

Your new pet has much to absorb when he leaves his mother and siblings to come home with you. He's still a baby and won't understand what's happening. And nobody can explain it to him.

To make the transition easier on your puppy, take some time to play with him while he's still at the breeder's.

Take some time to play with him and become acquainted while still in the comfort and familiarity of his first home. That can help ease the initial transition. It can be tempting to cuddle and hold your new puppy in the car ride home. However, containing him in a crate that is seat-belted in the back seat will be safer for all involved, for several reasons.

A loose dog in a moving car, especially a pup that may become panicked, could cause an accident. Further, if an accident should happen, the airbags that save your life could crush the puppy. He also could get out of the car and become lost. In most cases, there won't be any car accident, but the puppy could have other kinds of "accidents" during the car ride home, either from stress or from car sickness. You do not want the new pet to associate sitting on your lap with feeling sick or scared. And, in fact, trying to comfort a distressed puppy with baby talk can actually make him believe he really does have something to cry about and can reward the behavior.

Instead, bring a small hand towel with you to the breeder's. Before leaving, as you play with the puppy and his littermates, rub the towel over all the puppies. Ask the breeder to use the towel to pet the mother dog as well. When you leave, place the scented towel inside the pet carrier so the puppy has a comforting reminder for the car ride home and for his sleeping spot once you arrive.

What to Expect

It will take time for you both to become used to the new routine. Expect the puppy to cry, especially at night when you want to sleep and can't give him attention. Set up his sleeping area, such as his bed or crate, near your own bed so that he smells you and knows you're near. It may take several days or even a couple of weeks before he'll stop crying when separated from you at night. A canine pheromone product that reduces stress can prove helpful with the transition, since it signals the puppy not to be afraid.

Being nearby also allows you to monitor his nighttime bathroom needs, as young puppies won't have the capacity to hold it for a full eight-hour sleep. You may wish to set an alarm to anticipate when he needs an outdoor potty break. A good rule of thumb is that you can expect your puppy to "hold it" for one hour for how many months old he is. So a two-month-old puppy can hold it for two hours, a three-month-old for three hours, etc.

Some owners wish to sleep with the new puppy, and that's certainly up to you. This may prompt him to indulge in play behavior you

don't appreciate, though, such as chase-the-feet-beneath-the-covers.

The first several weeks, the new puppy will take turns playing, sleeping, eating, and eliminating. He will be curious, loving, funny, and frustrating. These early days, perhaps more than any others, help forge strong bonds that sustain your love for each other for the rest of your life together.

Purchase dog toys that are safe and durable for your rambunctious puppy.

CHAPTER 3

CARE OF YOUR AMERICAN PIT BULL TERRIER PUPPY

What you do today to care for your American Pit Bull Terrier puppy has an impact on his health and well-being for years to come. It's hard to imagine, when you look at that bundle of energy, what he'll be like a decade from now and beyond. But what you feed him, the way he's handled, and the preventive veterinary care he receives at your hands determines how long he lives and whether that life will be full of fun and joy, or the opposite.

FEEDING A PUPPY

Puppies grow very quickly and require the equivalent of rocket fuel to keep up with nutritional needs. But feeding your puppy takes more than just filling the bowl. The right food depends on his lifestyle, age, and activity level. The active dog typically requires more calories than the couch potato pooch, for example. And a tiny pup only recently weaned from nursing may do better on a soft food, while older pups relish crunchy dry kibble. Food choice also depends on your pocketbook—what you can afford to spend—as well as the time you have for food preparation. Finally, the food must be acceptable to your pup. If he won't eat it, or

it upsets his tummy, it doesn't matter if it's "perfect" in the can or bag.

What to Feed

A two-month-old puppy needs about twice the number of calories per day as that of an adult dog. Puppies also need more protein, fat, calcium, and phosphorus. Nutrients must be in the proper balance, because too much or too little can cause problems. Commercial foods make this easy for you by preparing formulations specific to the needs of a growing puppy. Just make sure the label specifies that it is complete and balanced for a puppy or for "all life stages."

Avoid upsetting the puppy's tummy when you first bring him home. An abrupt change of food often prompts diarrhea, so ask the breeder what he's used to eating, and have that food handy. You can later transition him to a new food by mixing the old with the new in a 50/50 mix, and gradually over the first week, reduce the old and increase the new percentage.

The American Pit Bull Terrier is considered a large-breed dog. Growing too fast can result in obesity or joint problems later in life for big breeds. So experts recommend that you feed a food designed specifically for a large-breed puppy. These adjust the calcium and phosphorus ratio, calories, and protein to slow the growth rate. Your puppy will end up just as big but will take longer to mature. That's healthier, because it allows his joints to develop and stabilize before he gains too much weight that can strain immature bones and joints.

Commercial Pet Food

Commercial pet food falls into three broad categories: super premium, premium, and low-cost products. Although there aren't any legal definitions, in general terms the super-premium foods tend to be highest in nutrient density and digestibility; use high-dollar, quality ingredients; and therefore are the most expensive. More fat makes foods very tasty, nutrient density means the pup doesn't need to eat as much, and high digestibility allows puppies to use a high percentage of nutrients—there's less waste ending up on the lawn. Super-premium foods are marketed primarily through specialty pet stores or veterinary clinics. If you have a picky eater who has trouble eating enough to maintain normal weight gain, a super-premium food may be the best choice.

Puppy Food

Choose a puppy food that has been specifically formulated for large-breed dogs. The APBT will be a powerful adult dog, and growing too fast could cause joint problems when the hips or knees haven't matured enough to support the dog's weight. That's especially important for dogs with competition in their future.

Grocery stores tend to offer premium name-brand products and are less expensive but good quality for the average dog. Specialty brands may be very good but often are regional distribution only. The least expensive foods are typically sold in grocery stores or discount chain stores as the "store brand." Cheap ingredients result in less tasty food and lower digestibility—food that isn't useable ends up on the lawn. House-brand products claim nutritional value equal to national name-brand products but at a lower cost. Some adult dogs may do fine on these foods; however, they are not appropriate for puppies. Stick to the super-premium and premium foods.

Feeding Schedule

How often to feed depends on the puppy's age and can change over time. Most pups should be fed at least three times a day until six months of age. However, there are some puppies who can't (or won't) take in enough calories when fed one or two meals a day. Multiple smaller meals are a kinder way to treat a developing gastrointestinal tract.

Feed three or four separate meals to young puppies during the first few months at home. Then gradually wean them to one or two meals daily by the time they are six months of age. Base the feeding times on your schedule and what you can do consistently. A first meal might coincide with your own breakfast, the second when the kids come home from school in the afternoon, and the third coordinated with your evening meal. If you're not able to be there to feed at proscribed times, you can provide one of the puppy's meals in a treat-toy, like the ones Nylabone makes, and leave it with him in his crate or play area while you're gone.

Puppies should be fed three or four separate meals during the first few months at home.

GROOMING A PUPPY

Your American Pit Bull Terrier is an "easy keeper" when it comes to grooming. His short coat requires little more than a quick touch from a slicker brush or chamois cloth. And unless he gets dingy rolling in the mud (and puppies *do* seem to attract dirt), he won't require baths too often.

But grooming goes beyond coat care. You'll need to monitor his eyes, ears, and nails. And some individual dogs have more problems with anal glands—situated on each side of the anus—that may require regular expression.

Grooming also is a great opportunity to bond with your puppy while at the same time giving him a routine health check. Simply petting him from head to toe feels good to the dog and allows you to learn what's normal for

your puppy, so you can be alert to any changes that need veterinary attention.

Get Your Puppy Used to Grooming

Create a grooming ritual that's always the same, so your dog knows what to expect. Groom him in the same time and place, and always finish with something pleasant like a game or treat, so he'll equate the experience as positive. If he objects to being touched or groomed in sensitive places, pair the exercise with a special treat so that he associates good stuff with the action.

For routine care, always begin by allowing your dog to sniff and investigate the grooming tools, especially if the experience is new to him. Then pet your dog to familiarize yourself with the contours of his body and discover any

Avoid bathing pups until they're older than four weeks, because they have trouble regulating body temperature and can become easily chilled. If they get grubby, a damp cloth is adequate for cleaning up the worst in tiny pups.

problem areas ahead of time. Start with the face, look in his eyes and ears, and touch all over his body. You can use the flat of your palms or the tips of your fingers, and lightly scratch him if he enjoys that. Handle his feet and toes, look under his tail to be sure he's clean, and open his mouth to look inside. Then use the brush and repeat touching him but with short, light strokes in the direction the fur grows. Always be careful not to press too hard, though, or you risk hurting tender skin.

It's helpful to regularly handle your puppy's paws and trim just the tip of his nails, even if they don't need it. "Pay" him with special treats for allowing you to touch the paws and individual toes or nails. Similarly, look inside his ears by first rubbing the outside base area that feels good and that the puppy welcomes. This gets him used to the idea. What he learns to accept as a puppy is more easily endured as an adult. This is particularly helpful with large-breed dogs who can be handled more easily while puppy-size.

Grooming Supplies

You will need to keep general grooming supplies on hand. Most of these are available from any pet product store. Your breeder or veterinarian may recommend particular brands.

- Rubber curry or bristle brush, and chamois for polishing the coat

- Grooming shampoo. If you choose one with flea preventive additives, be sure the label specifies that it's safe for the age of your puppy.

- Ear-cleaning solution (if recommended by veterinarian)

- Saline solution (for eyes)

- Fur whitener product for tear stains on white-faced pups

- Cotton balls or makeup-remover pads (for eyes and ears)

- Nail trimmer—guillotine type or scissor action. Small size works for puppies, but you'll need a large size once he grows to adulthood.

- Canine toothpaste (flavored with meat) and dog toothbrush (or human baby toothbrush)

HEALTH OF YOUR PUPPY

Taking care of your APBT puppy's health needs now can help ensure his health as an adult.

Finding a Veterinarian

People become veterinarians because they like and care about animals. There are 28 schools and colleges of veterinary medicine in the United States, where students study for eight to ten years before they receive their "doctor of veterinary medicine" degree (DVM) or *veterinariae medicinae doctoris* (VMD) degree.

Unlike human medical doctors who care for a single species, veterinarians must understand and care for all sorts of animals. Some may specialize in dogs and cats, or horses, or even exotic species such as parrots and lizards. It's best to work with a veterinarian who is comfortable working with and treating dogs in general and American Pit Bull Terriers in particular. It's important to find someone comfortable with APBTs—there may be some vets who have a negative view of the breed, but in many cases Pit Bulls are actually welcomed by many doctors because of their stoic and accepting nature during treatment.

Ask your puppy's breeder for a recommendation. In the ideal situation, you can continue taking your pup to the same doctor who cared for his mother during the pregnancy and already has a history on your little guy.

General-Practice Veterinarians

Most dogs receive optimum care their whole lives from general-practice veterinarians. The ideal veterinarian should offer the following: office hours and location convenient to your schedule, a fee and payment structure you can afford, emergency services either through their clinic or shared with other facilities, and a knowledgeable and personable staff. Some practices include boarding, grooming, or training facilities. Consider making an appointment to visit a potential veterinary clinic ahead of time. The doctor's office is a busy place, so avoid times when the staff must deal with regular appointments or surgery.

Veterinary Specialists

For special care issues, a veterinary specialist may be your best choice. More than 20 veterinary specialties now are available, from cancer specialists and internal medicine doctors to orthopedic surgeons, dentists, and veterinary ophthalmologists. Your local veterinarian can refer you to appropriate specialists when needed, and you can learn more about them at www.avma. org by clicking on "veterinary specialty organizations."

Respect Is Key

Some individuals or practices may suit your needs better than others. Personality of the doctor certainly can be an issue. You should like or at least respect each other, and the doctor should care about your pet and be willing to explain treatments and answer your questions. Conversely, you must be willing to provide necessary information, respect the doctor's time and expertise, and trust her judgment.

Take the time to develop a positive relationship with the people who care for

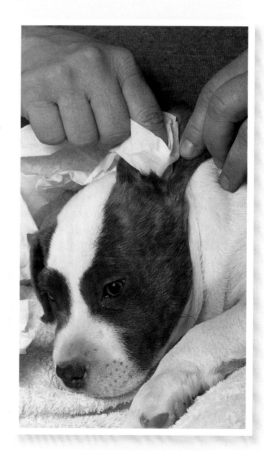

Get your puppy accustomed to a grooming routine as soon as possible.

your puppy. After all, you're on the same team and want the same things—to create the pet of your dreams.

First Checkup

Your puppy's first exam is a great opportunity for you to show him what a terrific, fun place the veterinary clinic can be. Be sure to take along a favorite blanket or toy. The blanket or towel that smells like home can be placed on the examining table. The familiar scent can be comforting. A toy that he can chew also helps the pup associate the location and handling by the veterinarian as a fun experience.

The doctor will look at the puppy all over, touching and gently squeezing (palpating) the tummy and other body parts to ensure he's developing normally. The skin will be examined to see that it's clean and healthy, with no sores, fleas, or other pests. For a boy puppy, the doctor will check to see if his testicles have descended or are retained in the abdomen.

Training Tidbit

Teach your puppy to accept nail trims by "paying" him for each toenail. Begin by simply handling his paws, one at a time, without forcing the contact. When he allows your touch, offer a toy or treat as a reward to associate good things with the experience. Gradually progress to snipping just the end off of one nail before rewarding him and throwing a puppy party. One nail trimmed a day results in a full pedicure in two weeks.

The veterinarian also will check the eyes to be sure they're clear, with no redness or discharge that might be a sign of illness. The inside of the ears will be examined with an otoscope that magnifies ticks and debris that point to ear mites or infection. The mouth also will be opened to check for the color of your puppy's gums. A pale color might indicate anemia, possibly from a parasite infection. Checking the progression of tooth eruption also tells the veterinarian information about health.

After examining the outside of the puppy, your veterinarian will listen to his heart and lungs with a stethoscope. The baby's temperature also will be taken, most often with a rectal thermometer, which some dogs find to be quite a rude procedure. Distract your puppy with the toy while the thermometer percolates in his nether regions, and offer a treat afterward. A puppy's normal temperature ranges between 100° and 102.5°F (38° and 39°C). A fever may indicate infection brewing, in which case the veterinarian may wish to perform additional tests.

You may be asked to bring a stool sample, or the doctor may be able to acquire a sample from the thermometer or a fecal hook—small instrument inserted like the thermometer that collects a sufficient sample when withdrawn. This will be examined to ensure that it looks normal (is not runny, is a normal brown color, has no blood or mucus). It will also be tested for intestinal parasites. Nearly all puppies are either born with or develop worms, and they can be treated with liquid oral medication or sometimes pills or injections. The doctor needs to determine what type of parasites the puppy may have in order to treat them.

Vaccinations

The specialized cells of a pet's immune system protect against disease. Vaccinations help "program" these cells to recognize, seek out, and eliminate viruses, bacteria, and other pathogens that are found either in the bloodstream or at the cellular level (as in the nose or eyes) before they cause disease.

Puppies born to vaccinated mothers receive some temporary protection, called passive immunity, simply from nursing. A pet's individual immune system doesn't mature and take over until about eight weeks of age. However, passive immunity not only protects the youngster, it also attacks vaccinations, as if they were real viruses, and neutralizes the vaccine. Because it's hard to predict when Mom's protection fades and baby's takes over, a series of boosters are recommended to cover all bases.

Today, vaccinations are available to protect against a wide range of dog illnesses. You simply cannot scrimp on the series of puppy vaccinations. In fact, this earliest protection can be your best health care investment and potentially last for years.

It is absolutely inappropriate that all dogs get every vaccine every year. The most recent canine vaccination guidelines use the terms *core*, *non-core*, and *not recommended* to categorize vaccine types. These criteria measure health risk associated with infection, incidence and severity of the disease, and efficacy of the vaccine.

Core Vaccines

Core vaccines are needed by all dogs at some point in life. They should be administered to every dog who is six months old or older or has not received vaccinations before. Core vaccines prevent diseases that are particularly dangerous, have a wide distribution, or are contagious to people (zoonotic). The core vaccinations have been shown to provide protection for (on average) about five to seven years—but a minimum of every three years

Heartworm

The heartworm parasite requires about six months from initial infection to become mature enough for common tests to detect its presence. Young puppies can be safely put on preventive medication without the test.

revaccination provides the best insurance on the core vaccines. Based on the latest vaccination recommendations, puppies and adult dogs should receive the following core vaccinations on the indicated schedule:

- Canine Adenovirus-2, Distemper, and Parvovirus: begin at six to eight weeks of age, then every three to four weeks until 12 to 16 weeks of age; booster at one year of age, and then every three years

- Rabies: one dose at three to six months; one year later; then annually or every three years (per local law requirements)

Canine Adenovirus-2

The canine adenovirus-2 (CAV-2) is one of the infectious agents that can cause kennel cough. See section on "Kennel Cough" under "Non-Core Vaccines" for more information.

Distemper

Canine distemper (CDV), first recognized in Europe in the 18th century, is still considered the most important viral disease of dogs. Similar to the human measles virus, in dogs distemper rates as the most commonly known infectious disease of the nervous system. This highly contagious, often fatal virus is excreted in the saliva, respiratory secretions, urine, and feces and is transmitted through the air (sneezing and coughing) and by contaminated objects the same way a cold virus spreads in people. Rarely,

Core vaccines are needed by all dogs at some point in life.

unborn puppies are infected by their mother. That results in stillbirths, abortions, fading puppy syndrome, and central nervous system signs in four- to six-week-old puppies.

Puppies are more susceptible than adult dogs are, but during their lifetime, most dogs will be exposed to distemper. Dogs who are kenneled or regularly boarded, and those routinely shown or hunted, have a higher risk because of increased exposure to other dogs. Dogs obtained from shelters or pet stores, particularly at 9 to 12 weeks of age, are often affected. They may appear healthy but be incubating the disease when adopted (even if they've been vaccinated), then become sick once in their new home.

The virus attacks various body tissues, especially the epithelial cells that line the surfaces of the body, like the skin, the conjunctiva of the eyes, the respiratory and urinary tracts, and the mucus membranes lining the gastrointestinal tract. It also infects the lymph nodes, kidney, liver, spleen, and brain and spinal cord. Whether or not the infected dog survives depends on the effectiveness of his individual immune system.

Within two days following infection, the virus spreads to the bronchial lymph nodes and tonsils, and then throughout the bone marrow, spleen, and other lymph nodes. Within five days, virus infects and begins destroying the white blood cells. By 9 to 14 days following infection, 75 percent of dogs that have competent immune systems will kill the virus and won't become sick. Dogs who aren't able to mount an early immune response develop sudden devastating signs of disease. Diagnosis of CDV is usually based on the signs of the disease.

The first sign is a fever of 103° to 105°F (39° to 41°C). Within a few days, the dog refuses to eat and has yellowish diarrhea, trouble breathing, and central nervous system signs such as seizures, behavior changes, weakness, and poor coordination. A characteristic thick, white to yellow discharge from the eyes and nose looks similar to a cold. This is a serious warning of illness.

Other symptoms vary, depending on what organs are affected by the virus. Infection of the respiratory system may prompt the dog to cough and develop pneumonia. Gastrointestinal infection can cause bloody or mucoid diarrhea. The eyes may ulcerate or even become blind. The skin (particularly the footpads) may thicken, crack, and bleed. Pus blisters appear on the abdomen. Because of an impaired immune system, dogs suffering from distemper may also develop bacterial, fungal, or parasitic infections that can make him even sicker and increase the risk of death. Without veterinary intervention, dogs experiencing severe symptoms usually die within three weeks.

There is no cure for distemper, only supportive treatment that addresses individual symptoms to make the dog more comfortable until (if) his own body overcomes the infection. Stricken dogs receive antibiotics to combat infections, along with fluid therapy and medications to control diarrhea and vomiting and to counteract dehydration. Anticonvulsant medication may be necessary to control seizures. No one treatment always works, and it may take ongoing therapy for up to six weeks to conquer the disease.

Dogs sick with CDV also shed the virus for up to 90 days and are sources of infection for other healthy dogs. Sick dogs must be quarantined from healthy animals. The virus can live in a frozen state for many years, thaw out, and still infect your dog. However, it is relatively unstable in hot or dry conditions and can be killed by most disinfectants such as household bleach.

The decision to attempt to save the dog is based on his overall health, the seriousness of the disease, and the potential for permanent health problems. Each dog responds differently to treatment. For some, symptoms get better and then worsen before recovery. Other dogs show no improvement despite aggressive treatment. Often, after consulting with their veterinarian, owners make the difficult decision to euthanize the sick dog.

Dogs who survive infection during puppyhood may suffer enamel hypoplasia— poorly developed tooth enamel that's pitted and discolored—as adults. Even dogs who recover from infection may suffer permanent damage to the central nervous system, which results in seizures or palsy for the rest of the dog's life.

If your APBT puppy seems to be unusually lethargic or out of sorts, take him to the vet.

The distemper vaccination, considered a core treatment, is virtually 100 percent protective. All puppies should receive this protection by eight weeks of age.

Parvovirus

This highly contagious and often lethal virus was first identified in 1978 and is found throughout the world. Parvovirus affects dogs of any age. However, puppies are the most susceptible, with up to a 20 percent mortality rate even in pups who receive treatment. Pups who are already stressed from parasites or from surgical procedures like neutering or ear cropping are at highest risk for severe disease. The highest incidence occurs in kennels, pet stores, shelters, and poor-quality breeding facilities. The APBT breed in general is considered "highly susceptible" to parvovirus, but the cause of this susceptibility is unknown.

Infected dogs shed the virus in their droppings for about two weeks, and the disease spreads by direct contact with this infected material. Following exposure, symptoms usually develop in 5 to 11 days. The tonsils are infected first, and from there the virus travels to the lymphatic system, which routes it to the bloodstream. Then the virus travels throughout the body, ultimately infecting the crypt cells of the intestinal lining.

The hill-shaped villi that line the small intestine contain tiny hair-like projections called microvilli, where digestive absorption takes place. Crypt cells down in the "valleys" replace the microvilli every three to four days, but parvovirus kills the crypt cells that make the nutrient-absorbing microvilli. It takes three to four days for crypt cells to heal and begin to repopulate the villi. During that time, the dog's body is unable to effectively process food and water.

Dogs die from dehydration, electrolyte imbalance, shock, or secondary infections. Puppies often collapse and die in as little as 12 hours following the onset of symptoms. Parvovirus should be considered a medical emergency.

Signs of illness include depression, fever of 104° to 106°F (40° to 41°C), refusal to eat or drink, and severe vomiting along with diarrhea. Vomiting usually appears first, with diarrhea following within 24 to 48 hours. Vomit may be clear, yellow, or blood-tinged. Bloody diarrhea smells rotten and may have mucus present. The acute form of the disease, however, may result in sudden severe stomach pain and depression, followed by shock and sudden death before any other symptom appears. Dogs typically either recover quickly, or they die.

In most cases, parvovirus is suspected in any young dog with vomiting, bloody diarrhea, and a fever, especially unvaccinated dogs under 12 months of age. Early detection and treatment increases chances for survival, with therapy centered upon good nursing and supportive care. Essentially, a sick dog must be kept alive long enough for his own immune system to suppress and clear the virus from his body. Dogs that survive for three to four days following the onset of vomiting and diarrhea generally recover rapidly and will become immune to the enteric form of the disease.

Food and water are usually withheld for

Want to Know More?

For information on the health of an adult APBT, check out Chapter 8: APBT Health and Wellness.

two to four days to give the digestive system a chance to rest. Fluid therapy helps counter the devastating dehydration and returns electrolyte balance to normal. Antibiotics may be administered to fight secondary infection, along with medications to control vomiting and diarrhea.

Once vomiting and diarrhea have subsided, water and a bland food, like cottage cheese and rice or a veterinary-prescribed diet, are offered in small amounts several times daily. The normal diet is reintroduced gradually as the dog recovers over the next several days.

Parvovirus can live in the environment for at least five months and sometimes for years. Direct dog-to-dog contact isn't necessary for spreading the disease. The virus can be picked up simply by walking through a yard contaminated with infected feces or by contact with kennels or other objects that have been contaminated by an infected pet. The virus resists most common disinfectants and household detergents, but thorough cleaning with household bleach will kill it. A dilution of 1 part bleach to 30 parts water is recommended.

Strict isolation helps control the spread of disease. Sick dogs should remain isolated for 30 days after recovery and be bathed thoroughly before being brought into contact with other dogs. Everything that comes into contact with the infected animal, including owners, must be disinfected with the bleach solution.

The latest vaccinations cross-protect against the various strains of parvovirus. Because of its widespread and deadly nature, parvovirus vaccination is a core vaccine.

Rabies

Rabies, caused by a bullet-shaped virus, is a devastating neurological disease that affects the brain, resulting in symptoms that are similar to those of meningitis. Once symptoms develop, the disease is always fatal.

Rabies has been around for centuries and continues to appear throughout the world. The disease affects all mammals, most commonly wild animal populations, but also afflicts dogs, cats, and people. The disease appears today in pets or people as a result of disease "spillover" from wild animals, and parallels the incidence of rabies in these feral reservoirs. Animals most often associated with the disease include raccoons, coyotes, foxes, skunks, and bats. Dogs allowed to roam risk encountering a rabid animal and getting sick. Because rabies also affects people, laws require vaccination of your dog against the virus.

Infection requires direct contact with an infected animal. Usually, a bite introduces infective saliva into the wound. There, the virus proliferates until it reaches the nerves, which carry the infection to the spinal cord. Ultimately, the virus reaches the brain, whereupon symptoms develop.

Rabies has three recognized states of clinical disease: 1) incubation, 2) clinical signs, and 3) paralysis terminating in death. The

If a dog contracts parvo, food and water are usually withheld for a few days.

incubation period, the time from the bite until development of symptoms, takes 14 days to 24 months, with an average of three to eight weeks for most species. From the brain, the virus spreads to other tissues, like the salivary glands.

Clinical signs are mild to severe behavior changes. The first symptoms are refusal to eat or drink, and the stricken dog typically seeks solitude. The disease then progresses to one of two forms: paralytic (dumb) rabies and furious rabies.

In the dumb form, dogs act depressed, become insensitive to pain, and develop paralysis of the throat and jaw muscles. They salivate and drool. Because they can't swallow, it looks like something is stuck in their throat. Pets with dumb rabies usually fall into a coma and die within three to ten days of initial signs.

Furious rabies presents with the classic "mad dog" symptoms. Dogs become extremely vicious and violent, and any noise prompts attack. Such dogs snap and bite at real or imaginary objects and may roam for miles attacking anything in their path. They lose all fear of natural enemies and commonly chew or swallow inedible objects like stones or wood. Death occurs four to seven days after onset of clinical signs as a result of progressive paralysis.

Diagnosis of rabies can be accomplished only by microscopic examination of brain tissue from the suspect animal. This cannot be done while the animal is alive. Wild animals that act suspiciously, or attack humans or pets, should be euthanized immediately and the brain examined for evidence of rabies. Dogs bitten by an animal that cannot be tested for the disease should be considered exposed to rabies.

Each state establishes rules regarding rabies exposure in pets. Animals are thought to be infectious only shortly before and during the time they show symptoms. Therefore, animals capable of transmitting disease at the time of the bite will typically develop signs within a ten-day period. For that reason, ten days is the recommended period of quarantine.

Human health officials may require that any unvaccinated pet that bites a person be euthanized and tested for the disease. However, some local or state laws may allow an exposed pet to live under stringent quarantine for six months and, if no signs develop, be vaccinated prior to release. Recommendations for pets current on rabies vaccination who are exposed to the disease include immediate revaccination and strict owner control/observation for not less than 45 days.

Dogs who are fed a nutritious diet are more likely to lead healthier lives.

Non-core vaccines are elective, so your puppy is not required to receive them.

Prevent exposure and protect your dog and yourself by restricting roaming and keeping his rabies vaccination current. Any contact with wild animals acting in an abnormal behavior, including stray or feral cats or dogs, increases your risk. The core rabies vaccination not only protects your dog from possible disease, it also offers insurance that he won't be euthanized simply due to a suspicion of exposure.

The rabies virus is sensitive to many household detergents and soaps. Should you or your pet suffer a bite, thoroughly wash the wounds with soap and hot water to kill as much virus as possible, then consult a doctor/veterinarian immediately. The post-exposure vaccine available for people is virtually 100 percent effective when administered within the right period of time.

Non-Core Vaccines

Non-core, also called "elective," vaccines include vaccines that protect dogs against less common or less severe infections that are either self-limiting or treatable. Non-core vaccines should be given only to those individual dogs who have exposure to that given infectious agent. Deciding factors include age of the patient, such as puppy versus adult, geographic distribution of the disease, and lifestyle that varies from strict indoor to free-roaming animals. Most bacteria-protective vaccines give only about six months protection, which means these are not suited for a three-year protocol. The shots your pet receives must also be based on exposure risk. If your pup is never exposed to ticks, he'll likely not require a

Kennel cough can be contracted when dogs are exposed to crowded conditions or even just to another dog who has the illness.

Lyme vaccination. The guidelines encourage individual veterinary practices to designate which vaccines constitute core and which constitute non-core for their practice, based on a defined health risk assessment.

Based on the latest vaccination recommendations, puppies and adult dogs who are candidates for the following non-core vaccinations should receive them on the following schedule:

- **Bordetella:** begin at six to eight weeks of age, a second dose at 10 to 12 weeks; then annually

- **Combined Intranasal Parainfluenza and Bordetella:** first dose as early as three weeks, and second dose two to four weeks later; then annually

- **Leptospirosis:** one dose at 12 weeks of age, a second dose at 16 weeks; annually thereafter

- **Lyme Disease:** one dose at eight weeks of age, and a second dose at 12 weeks; annually thereafter

- **Parainfluenza:** begin at six to eight weeks of age, then every three to four weeks until 12 to 16 weeks of age; booster at one year of age, and then every three years

Many vaccines are combined for convenience, so that the puppy receives protection against several diseases with a single injection. The most common combinations are the DHPP or DA2PP, which stands for "distemper, hepatitis, parvovirus, parainfluenza" and is commonly used for the puppy's first series of vaccinations.

However, since not all these vaccines are necessary every year, the trend has become to vaccinate adult dogs with single-dose vaccines as needed. The vaccinations may be alternated so that the dog receives rabies one year and distemper and parvovirus vaccinations the next, and so on. The dog will need an annual wellness check whether vaccinations are due or not.

Kennel Cough (Bordetella, Parainfluenza, Adenovirus-2)

Canine infectious tracheobronchitis, generically referred to as kennel cough, is a highly contagious and common condition affecting dogs. The disease causes an inflammation of the dog's larynx, trachea, and bronchi (tubes leading to the lungs).

All dogs are susceptible, but the disease most often affects dogs exposed to crowded conditions, such as kennels (hence, the name), shows, or other stressful situation. Most cases cause only mild disease, with signs that tend to be more aggravating to owners than dangerous to the dog. But kennel cough in puppies can cause stunted lung development and/or develop into life-threatening pneumonia.

The disease can be caused by any one or a combination of several different infectious agents. The most common culprits are bacteria called *Bordetella bronchiseptica*, the canine parainfluenza virus, and the canine adenovirus-2 (CAV-2).

These agents, alone or in combination, attach themselves to the delicate hairlike cilia in the dog's trachea or actually cause the removal of the cilia. Cilia normally protect the tracheobronchial tract by clearing away irritants like bacteria and other microorganisms with wavelike motions similar to wind moving a grassy field. When they are destroyed, or the agent can't be dislodged from the remaining cilia, the protective mechanism breaks down, resulting in further irritation to the dog's respiratory tract.

Dogs with the disease suffer a chronic high-pitched honking cough. It can easily be prompted by excitement, drinking, or gentle pressure applied to the base of the dog's neck. The dog tugging at his leash may result in a paroxysm. Rarely, you'll also see nasal or eye discharge, and dogs may suffer a slight fever or loss of appetite. The signs can last from a few days to several weeks.

Infection spreads through the saliva and nasal secretions and may occur by direct nose-to-nose contact. However, coughing also transmits the agents through the air from one dog to another. Signs develop four to six days following exposure.

Diagnosis is based on the dog's recent history and clinical signs. Because the disease results in a vicious cycle of irritation that causes the cough, and coughing that causes further irritation, cough suppressants to relieve persistent coughing are very important. Antibiotics may be required when bacterial infections are involved. Anti-inflammatory drugs and bronchodilators that open breathing passages can help the dog breathe.

Bordetella usually isn't dangerous by itself but can predispose to secondary infection with other bacteria and result in pneumonia. Dogs can be infected without acting sick, yet transmit the organism simply by breathing, and infect other dogs. The bacteria can be cultured from nasal swabs. Treatment of this agent may require antibiotics given by nebulizer, because the bacteria attach to mucosal surfaces of the respiratory tract and can be difficult to reach.

Parainfluenza more often is involved in kennel cough. The vaccine will decrease the prevalence and severity but won't prevent the disease and probably will not be protective for a full year. It also won't eliminate the virus from nasal secretions, so dogs can still transmit infection to other canines.

The parainfluenza vaccination can combine with the distemper vaccination. An intranasal (nose drops) vaccine that includes the bordetella agent also is available. Because infection depends upon exposure, and the vaccine has limited protection, the bordetella

Multi-Dog Tip

Dog society is not a democracy, and treating all your canines equally could cause trouble in your peaceable kingdom. Be sure to give preferential treatment to the oldest resident dog in your home to communicate that the puppy should defer to him and not argue or cause problems. Do this by feeding the resident dog first, giving him attention first, and offering best/first access to prime resting spots, such as the sofa beside the owner.

and parainfluenza vaccinations are considered non-core.

Canine adenovirus-2 vaccination, however, is considered a core vaccine. In addition to some protection against kennel cough, it also cross-protects against canine adenovirus-1 (canine infectious hepatitis), an uncommon but devastating contagious illness that can kill puppies within hours.

Leptospirosis

This disease is caused by a spirochete, a type of spiral-shaped bacteria. Several varieties can cause leptospirosis in dogs: canicola, icterohemorrhagiae, grippotyphosa, and pomona. Dogs may be infected when livestock or wild animals pass the agents in their urine, contaminating food, soil, or water. Most infections are mild and cause no problem. However, leptospirosis is extremely contagious and can be transmitted from infected dogs to people. Fortunately, canine leptospirosis is relatively uncommon.

The bacterium infects the dog by entering through a break in the skin or when the dog swallows contaminated water or food. Drinking from standing water in a cattle pen or from mud puddles is a common route of infection.

Owners probably won't notice signs of mild disease. But following recovery, untreated dogs can become carriers, and they'll shed bacteria in their urine for as much as a year.

Common symptoms include low-grade fever with mild to moderate listlessness, loss of appetite, increased thirst, and increased urination. Pain in the kidneys causes the dog to walk in a hunched posture. In severe disease, diarrhea and vomiting develop, and mouth ulcers can make eating painful. The dog may have bloodshot eyes, reddened gums, and a brownish coating on the tongue. In rare cases, leptospirosis causes a generalized bleeding disorder that also affects the kidneys and liver, causing jaundice (yellow tinge to the eyes). The canicola and grippotyphosa serovars result in kidney damage most often, while the pomona and icterohemorrhagiae affect the liver. However, young dogs often show liver damage with any of these agents.

Diagnosis can usually be made by the signs themselves, and the disease is confirmed by finding the bacteria in the dog's urine or blood. When diagnosed early and treated aggressively, most dogs recover.

To reduce the chance for human infection, dogs usually must be hospitalized. When the dog returns home, owners should wash their hands thoroughly with soap and warm water after handling the dog. Confine the dog away from where you prepare and eat your meals.

The bacteria are killed and further organ damage arrested using a combination of antibiotic therapies, such as penicillin and streptomycin. Antibiotics may be required for several weeks to ensure that all the bacteria are eliminated. Diuretic drugs that promote urination help with the kidney failure. Supportive care such as fluid therapy to control dehydration, along with medication to help minimize vomiting and diarrhea, are often required. If hemorrhage is present, the dog may need a blood transfusion.

Vaccinations are available, but they do not combine all agents, and can be difficult to recommend based on geographic region. Only dogs at risk for infection are advised to receive this non-core vaccination. In addition, puppies less than 12 weeks of age may suffer mild-to-severe vaccination reactions, so vaccination is not recommended until after this age.

The best way to prevent leptospirosis in your dog is to prevent his opportunity for infection. Don't allow him to roam unsupervised, and provide fresh drinking water so he's less tempted to drink from contaminated puddles.

Lyme Disease

Lyme disease was first identified in 1975, when a cluster of childhood arthritis cases were reported in Lyme, Connecticut. It's caused by a spirochete bacteria, *Borrelia burgdorferi*, which occurs naturally in white-footed mice and deer. The organism is transmitted to people and dogs by ticks.

A number of tick species can carry the organism, but the deer tick is the most effective transmitter of the Lyme bacterium. It's found most commonly in the northeastern, north central, and Pacific Coast states.

Deer ticks mature in a two-year cycle, progressing from egg to larvae, nymph, and then adult. Adult ticks prefer to feed on deer, but immature stages feed on white-footed mice and sometimes other warm-blooded animals. The Lyme bacterium makes its home in deer and mice, which don't become sick but spread the disease to ticks at any stage when they feed on infected blood. Both the nymph and adult tick are able to transmit the disease to people and dogs and will make do with such victims when a preferred host isn't available.

Most dogs exposed to Lyme disease won't get sick. Blood tests can reveal if the dog has been exposed or is indeed infected. The most common sign of Lyme disease in dogs is a sudden lameness (limping) from painful, swollen joints. They may also run a fever. Diagnosis is based on the presence of these signs, a history of being in an endemic region, and blood tests. X-rays of the joints reveal swelling and fluid but without degenerative joint changes typical of arthritis. Antibiotics are most effective when given soon after onset of the symptoms and may be required for two to four weeks.

Deer ticks are found in high grass and weeds between the lawn and the woods, and pets and people that roam these areas are more likely to pick up ticks. Use veterinarian-approved tick repellents or insecticides. The tick must feed for 5 to 20 hours before the organisms will be transmitted into the host, so inspect your dog for ticks, and remove them promptly with tweezers to avoid exposing yourself. People don't become infected from their pets, but you can become sick by touching infected ticks, so wear gloves. The preventative non-core vaccine available for dogs may be recommended for those living in a Lyme disease endemic area.

Not Recommended Vaccines

Vaccinations may fall into the not recommended category if the disease is uncommon or not considered a problem, or if the vaccine has been shown to be dangerous or ineffective.

Coronavirus

Canine coronavirus (CCV) is a gastrointestinal disease most common in kennel situations,

Examine your dog for fleas and ticks after he's been playing outside.

and which usually causes only mild symptoms. The signs are most severe in puppies and may develop suddenly. Dogs become infected when they come into contact with sick dogs via oral secretions or droppings. Once the virus is swallowed, infection develops within one to three days. Many dogs show no signs, and the most serious cases occur when the puppy becomes infected with parvovirus at the same time.

Early signs include loss of appetite, vomiting, and depression. This is followed by loose to liquid diarrhea that may contain blood or mucus and that has a characteristic yellow-orange color and foul odor. Dehydration can develop quickly.

CCV infects a specific part of the lining of the small intestine. These hill-shaped structures, called villi, are covered with tiny hairlike projections (microvilli) that absorb nutrients. CCV infects the "hilltops" of the villi, compromising the body's ability to process food, which results in the diarrhea. The "valley" portion remains unaffected and is able to replace the tips about every three or four days. For that reason, the virus tends to produce only a mild to moderate, usually self-limiting disease. In most cases, dogs will recover within seven to ten days. The disease by itself rarely kills. However, dogs with intestinal parasites or parvovirus along with CCV can have up to a 90 percent mortality rate.

Diagnosis relies on symptoms, as no test can easily identify the virus. There is no specific treatment for CCV, but supportive care speeds recovery. Fluid therapy helps combat dehydration that often results from the vomiting and diarrhea. Antibiotics aren't generally prescribed because of the mild nature of the illness. Medication can help control the diarrhea and vomiting.

Prevention of the disease is best managed by avoiding contact with infected animals and their droppings. Sanitary procedures, such as picking up the yard and kennel area, help a great deal. The vaccine is not recommended, because coronavirus responds well to treatment and rarely is fatal.

Spaying or Neutering

Neutering, also called altering or sterilizing, is the surgical removal of an animal's reproductive organs. Neutering more specifically refers to males, while spaying refers to females. A male's testicles are removed in surgery, called a gonadectomy or castration. Spaying surgery (ovariohysterectomy) removes the female's reproductive organs.

Benefits of Neutering and Spaying

Neutering not only prevents the births of unwanted puppies, it reduces and in some cases eliminates certain health and behavioral problems. Excessive roaming and aggression, which can result in abscesses, excessive marking behavior, and embarrassing "mounting" behavior, are all greatly reduced in neutered dogs, making them better pets. Castration also eliminates any chance of testicular cancer, which accounts for up to seven percent of all canine tumors. Prostate problems are suffered by more than 60 percent of sexually intact male dogs over the age of five; neutering drastically reduces the chance of your dog ever having these problems.

Female dogs go into season, also called heat or estrus, twice a year, during which time they can become pregnant. Spaying eliminates the messy, bloody discharge as well as the dog's urge to jump the fence and seek out canine Romeos. It also removes the chance of cystic ovaries, false pregnancies, pyometra (uterine infection), and uterine cancer. In addition, spaying your dog before her first heat reduces the potential for mammary cancer by 90 percent or more.

APBT dogs do not need to become parents to feel "fulfilled," and the surgery won't change your dog's great personality or the breed's basic instincts. He'll still be a people-friendly, weight-pulling, varmint-chasing fool. Surgery may temper the dog's desire to aggress toward other dogs, but neutering and spaying should not be considered a magic cure-all.

To reap the greatest benefits, avoid behavior problems, and prevent unplanned puppies, dogs should ideally be neutered before reaching sexual maturity. Timing varies from dog to dog, but most male APBTs are able to reproduce by six to nine months of age. Females more likely go into season for the first time at about six months old but rarely are bred by the professionals until after two years of age (when proper health testing can be done).

Healthy dogs may be castrated or spayed at any time. The American Veterinary Medical Association (AVMA), American Kennel Club (AKC), and other organizations note that the procedure can be done safely on puppies as early as eight weeks of age. For puppies adopted from shelters, or for purebred pups not intended for the conformation ring, juvenile sterilization ensures that they will not be used for breeding, either intentionally or accidentally.

Research confirms that there's no adverse effect on the growth of the puppies. Those spayed or neutered prior to sexual maturity may grow a bit taller and leggier, though. Sexual hormones influence the way the dog's body matures and can promote the heavier musculature typical of the adult APBT. Veterinarians may recommend delaying sterilization until adulthood for performance/sporting dogs, which can be healthier for the joints.

Neutering and spaying are performed while the dog is under a general anesthesia. A combination of injectable drugs and/or inhalant anesthetics may be used. Depending on the pet, preanesthetic blood work may determine which anesthetic is best for the animal.

Your dog's stomach should be empty during the procedure to reduce the danger of aspiration. Inhaling foreign material can cause life-threatening complications, including pneumonia. For this reason, it's usually recommended that food and water be withheld for a period of time prior to the surgery. Should your dog sneak an unauthorized snack, tell the veterinarian so that appropriate precautions can be made or so the surgery can be delayed.

Puppy-Specific Illnesses

The APBT is a remarkably healthy breed. However, puppies can sometimes develop transient skin disease as a result of a tiny mange mite.

Demodex canis, a cigar-shaped microscopic mite, normally lives in the hair follicles of healthy dogs, and the immune system keeps the parasite in check. But in excess numbers, especially with immune-compromised dogs, the mite causes demodicosis, also called demodectic mange.

Puppies are infected the first two or three days after birth through close contact with an infected mother. You'll see one to five small, circular, red scaly areas of hair loss around the eyes and lips or on the forelegs, which may itch or not. It's diagnosed by finding the mite during microscopic examination of skin scrapings of affected tissue. Treatment may not be necessary, as most cases resolve by puberty.

Once the dog is anesthetized, the surgical site is prepared. Sterile procedures include removing the hair and disinfecting the area. The surgeon wears sterile gloves and uses sterile surgical instruments, and drapes the dog with sterile cloth or towels to keep the site clean.

Castration

The fur-covered sack seen between the male dog's rear legs is the scrotum, which contains the sperm-producing testicles. Each testicle connects to a spermatic cord that contains an artery and the spermatic duct. With small puppies, the veterinarian expresses each testicle through incisions in the scrotal sac. For larger dogs, a single 1- to 2-inch (3- to 5-cm) incision in front of the scrotum at the base of the dog's penis provides the exit from which each testicle will be expressed.

The doctor cuts free the testicles once the attached spermatic cords are tied with suture material to prevent bleeding. The stub of the spermatic cord recedes back into the surgical opening, leaving the scrotal sac empty. An antibiotic may be sprayed into the scrotal cavity, and scrotal incisions may be closed with internal stitches or skin glue. Male dogs that lick at the site may need an Elizabethan collar restraint that prevents them from bothering the incision until it heals. Other times, absorbable stitches close the incision from the underside and won't need to be removed. A routine castration takes 10 to 25 minutes of actual surgical time.

Spay

The spay constitutes major abdominal surgery. As with the boy dog, the procedure requires sterile techniques. Surgery is performed through an opening in the sterile drape positioned over the dog's shaved and scrubbed abdomen.

An inch-long incision below the "belly button" at the midline goes through the surface skin, a thin layer of fat, and then

Spaying a female dog will keep her from having puppies and has certain health benefits.

directly through the abdominal wall. Special instruments hold the incision open so the surgeon can see into the abdomen. A dog's Y-shaped uterus consists of an ovary attached to the top of each "horn," and an ovarian artery, vein, and nerve attached to each ovary. The spay hook (a long smooth metal instrument) inserted into the abdomen retrieves the uterus. The ovaries must be secured to prevent bleeding before being cut free, so that the stumps containing the artery, vein, and nerve fall back into the abdomen. Then the surgeon ties off the uterus just ahead of the cervix, cuts it free just beyond the tie, and removes the uterus and ovaries in one piece. Once the doctor ensures no bleeding, the uterine stump falls back into the abdomen and the incision is stitched closed. A routine spay takes about 15 to 25 minutes, possibly longer in large dogs, especially if they are already in heat, which can make bleeding worse.

Following the surgery, dogs may be held for only a few hours, or overnight for monitoring by the veterinarian. Until the anesthesia wears off, dogs often act drunk or disoriented but typically are fully awake and functional within an hour or so of the surgery. Your dog's activities should be restricted for two or three days following the surgery. Outdoor dogs should be kept inside for several days and then prevented from lying in dirt until the incision has healed. The neutered dog doesn't need to see the veterinarian again unless there's a problem.

Postneutering difficulties are rare, but monitor the incision site for inflammation or swelling. See the veterinarian about any discharge or puffiness at the surgery site. Most problems are minor and involve the dog licking the incision. Puppies tend to bounce back much more quickly from spay and neuter surgery than adult dogs do.

Ear Cropping

Otoplasty, commonly called cropping, refers to the practice of surgically altering the shape of the dog's pinna—the external ear flap. The procedure may be done to correct congenital defects or damage from injury or disease. More commonly, the procedure simply alters the dog's ear for purely cosmetic reasons when the breeder or owner prefers a particular look.

Ear cropping has been banned in many European countries but continues to be

Retained Testicles

The testicles of male puppies are generally descended from the abdomen into the scrotal sack by ten days after birth. Puppies that fail to have their testicles descend by eight weeks of age are said to be cryptorchid. Having only one testicle retained is called monorchid. Occasionally, the organs will descend by six months of age.

Cryptorchid dogs are sterile, but monorchid dogs may be able to father puppies. This isn't considered a good idea, though, since the condition can be inherited. Dogs with a retained testicle cannot be shown in conformation, and surgically moving the organ into the scrotum is considered unethical.

Dogs with this inherited condition have a 13 times greater incidence of tumors in that retained testicle. Both testicles must be removed to prevent unwanted sexual behaviors. The veterinarian must go into the abdomen to remove retained testicles.

Today, the APBT's breed standard accepts dogs with natural ears.

performed in the United States on select dog breeds in order to fit the historical or preferred standard. In terms of APBT history, the dogs had their ears cropped short to reduce the chance of them being injured during fights. The procedure also served to accentuate the broad look of the muscled cheeks and head. Today, the APBT breed standard accepts dogs with either natural or cropped ears.

The surgery, typically performed on eight- to ten-week-old puppies once they've had two or three of their puppy shots, requires general anesthesia and the expertise of a veterinary surgeon familiar with APBT standards. Once trimmed, the cut edge of the ear receives stitches, and ointment must be applied until the stitches are removed.

Aftercare (also known as splinting, racking, or wrapping) trains the ear to properly stand up and can be expensive and labor-intensive, especially for a "show" (tall) crop. Poor management after the surgery can ruin the ears. Medication to relieve postoperative pain is recommended.

The practice of surgically altering the conformation of a dog's ears is expensive and painful and, frankly, is unnecessary. Unless you plan to show your dog, ear cropping shouldn't even be considered. Please consult with your veterinarian, and consider your own motives, before putting your puppy through this elective procedure.

CHAPTER 4

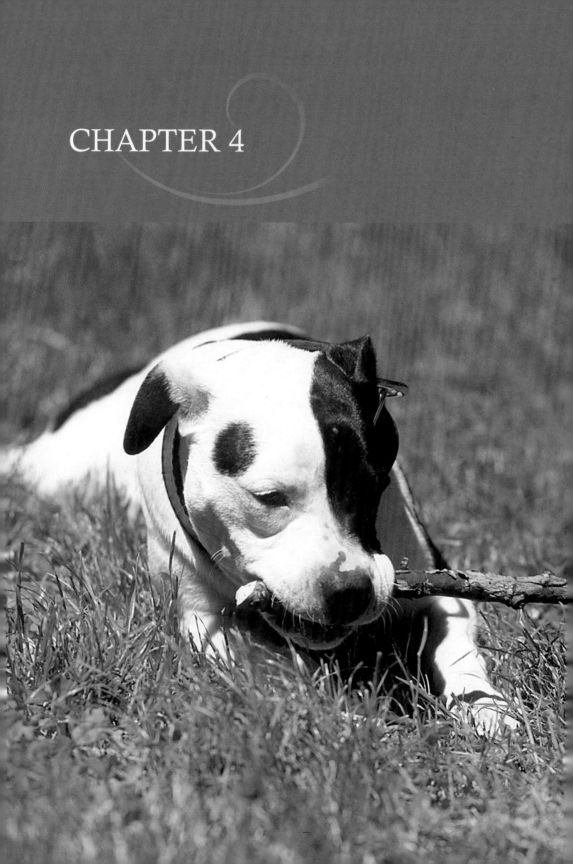

TRAINING YOUR AMERICAN PIT BULL TERRIER PUPPY

We've all fallen in love with a particular dog and as a result have chosen to bring that breed into our life. It goes beyond the regal good looks of the American Pit Bull Terrier, or the goofy clownlike grin, or the nonstop playful attitude. The APBT dogs who have impressed you most likely have terrific canine manners, have at least some basic training, and are great ambassadors of their breed. Your puppy has that same potential, but no baby dog comes preprogrammed.

Despite what you may have been told, dogs are not born willing to please us. In order for your puppy to want to please you, he needs to know there's something good in it for him. That might be a treat, or extra attention, or a game—but once you've connected and he figures out there's a great benefit to being around you and pleasing you, he'll want to find ways to make you happy. That makes him happy, too.

It takes effort and energy to raise an APBT puppy right. And because of breed prejudice and preconceived negative connotations of the breed, you must be even more conscientious to help your puppy become the best behaved and well-trained dog he can be. Training not only allows him to become a better companion, but it could also save his life.

INTRODUCTION TO TRAINING

The word *training* conjures images of a dog able to fetch a beverage from the refrigerator, win an obedience match, or bark protectively at an intruder. That's too narrow a focus, however. Even dogs who will never compete in a training contest require training—yes, I said "require." This isn't up for debate. Every single dog on the planet, and American Pit Bull Terriers in particular, need training to learn how to be good companions.

Training simply means acceptable behavior. What's acceptable to you may be different from what's acceptable to me or to your neighbor. You have a responsibility to first train your APBT puppy so that he fits your expectations of a good companion. And second, he should be trained to meet your community's standards of what constitutes a "good dog." At the very least, that should include walking nicely on a leash and following your voice commands for restraint and polite behavior.

Why Is Training Important?

When he's still a baby, it may be hard to imagine that someday very soon he'll tip the scales at 60 pounds (27 kg). An American Pit Bull Terrier is a powerful canine. And despite his intelligence, you don't want him making decisions for you. That would be like allowing your four-year-old child to run the household. It's vital that you be in charge, establish guidelines, and teach your dog what's expected.

Even a sweet-tempered dog can be dangerous if he doesn't have good dog manners. The sweet little old lady next door won't appreciate

Training not only allows your APBT to become a better companion, but it could also save his life.

being mugged by a leaping canine intent on kissing her cheek, especially if he knocks her down and breaks her hip in the process.

It's all about expectations and what I like to call *p'etiquette*. Your dog doesn't have to be an obedience star, but he certainly should understand the house rules and abide by them. A dog who swipes food off the table isn't welcome as a visitor. He may seem cute when he rushes out the door at eight weeks of age, but an adult who pushes you off balance is at best rude and at worst a potential cause for injury. The "cute" factor only protects puppies, and you want your dog to be welcome and an enjoyable member of the family all his life. Puppies learn very quickly, and teaching your dog at this age sets him up for a lifetime of success. Training him and rewarding your pup for doing the right thing can be a powerful bonding experience for you both. He learns how to please you—and training gives you both that opportunity to enjoy how smart he is.

More than that, a big dog can pull you off your feet if he hasn't learned how to properly walk on a leash. Training commands such as "stay" and "come" could save your dog's life by keeping him out of a busy street where he could be hit by a car, or for calling him away from dangerous temptations. He'll also need to be handled by your veterinarian for routine care. Training not only is a safety issue for you but also for your dog.

Finally, every time your American Pit Bull Terrier appears in public, he's being judged as an example of the breed. Sadly, these days the public often looks for the worst in any Pit Bull. It's vital that your puppy not only have good basic manners but that he be able to conduct himself well in public. Whether or not he makes a good impression can impact his own well-being and that of other APBTs in your community.

Positive training rewards a dog for performing a command correctly.

The Importance of Positive Training

In the past, we trained dogs by waiting to catch them doing something wrong and then punished for the behavior. For instance, we'd yell, slap, or otherwise punish the puppy for wetting on the carpet. This old style incorporated coercion and physical techniques that pushed or pulled a dog into the "sit" position or jerked a choke/slip collar to make him follow on leash. Some even employed electronic collars that use a remote-controlled shock to "tell" the dog he'd done something wrong.

Technically, a "punishment" reduces the frequency of a particular behavior, and the type that most people think of is "positive punishment"—which adds something that the dog hates, like being slapped or shocked. Theoretically, using positive punishment teaches the puppy when his behavior is unacceptable.

Over the years, though, we've learned that dogs taught using positive punishment tend to mind only when on leash or wearing the shock collar, out of fear of reprisals. They learn something you never intended—to dislike training and maybe even dislike the trainer (you!). Depending on the temperament of your puppy, corporal punishment also can prompt him to fight back out of fear or retaliation. That's training that no APBT (or any dog!) should experience.

Positive punishment also teaches "avoidance behaviors." The puppy who gets yelled at or hit for not coming when called learns to stay away so he won't get slapped. Being punished for pottying in the wrong place teaches the pup to "go" only when you aren't around to see it, and to hide the deposit better.

However, there's nothing wrong with including consequences with training. For instance, "negative punishment" can be used very effectively and humanely because it involves *depriving* the dog of something he likes. That's no different from taking away your children's cell phones if they don't behave properly. So, for instance, you might ask your puppy to "sit" before you open the door—and each time he gets up, you close the door (negative punishment) until he's able to stay in the sit. Then you reward him by opening the door.

Force Isn't Necessary

The best way to train your dog is to encourage him to want to please you. Don't you learn things more easily when you enjoy the process and want to learn? Dogs are no different. Rather than focusing on coercion and forcing the dog to do our will, owners should teach puppies they get good things (praise, attention, toys, treats) by behaving well. You become the leader in your household when your dog chooses to follow your requests without any need for intimidation or force.

On top of that, dogs don't have the same memory of a "bad" behavior as people do. To him, stealing your peanut butter sandwich isn't wrong—he just took advantage of the opportunity when you left it within reach on the coffee table. And after he's snarfed it down and runs to meet you coming out of the bedroom, if you express anger, he'll think it's for running to meet you, which he just did (not for eating the food, which is already in the past). It's your fault, actually, because you failed to supervise and keep him from making the mistake. Preventing problems is the best choice, and giving your puppy every excuse to do the *right* thing is even better. Create opportunities for him to succeed, and he'll thrive.

How to Find a Trainer

One of the best ways to find a dog trainer is to ask for recommendations and then visit the facility and watch the trainer in action. Your veterinarian may be able to recommend someone in your community. Veterinary behaviorists who deal with problem behaviors may also be good candidates for helping with training, or they may be able to recommend professional trainers they work with.

There is no universal accreditation for dog trainers. Anyone can set up a dog training business and call themselves an expert. Every dog is an individual, and a cookie-cutter approach to training may actually limit your dog's potential. Avoid those who use shock collars or other coercive punishment methods. Unrealistic promises ("will train in one visit!") should raise a red flag. You're training your puppy for a lifetime together, and it takes commitment and time—a magic wand approach to training will disappoint.

Multi-Dog Tip

Dogs pattern behavior by watching other canines. If your adult dogs behave nicely, and you put them through their training paces in front of Junior, the puppy learns more quickly. But adult dogs also can teach bad habits, so brush up on the resident dog's manners, too.

You'll want someone who has experience with American Pit Bull Terriers and who takes a positive approach to training. Figure out what you want out of the training: basic good manners? Or to eventually compete in canine trials? Fit the trainer to the skill set you wish for your dog. A number of highly skilled trainers are able to take your puppy into their program on a "send away," in which he lives with them for a period of time and is trained. However, for a pet dog, the best programs teach *you* how to train. After all, you must live with your dog and will need to know how to motivate him to behave correctly, even when the professional isn't there.

A training class may benefit your new APBT puppy.

Some of the pet product chain stores offer training classes. These trainers typically go through the company program to learn how to train. Your local animal welfare or APBT rescue organizations also may provide trainers to work with dogs privately or in classes.

Professional Associations

Two professional dog-training associations also can provide a list of member trainers in your area. The Association of Pet Dog Trainers (APDT) (www.apdt.com) promotes "dog friendly training techniques" and the National Association of Dog Obedience Instructors (NADOI) (www.nadoi.org) promotes "humane, effective training methods." In addition, the dog division of the International Association of Animal Behavior Consultants (IAABC) (www.iaabc.org) includes many members who not only specialize in behavior issues but also offer training classes. These organizations certify members by measuring competency, holding them to specific standards, and requiring continuing education.

When you visit prospective trainers, ask if they hold membership in a professional organization such as APDT, NADOI, or IAABC. Ask about continuing education. While a trainer with many years' experience can be a great benefit, you also want the trainer of your dog to be current on canine learning science.

SOCIALIZATION

To be good pets, all puppies require early-age "socialization." That's a fancy way of describing how they learn to interact with the world around them, including with other pets and people. Puppies need to know how to develop positive relationships with other animals and the humans in their life.

The prime socialization period is a narrow window during babyhood when learning the "wrong" lessons or failing to learn the right lessons can emotionally cripple the pet. Proper socialization teaches dogs social and communication skills and how to identify acceptable and unacceptable members of the canine clan. The age when pups are most

Socialization with other dogs is critically important for your APBT.

receptive is six to eight weeks old. During this time, mother animals teach many lessons by example. For instance, if Mom-Dog becomes hysterical around men, her pups pay attention and copy her behavior. Socialization continues on through 16 weeks and even up to eight months in some cases.

Your puppy needs to have a comfort level with what he'll experience in life. If he feels fearful, a dog reacts either by running away or attacking. Neither is a good option. Socialization gives him the experience he needs to handle even strange or uncomfortable experiences in a positive way.

People raising litters must begin positive lessons before the babies go to new homes. Youngsters have an increased capacity for learning when they're young, so it's helpful for new owners to continue these lessons for several weeks after adopting a pup. It's vital that the babies be exposed to positive experiences with other pets and people if they are to accept them as part of their "family" and become loving, well-adjusted pets. But socializing never ends—reminder lessons must be taught throughout the rest of your dog's life.

How to Socialize

Random experiences are not enough to accomplish good socialization. It needs to be a priority in your puppy's training, and set up in a methodical way. The key is to provide your puppy with repeated, reproducible positive experiences. Use toys, treats, and games to ensure that the baby understands that these events in his life mean good stuff, especially for him—and in that way, he'll generalize the experience for the future.

If you have more than one puppy, be sure to socialize individually. Certainly they can play together, but they'll need independent training to most benefit from these exercises.

Exposing the pup to new things does not mean you force him into a frightening situation. If he tries to run away, tucks his tail, or snaps at you, *do not* try to comfort him. That actually rewards him for acting scared. Instead, change his attitude by tossing a toy or getting him interested in a game. You want to start out at a distance from a potentially scary thing and gradually move him closer, while encouraging with praise and treats. If he's scared, back away and take the process more slowly. End the experience with a paaaarrr-teeeeeeee of special treats and happy praise!

Keep a pocketful of special treats handy that he gets only during socialization exercises. Or if he's particularly toy-motivated, reserve a favorite toy for the exercises. Then each person he meets should be given the toy or treat to offer to your pup—and suddenly, he learns that meeting a new person isn't scary but is a marvelous adventure with fun just for him.

Think about all the different situations he'll encounter, and plan for them. You'll want him to meet all different kinds of people: people of various ages (infants, toddlers, adults, old people), ethnic backgrounds, and sexes; bald people and people with beards; people who speak with accents or in another language; people wearing hats, long skirts, and uniforms (postal workers, police); people with canes and people moving in wheelchairs; and on and on. For your APBT puppy, socializing to a mix of different people is vital, so that he recognizes them all as safe and fun to interact with. Once he's interacting happily with individuals, you'll want to have him meet several people at once

so he's also used to that experience.

Build on your puppy's natural curiosity. If you react in a positive way with a "look at that! Isn't it fun?!" attitude, he'll be more likely to be willing to explore that bicycle, or the vacuum cleaner. Give him opportunity to sniff all kinds of things and to walk on and explore a variety of surfaces, from grass to gravel, from sand to pavement, from carpet to linoleum. Don't forget stairs or trips in the car. Expose him to interesting sounds, from soft to loud. Many dogs develop a fear

Expose your APBT puppy to a variety of experiences and situations to better socialize him.

of fireworks or thunderstorms, for example. So when the thunder booms, jolly him along and throw a party with lots of treats for each loud noise.

Similarly, ensure that your APBT puppy gets to meet and play with other dogs during this period. This is the time to get him used to interacting with his own species, learning dog "language" and respect for his elders. While the breed tends toward dog-on-dog aggression, most youngsters are tolerant at this age and can learn how they're expected to act and react around other canines. During puppy socialization, you can help moderate his tendency toward aggression. Have him meet puppies his own size and age, as well as friendly adult dogs. The key is that the other dog (or cat—don't forget other pets!) must be friendly. A bad experience with another dog at this age could cause problems for him in the future. A good puppy kindergarten class can be very helpful for socializing him to other dogs.

PUPPY KINDERGARTEN

A puppy class can be a wonderful benefit for your new American Pit Bull Terrier baby. Puppy kindergarten offers instruction in teaching basic commands. It may also provide help with housetraining. But more than anything else, puppy kindergarten offers structured socialization classes for your puppy.

Veterinary clinics often offer puppy kindergarten classes to clients. Trainers also may provide classes for puppies. As when choosing a trainer, be sure you feel comfortable with the situation. Visit the organization and watch a class in session to see how the trainer interacts with owners and the puppies. Often the pups are divided into age and/or size groupings

so that very large pups don't overwhelm smaller breeds.

Because puppies are more susceptible to contagious diseases, cleanliness is vital. Floors should be kept clean and disinfected before and after each class. The training center should also require proof of vaccination and good health from the veterinarian. It's best for your puppy to have received at least two boosters in the series of puppy shots before interacting with other dogs. For a kindergarten class, the pups shouldn't be older than about 18 weeks.

The class should be run by a trainer who understands dog behavior, how socialization works, and positive ways to teach the babies as well as the owners. You know how much trouble your little pup can generate, and just imagine a room full of juvenile delinquent puppies. Be sure that the class you choose has enough trainers for all the dogs. One trainer for every three to five pups is about right.

When introduced correctly, your puppy will enjoy spending time in his crate.

CRATE TRAINING

As dog owners, we hate the thought of "caging" our new puppy. However, most dogs actually feel more secure in a small, enclosed denlike area, and a crate can be a terrific tool for your American Pit Bull Terrier puppy.

When introduced correctly, your puppy will welcome and even enjoy spending time in his crate. It will be used as a bed, a retreat to get away from other pets or pestering children, and a safe place to keep him out of trouble when you aren't able to watch him. In addition, most dogs will be required to be confined at some point in their life—at the vet, for instance. So already knowing about and accepting a crate should be part of your puppy's training. It is one of the best tools available when housetraining your puppy.

How to Crate Train

The ideal crate should be just large enough for your puppy to go inside, turn around, and lie down to sleep. It can be a solid, hard plastic container or a wire mesh cage. Large crates are available with partitions for you to "shrink" it to puppy size and then enlarge the area as your puppy grows.

The best way to introduce your puppy to the crate is to make it the happiest place in your home. Open the door and leave it open so that he can explore the area. Toss a toy or treat inside, and encourage him to go get it. You want him to have positive experiences with the crate.

A great technique for making your APBT puppy want to spend time inside is to use a toy that can be stuffed with a smelly, tasty treat. This should be a special treat that he gets *only* when inside the crate. Show it to him, let him smell and taste the treat, and then toss it inside the crate and shut the door—with the puppy *outside* the crate. You want him to know that

By the Numbers

When housetraining, timing is key. Simply take the baby to an appropriate place to eliminate after each nap, meal, and playtime, and praise him when he produces. Puppy capacity varies by age, so remember that a two-month-old pup needs a break about every two hours; at three months, take a break every four hours; four-month-old pups can wait five hours; five-month-olds about six hours. By the time your dog is seven months old, he should be able to wait about eight hours.

the most scrumptious thing in the world is inside, out of paw-reach. And after he's begged and scratched and whined to get inside, open the door and let him get the toy. Allow him to chew and enjoy it for five minutes with the door shut.

If he fusses and wants to get out, he can come out—but the treat stays inside. Over a week's period or so, increase the length of time that puppy stays inside the crate with the treat toy.

HOUSETRAINING

Your puppy, like all animals, needs to eliminate. Housetraining simply teaches him the proper location to defecate and urinate (outside the house) and how to tell you he needs a potty break.

Puppies aren't born knowing what's right and wrong regarding elimination. All he knows is that his body tells him he must squat and pee or poop in order to feel good. Without proper instruction, he'll simply empty himself whenever his body signals "now," and never mind that he's on your bed at that moment in time.

Bathroom accidents might not seem a terrible problem while he's a baby. But an adult leaves much larger deposits. It's unsanitary and plain bad manners to "go" inside the house.

How to Housetrain

By three weeks of age, most puppies instinctively begin eliminating away from the "nest" on their own. Five-week-old puppies choose a general area for their potty, and by nine weeks, they return to an even more specific place time after time.

The best way to train good potty behavior is to predict when he needs to go, get to the right spot on time, and confine and/ or supervise him to prevent "accidents." Young pups need to "go" right after waking up, eating, drinking, playing, or being released from confinement. To prevent night accidents, the last meal should be finished three to five hours before bedtime.

A two-month-old pup needs a break about every two hours. At three months, every four hours should be adequate. Four-month-old pups can wait five hours, five-month-olds about six hours, and by the time your dog is seven months old, he should be able to wait about eight hours.

If you're not able to watch the puppy, confine him to prevent accidents. Because pups are naturally clean and don't like sleeping or living with their own waste, he'll learn very quickly to tell you when he needs to get out of his crate. Use the crate as a bed, and confine your puppy when he can't be watched, and he'll be more likely to cry and "tell" you he needs to use the bathroom so you'll let him out. An alternative is to hook a leash to his collar and the other end to your belt, so he can't sneak off to do a dirty deed in a hidden room.

Circling and nose-to-ground sniffing mean he needs to go. If necessary, carry the puppy to the right spot. Pups tend to "hold it" as long as they're being held but may dribble or make a deposit on the way to the door if moving under their own power. Even if he doesn't act like he needs to potty, make sure he's in the designated area within 15 minutes of eating, awaking from a nap, or playing, or he's likely to find a handy spot under your piano bench when you aren't looking. Designate one specific area of your yard for the pup's toilet, and be sure to take

Take your puppy outside as soon as he gives you a clue that he has to potty.

him to the same spot every single time. The scent will help cue him as to what he needs to do.

As he poses, give him a cue word to learn, something like "potty" or "hurry," so he associates the command with doing his business. Trainers swear that pups eight weeks and older can learn a "potty" command within a week. Once he's productive, praise him profusely! Tell him what an intelligent, beautiful dog he is, so that he has no doubt you're pleased. Once the pup has gone to the bathroom, allow some playtime as a reward. You can even have a special treat or toy reserved for him being successful, so that you can pay him for emptying his bladder or bowels in the right spot.

After play, bring him back into the house. It's a good idea to have a designated "safe area," such as the kitchen or a small bathroom with floors that are easily cleaned, for his indoor play area.

Don't punish your puppy for housetraining mistakes.

Accidents

If you find a puddle or pile but didn't see him leave it, roll up a newspaper and hit *yourself* in the head three times for not paying attention. Puppies won't know why you're upset—they won't connect the deed with your concern—unless you catch them in the act. Angry shouts or punishment makes dogs fearful, so they hide deposits, because after all, a puppy has to go. So the best way to handle accidents is to simply clean them up without comment to the dog—no treat, no attention. And then promise yourself to pay closer attention so that the pup doesn't have the opportunity to make a mistake.

Puppies learn very quickly, and it's less "mean" to teach him rules to live by while he's a youngster. The same housetraining rules work for adult dogs, but it can take months rather than days or weeks for untrained adult dogs to become faithful to an outdoor bathroom.

Dogs can detect minute chemical scents humans can't fathom. Simply mopping up the mess may satisfy your nose, but the smell lures pets back to the scene of the crime to repeat the dirty deed, time after time. Urine soaked into carpet proves particularly difficult to remove.

Training Treats

A treat for a puppy needs to be only a tiny taste, perhaps the size of the tip of your little finger. Rewards are as much about positive attention as they are actual food rewards. The ideal treat smells and tastes very strong so that size doesn't matter.

With fresh accidents, pick up the solids and blot up as much liquid as possible. Then use a product that neutralizes the chemicals that smell bad. Urine is composed of sticky urea, urochrome (the yellow color), and uric acid. The first two can be washed away, but uric acid is nearly impossible to dissolve and remove from surfaces.

A number of excellent products are available from pet product outlets or your veterinary office. Some of my favorites include products that use live bacteria to eliminate any organic material left behind by your pets. Others employ an enzyme that breaks down and neutralizers the odor, digests urine molecules, or "encapsulate" the odors.

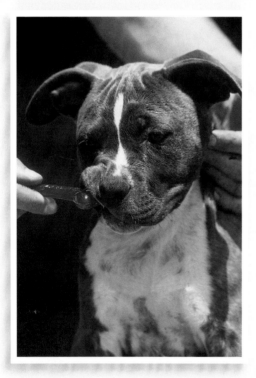

You can lure your dog to do what you want by tempting him with a favorite toy or treat.

BASIC TRAINING

Puppies are little sponges, absorbing information and learning at an incredible rate. Don't waste this wonderful opportunity to teach your Pit Bull baby. Whether you set up formal training sessions or not, a puppy begins to learn from the moment he sets paw in your home. So make sure you're dishing up the good stuff, so that he has basic obedience commands learned as quickly as possible. It's as much about him learning how to learn, and enjoying the process, as becoming adept at specific commands. And by six to eight weeks of age, your puppy can easily learn basic commands and wow your friends.

Use of "No"

While it's very tempting to use negatives—to shout "no!" when he does something wrong—try to avoid using this word. It's so overused that some puppies begin to believe that "no" is their name. Instead of resorting to a "no," try to find opportunities to say "yes!" and encourage the puppy in an alternate behavior. For instance, if he grabs your shoe and runs to get you to chase him, be strong. Instead of yelling "no" and giving him what he wants (a game of keep-away), pick up one of his toys and run the other way, pretending it's the very best thing in the world. As soon as he drops your shoe and approaches, say "Yes!" and give him the legal toy. Look for opportunities to reward good behavior and replace bad choices with acceptable ones.

How Long?

Puppies have short attention spans. Several short training sessions of about five to ten minutes each will be more successful than a single marathon training time. Set up a schedule so that you know your puppy has the energy and eagerness to learn. A good time is

All dogs should know the basic obedience commands.

before meals, because you can use a portion of his meals as treat rewards during training, without upsetting his nutrition.

Lure and Clicker Training

Your baby may not look like it now, but when he's an adult, your APBT will be so strong that if he doesn't want to sit, down, stand, or stay, you can't make him. Trying to push or pull your dog into a particular posture gets you canine looks that translate, "Are you nuts?" Think about it—what do you do if somebody leans or pushes against you? Or heaven forbid, hits you or jerks you by the neck? To keep from giving ground, the natural tendency prompts you to counter the pressure and push back. Pull on the leash, the dog tugs against the effort. Besides, the APBT's eagerness to please makes punishment training unnecessary.

So how do you get your puppy to assume the position? You let him think it's *his* idea. And instead of arguing or trying to force him to do something, find out what he wants most, and then control access to that treat, toy, or water-hose. You can be the natural leader by controlling access without acting bossy or mean.

Luring

A highly effective and positive training method employs luring the dog into the desired behavior. This works very quickly. Instead of waiting for the puppy to "sit," you use a toy or favorite treat to lure him into position—and then reward with the toy or treat once he's done what you request. The technique teaches dogs to respond to commands, listen, and react to people; it teaches you to watch and react appropriately to your dog. Require your dog to earn privileges and positive rewards, and he'll turn himself inside out to please you. He'll want to learn and will enjoy interacting with you, and your relationship with your dog will blossom.

Clicking

Another effective and humane training technique allows your puppy to teach himself, somewhat by trial and error. Instead of waiting for your APBT to do something wrong, look for opportunities to catch him in the act of doing something *right*, and then reward the behavior with something he likes. Trainers "capture" the desired behavior with a cue word or sound—such as "yes!" or a click-sound from a clicker. This requires "loading" the clicker so that the dog quickly identifies the sound with a forthcoming reward.

1. Fill a small bowl with high-value treats, such as liver bits or tiny slices of hotdog. These don't have to be large—the smaller the better, so that you don't unbalance the dog's nutrition. Mostly, you want him to appreciate the smell and flavor but leave him wanting more.
2. Sit on the floor with the bowl between your knees to control access. Hold the clicker in one hand, while readying a treat in the other. Click the clicker, see that the dog's ears twitch or he otherwise acknowledges the sound, and immediately give him a treat.
3. Repeat a dozen or more times. Click-treat. Click-treat. Click-treat. Very quickly, the dog will start to look to your treat hand as soon as he hears the click—and that means he's made the connection. He's learned that the sound of the "click" means a treat for him.
4. Now you can use the sound of the "click" to communicate with your dog. The sound tells him a "sit" (click-treat) is the behavior

The sit command is one of the easiest behaviors to teach a dog.

you want.
5. Dogs learn to understand cause and effect (their action makes you click-treat) very quickly. Before long, your dog will volunteer all sorts of behaviors in an attempt to make you click and give a treat. He wants to learn, because he knows that *he* controls the treat and can turn you into a treat-dispenser once he figures out what you want. So the dog spends time doing just that—trying to please you. Don't you perform better when you anticipate being paid for a good effort?

BASIC OBEDIENCE COMMANDS

There are four must-know commands for all dogs, and they're quite easy to train. It's a good idea to teach one command at a time, until your puppy understands the concept, before moving on to the next challenge. Thereafter, you can use the skill he already knows to end each training session on a positive note.

Automatic Check-In

A great exercise that proves helpful in teaching any command is an automatic check-in. Some trainers teach a "look-at-me" command, but it can be even more effective when your dog learns to do this on his own without prompting. Dogs should look to owners and pay attention, frequently checking in to be sure they're following the owner's direction. A puppy or dog who goes his own way is more likely to get into trouble and not know how to handle unexpected situations. The automatic check-in can be taught pretty much anytime, anywhere, but it's best to try for three to five repeats at a time. That way your puppy actually has the light bulb go off and realizes that his action has a consequence. Your puppy can control what happens.

1. Find what floats your puppy's boat—toy or special treat. It can be the same reward you use for other training exercises.
2. Choose a word or sound—"Yes!" or the click from a clicker—to act as the marker for your puppy having done the exercise correctly.
3. As you walk around the house or the yard, watch your puppy. The minute he makes eye contact with you (and I mean the *instant!*), mark the behavior with a "click" or "Yes!" and then give him the treat or toy.
4. Continue the exercise. Remember, this is an automatic behavior that your puppy controls. Don't say his name, or squeak the toy, or otherwise draw his attention. You want this to be purely at the pup's discretion—and when he makes eye contact, *immediately* mark the behavior and reward.
5. He can make eye contact from a distance, but more likely he'll come close to you to

Teaching your puppy to pay attention to you will help with his training.

be near the reward. And that helps him learn that there are great benefits for him to constantly return to you (even without being asked to "come") and to make eye contact. This comes in handy when teaching the "come" command.

Come

A solid recall—coming when called—can be a safety issue for your puppy. Baby dogs can be incredibly curious, and without constant supervision and direction, they can get into life-threatening trouble. You need to be able to call him away from danger. For instance, if the neighbor child stops by to play and forgets to latch the gate, your puppy could wander onto the highway or chase a squirrel out of the yard. Since those four little puppy legs move much faster than you, there's absolutely no way to catch him if he wants to run away. So teaching him to come when called keeps him safely within reach.

Dogs fail to come for a variety of reasons. They may not know their name or don't understand what "come" means, or running and playing or chasing that squirrel simply is more fun. Too often, we teach them *not* to come, because when they finally do, we act upset or (horrors!) punish them. Never punish when your puppy comes no matter how long it's taken him to respond. Here's how to teach your puppy to come on command.

1. Find what type of incentive (toy, treat) gets him excited. If your puppy would rather be rewarded with a game of tug or chase the squeaky toy, reserve that game for your training reward and don't offer it any other time.

2. It's best to have a training session when he has no other distractions, at least initially. Find a time when the kids aren't around and the yard or house is quiet.

3. Call his name to get his attention, and let him sniff the treat or hear the toy squeak.

4. When you practice a command that requires your puppy to move, it's a good rule of paw to use his name. That not only gets his attention, it can help cue him to the type of request you'll give. For commands that don't require him to move or that actually need for him to stay in a particular position, use only the command. Again, doing this consistently helps him identify the type of request you give him.

5. Once he's focused on you and the reward, say "[Name], *come!*"—and then *run* away from him in the opposite direction. Puppies can rarely resist the urge to chase.

6. When he gets close enough, either hand or toss him the treat, and praise him for being such a smart doggy. Throw him a party, with petting and happy talk, so he knows without a doubt that he's pleased you.

7. Repeat the exercise three to five times in a row, and stop before he gets tired of the game. You want to leave him wanting more.

Sit

A "sit" is a great default command that every puppy should know. It's easy for the dog to learn and can be a great way to control otherwise exuberant outbursts. As long as his tail sticks to the ground, he can't get into trouble by wandering around and sticking his nose where it doesn't belong. Teach your puppy a "sit" as a polite greeting and as puppy currency for paying his way for bigger rewards. In other words, your puppy should understand that nothing in life

Want to Know More?

For advanced training commands, see Chapter 9: American Pit Bull Terrier Training.

A dog in the down position is signaling that he's calm and means no harm.

s free and he must be willing to play by your
ules to get what he wants. So if he wants to go
out the door, he should pay with a "sit" first.
Before he gets his bowl of food, have him sit and
then reward with the meal. If he wants to play
etch and brings his ball, ask for a "sit" before
ndulging in the game. This keeps you in control
and subtly reinforces your dog's position as a
amily member that must get along with you and
other humans. There are a couple of ways you
an teach a "sit."

Lure Training

Lure training uses a high-value reward (treat
or toy) to gently guide your puppy into the sit
position.

1. For lure training, stand in front of your
   puppy and say, "Sit."
2. Lift the lure upward, right in front of
   his nose and over the top of his head so
   that he must lift his head to follow the

movement. As his nose follows the treat,
his butt must hit the ground to keep from
falling over.

3. As soon as his tail touches down, give him
   the treat or toy reward.
4. Repeat this exercise multiple times
   each day. Within a short time, the pup
   learns that he can shortcut to the treat by
   simply planting his bottom as soon as you
   say "sit," rather than waiting to be lured.
5. Eventually, use the word *sit* and the same
   hand gesture but without the lure. He'll
   recognize the action and word, do the
   behavior, and then get the reward from you.
   The goal is for him to learn to recognize the
   command and perform the action with or
   without a treat present.

Clicker Training

Clicker training/shaping the behavior allows
the puppy to naturally sit (as with the

automatic check in) and then rewards him for the action.

For clicker training:

1. Have your treats and clicker handy. Then simply watch for your puppy to sit on his own. Click as soon as his bottom touches, and toss him the treat.
2. He'll likely look confused after he gobbles up the reward. Don't offer any spoken words or lures, or other guidance. Let him figure it out on his own—he'll know that he did *something* that prompted the "click-treat," but it may take him several wrong moves before he once again happens to sit—and you immediately click-treat.
3. Now he really knows he's onto something! You can nearly see the wheels turning as he starts offering behaviors—pawing your leg, backing up, barking, biting an itch, falling into a "sit" by accident (click-treat!).
4. When the light bulb goes off, your pup may offer half a dozen or more sits in a row. Once he realizes the behavior prompts the click-treat, you can start associating the command with the action. As his

Training Tidbit

The most powerful way to train involves watching your puppy until he naturally performs a behavior you like, and then rewarding him. Telling him with a marker-sound, like a clicker, that when he sits (click!) he gets a treat, puts the power in the puppy's paws. He'll nearly do back-flips to figure out what behavior you want, so he can get that click/treat.

bottom hits the ground, say "sit" at the same moment you click, and then give him the treat. He'll soon figure out the word identifies the action.

Down

Dogs use certain postures naturally as ways to signal intent. A dog in a "down" (reclining) position signals to other dogs that he's calm and means no harm. Lying down actually helps your puppy calm himself as well. It's a great exercise in relaxation for an exuberant Pit Bull puppy as well as a way to practice self-control. The puppy who will "down" on command won't be jumping up on visitors, pestering the cat, or chasing other dogs and becoming an unwelcome aggravation.

Lure Training

1. Place your puppy in a "sit" position. Give the command "down."
2. Using his reward of choice, hold it in front of his nose, and lower it to the ground and slightly ahead of him, so that he must follow. Basically, you'll lure him into walking his front legs forward until he's in a down position. His nose should be in contact with your fingers and treat, all the way down.
3. Once he's in position, give him the reward.
4. After he's learned to "down" from a sitting position, practice having him "down" from a standing start.

Clicker Training

For clicker training (as with the "sit"):

1. Have treats and clicker ready, and watch your puppy until he assumes the "down" position on his own. Click and treat the behavior.
2. Allow the pup's brain to percolate until he understands the behavior you want. It may take 30 seconds, or 15 minutes, for him

to again "down" on his own. Immediately click-treat to reward him.

3. He won't take nearly as long to repeat the behavior the third time. Once he's "got it," you can begin using the command "down" at the same moment you click. Your pup will very soon associate the action with the word.

Walk Nicely on Lead

Laws in many communities require that any dog off your property must be confined on a leash. Knowing how to walk nicely on a leash offers your dog the freedom to safely explore the world beyond your front yard or backyard. Adult APBTs are so powerful they can pull the leash from your hands or drag you all over. That's not only dangerous for you, it allows them to be rude, unruly, and socially inept. A dog who's out of control will be perceived as scary and dangerous. You want your adult dog to have impeccable manners, especially off your property. Learning to walk nicely on lead is much easier to teach to a small puppy than a powerful adult, so begin immediately when you bring your dog home.

1. If your puppy hasn't worn a collar before, give him some time to get used to it. A flat nylon collar with a metal buckle that you can fit two fingers beneath is ideal.

2. Let the puppy sniff the leash, but he should not be allowed to chew or mouth it. A leash is not a tug toy!

3. Your goal is for him to walk nicely by your side on a loose (not tight) leash. That's actually counter-intuitive for a puppy—he wants to go! And if you keep the leash tight, he'll naturally pull against it. So hold the leash in your right hand, doubling up the extra slack so it doesn't drag. Make sure there's no tension, and hold that right hand at your belt buckle level.

4. Have treats or toys handy to dole out. Show your pup a treat as he sits or stands at your side. If you plan to eventually compete in obedience trials, it's traditional to have him walk on your left side. But if you don't care about competition, it really doesn't matter which side as long as you're consistent.

5. Once he's focused on the treat, say "let's go!" or another verbal cue, such as "heel," that you use consistently. Hold the treat right in front of his nose as you begin to walk, luring him to keep pace.

6. He should not be jumping up for the treat—hold it lower if he's trying to jump. You can also use a long wooden spoon with a sticky treat, or a commercial "treat stick" designed for that purpose, so you don't have to bend over.

7. After a few paces, stop and have your puppy sit. Reward him with the treat.

8. Repeat the leash walk exercise with the lure. Stop every few steps and place your pup in a "sit" or "down," and reward him.

By the time he's a young adult, your APBT should know how to walk nicely on a leash.

PART II

ADULTHOOD

CHAPTER 5

FINDING YOUR AMERICAN PIT BULL TERRIER ADULT

Many times, the dog of your dreams comes to you in a roundabout way. Rather than searching out that perfect puppy, an unexpected gift wrapped in adult fur comes along. While dogs of all ages and breeds have quite a lot in common, adult dogs—and especially "second hand" canines—have special considerations.

When is an American Pit Bull Terrier an adult? Although shown in competition in the "puppy class" until 12 months old, different lines of dogs grow up at varying rates, with physical and emotional maturity not necessarily taking place at the same time. Dogs may attain their adult height sooner, but muscle mass with broader cheeks, chest, and body—what's called their "spread"—may not develop fully until age two. Females mature physically more quickly than male dogs, but both can act like goofy adolescents even when they look like an adult.

ADVANTAGES OF AN ADULT APBT

While puppies can be lots of fun, they also are a great deal of work. Puppies go off the cute-scale for a reason—so owners won't throw up their hands in horror and give up on them after the juvenile delinquent dog eats the sofa! Think of that baby as a work-in-progress that you must mold into the dog of your dreams. Before that happens, the puppy won't know what you expect and likely will chew property, poop, pee, and otherwise wreak havoc in your life and home. You'll forgive him, of course, but not before you've spent a small fortune in puppy vaccinations, spaying or neutering, ear trims, microchipping, dog obedience class, and more. And while choosing a pup from a responsible breeder gives you the advantage of better predicting future looks and attitude, a puppy remains an unknown quantity until reaching maturity.

Adopting an adult dog allows you to know what you're getting—to a point. Depending on the source, some of the dog's history may remain a mystery. But usually an adult American Pit Bull Terrier has received most routine preventive care, such as vaccinations and neuter surgery. Medical costs are highest for puppies and senior dogs, so adopting a robust adult should be relatively economical. Adult dogs also should have some basic skills, such as being housetrained and perhaps even obedience trained. A female dog will already have been spayed or a male dog neutered.

In addition, you'll know if the adult dog acts friendly or shy with people, or aggressive or tolerant of other dogs, and previous owners can tell you of any health or other issues. Foster caregivers or shelter staff may be able to offer a good evaluation of the dog's temperament. Very nice adult dogs lose their homes through no fault of their own, when military owners are deployed, when owners change jobs and schedules, or when homeowners must downsize to an apartment that won't allow the pet.

CHOOSING AN ADULT

If you already have a resident dog, stick with opposite sex pairings if you are adopting an APBT. The worst dog-on-dog aggression develops between two males or two females, and a boy-girl combination stands a better chance of succeeding long term.

When choosing your new friend, be conversant with body language that can signal trouble: Raised hackles, hard stares, stiffening of the body, and/or low growls are cause for concern, whether pointed at you, other dogs, or other people. Any addition to your resident pets can change the social standing, and even friendly pets may get irritated.

The presence of prized chew toys, food, and even attention from you or your company can send arousal levels up and spark conflicts in

By the Numbers

Dog tolerance changes as pups mature. But an adult APBT offers a much more accurate read on how well he tolerates other dogs.

some dogs. Tasty fat trimmings in the trash or a cat treat out of reach under the sofa can be a trigger. Even friendly games of tag or tug can get the dogs too excited. Races to reach the guest at the door may be so exciting that dogs lash out at each other. Above all, a new dog entering the household—especially an adult who may feel entitled to be the top dog—may prompt behavior issues in all your pets. Take precautions, and be alert. A new friend can be wonderful but only when you remain vigilant to make the experience a happy one for all concerned.

ADOPTION OPTIONS

You can find an adult American Pit Bull Terrier in several places.

Breeders

Breeders sometimes need to make room for younger canines and want to place a retired show dog in a home where he can enjoy more attention with a family. Other times, the breeder may have a dog returned when the owner's circumstances change. When you adopt from a breeder, you'll have the advantage of knowing about the dog's breeding and details of his training and life experiences. These typically are wonderful dogs who may be acquired for little or even no cost. You can't do better than a retired show dog who you know has good breeding, has been well socialized, and has impeccable manners and a known history.

Ethical Sources

Adult dogs can be wonderful companions but also may come with baggage. Ethical sources disclose the good and the not-so-good about available dogs. The best of these groups stay in touch and offer support and resources to help ensure that the dog stays in the new home.

Newspapers

Newspaper advertisements probably are one of the most "iffy" places to acquire your adult American Pit Bull Terrier. It can be difficult to get an accurate assessment of the dog's health and behavior history in these situations. There certainly are honest and well-meaning folks interested in finding the perfect home for the animal. But a newspaper ad could also be placed by unscrupulous strangers willing to fudge the truth simply to get rid of a dog.

Shelters and Rescues

The media has conditioned us to think that every APBT with a scar or wound must be a fighting dog, or that a shy pooch must have

breeder may have a retired show dog available for adoption.

> ## A Lifesaver
> Adopting an American Pit Bull Terrier from a shelter often saves the dog's life.

been abused. Dogs of every breed get into trouble; scraps with a cat, for instance, or a run-in as a puppy with an adult dog—or even running into a fence that leaves marks on the dog. A beloved pet or prize show dog can become fearful and get into scraps with housemates. And while shelter staff can be forgiven for seeking sympathy and creating dramatic hand-waving stories to get attention for needy American Pit Bull Terriers, most dogs in shelters do not come from fighting rings.

Shelters and rescue operations are a prime location for finding an adult American Pit Bull Terrier. Be aware, though, that different organizations may have varied missions and focus. And depending on funding and the abilities and background of those in charge, shelters and rescues range from outstanding facilities to heartbreakingly bad. In almost all instances, shelters and rescue groups have many more animals to place than there are available homes, and their staff and/or volunteers may be stretched—and stressed—to the limit.

These facilities work hard to humanely manage an impossible situation but do not always have the resources to warehouse unwanted animals indefinitely or to rehabilitate and re-home them. Some larger programs include staff or volunteers who help evaluate animals to help you choose an appropriate pet.

Municipal Shelters

A *municipal shelter* accepts, on behalf of local governments, any stray or abandoned animal as well as animals that people can no longer care for. They also strive to address complaints about roaming animals. These organizations exist to "control" unwanted animal populations and temporarily house them until reclaimed, rehomed, or euthanized. Typically the old, injured, and sick pets are immediately euthanized, as are dogs deemed poor candidates for adoption. Some animal control facilities categorize any "pit bull" lookalike as unadoptable and automatically euthanize these dogs. Those judged to be good candidates for adoption usually are available for only a set amount of time (usually days or a week or two at most) because of space limitations, and then they also are euthanized to make room for incoming animals. Check with your local animal control to learn their policy regarding APBTs.

Private Shelters

Private shelters may be run by individuals or nonprofit groups who have a passion and mission for helping animals and who are not bound by the restrictions of local government. The quality of services and operations are highly dependent upon available funding, which can vary throughout the year. A "shelter" designation means the group has facilities to house adoptable animals on at least a temporary basis, pending reuniting the lost pet, rehoming, or euthanizing.

Some shelters now designate themselves "no kill," which indicates that they keep each pet until a home is found or it dies of natural causes. However, these shelters may selectively accept the most "adoptable" animals that do not require extensive medical or behavioral

Check with your local animal control to learn their policy regarding APBTs.

rehabilitation. Limited space also means that a no-kill shelter frequently runs at full capacity and must turn away needy animals when they run out of room.

Rescues

Rescue organizations also can be run by individuals or a group as a nonprofit organization. A rescue organization often focuses on a particular breed—such as American Pit Bull Terriers—and has no single building for housing the animals. Instead, a rescue employs a network of volunteer foster homes. Foster owners may also seek to correct objectionable behavior that lost the dog his home, or offer training, or otherwise help the dog become more adoptable.

Temperament Tests

Temperament tests pick up the main tendencies of a dog, especially those that are extreme. A number of shelters use protocols such as the ASPCA's Meet Your Match SAFER™ (Safety Assessment For Evaluating Rehoming), a tool for assessing the probability of future canine aggression, developed by Certified Applied Animal Behaviorist Dr. Emily Weiss. Mary Burch, Ph.D., a Certified Applied Animal Behaviorist, helped create another test called the ADOPT shelter protocol, which stands for "Assess Dogs on Practical Tasks."

Many professional APBT breeders volunteer at local shelters to evaluate dogs so they can offer potential adopters good information on temperament, training, and pet potential. Even dogs who have suffered terribly in the past have been shown, repeatedly, to have the potential to be rehabilitated with proper training and become wonderful pets. Behavior assessments often rate such things as:

- In-kennel and approach behaviors

- Leash/collar and on-leash behaviors
- Reactions to petting, handling, play, and distractions
- Reaction to other animals (e.g., dogs, cats)
- Guarding of food or possessions

Ask what kind of temperament test or evaluations have been conducted on the dogs who interest you. Only those dogs who have passed will be available for adoption from organizations that use these techniques. Shelters and rescues without "formal" tests should still be able to provide you with their assessment of the dog's potential. Those organizations that respond to your query about temperament assessment with a blank look should be avoided!

ETHICAL ADOPTIONS

Like-minded rescue organizations may organize into larger networking collaborations, such as MuttsandStuff.com and its Pit Bull Rescue Alliance (PBRA). PBRA is an alliance of independent groups dedicated to rescue, education, and advocacy of the American Pit Bull Terrier through mutual collaboration and networking. The

Training Tidbit

Often the adult dog comes with a name that may not appeal to you or seem to fit. Train the dog to recognize a new name by first partnering it with the familiar one. "Zeus" becomes "Buddy-Zeus," and over a period of days or weeks, it transitions to "Buddy" alone, particularly if you give the dog special attention when he responds to the new name.

group promotes ethical rescue practices and responsible ownership, and serves as a resource for information about the breed. One of PBRA's goals is to provide and encourage implementation of ethical practices related to rescue. While not all sources for an adult APBT will be able or willing to adhere to all these PBRA practices, the adoption option you choose should follow as many as possible.

Correct Temperament

They should place only sound Pit Bulls of correct temperament—that is, people friendly and dog tolerant. While dogs with aggression or other issues can be rehabilitated, such work takes experience and time that many pet owners won't be able or willing to provide.

Screening Adopters

The organization should screen potential adopters and their home, to ensure that the owners have the education and environment

able to successfully keep a Pit Bull happy and healthy.

Education

Adoption organizations also should be able to provide education or refer you to the necessary resources so that you have the correct informational tools. Ideally, the organization should continue to offer the new owner information, advice, and help with training (or a referral to a qualified trainer) after adoption.

Fostering

Animal shelters, especially municipally run facilities, tend to simply kennel the dogs, and there's not much time available to work individually with the animals. There also may not be enough space for adequate exercise, and APBTs really need to burn off energy. In a foster situation, a dog can be given time to adjust into the household so that the volunteer gets a more accurate "read" of the dog's normal temperament—and can work to improve problems, if revealed. The dogs also can be better exercised when in a savvy foster family's home.

Spay/Neuter

An adult APBT should be altered before being adopted from the shelter or rescue. When a breeder retires a show dog, usually the dog will be altered and/or the registration papers will be withheld. That

Want to Know More?

There are many senior APBTs in need of a good home. Go to Chapter 12: Finding Your American Pit Bull Terrier Senior for information.

An adult APBT should be altered before being adopted from the shelter or rescue.

emoves the temptation and risk of having an ccidental litter.

Health Issues

ny adoption facility should let you know bout known health issues and also provide asic preventive care such as vaccinations and eworming prior to placement.

Contract

ome facilities ask new owners to sign a ontract that stipulates specific obligations in egard to the dog. That could include training ecommendations or health care requirements. or instance, if the shelter organization cannot ind altering surgery for all the dogs, they ay instead require that the new owner have ne dog neutered or spayed within a specific period of time. Local veterinarians may work with an adoption facility to provide discounted surgeries.

If It Doesn't Work Out

To ensure that the dogs do not end up back in the rescue system, many organizations (professional breeders as well) mandate that if, at any time and for any reason, the adopter is unable to keep the dog, the adopter must first contact them for assistance. Some go as far as to stipulate by contract that the adopted dog may not be sold, euthanized, traded, given away, relinquished to a shelter, or rehomed in any other manner without prior consent of the rescue group. Be sure that you understand all the particulars of any agreement that you sign.

CHAPTER 6

AMERICAN PIT BULL TERRIER GROOMING NEEDS

The word *grooming* conjures images of poofed Poodles with little bows and varnished nails. Your American Pit Bull Terrier requires much less coat care and handles some grooming on his own. He scratches with his rear toenails, nibbles to remove dirt and burrs or fleas from the fur, and licks to clean his genitals. But he'll rely on you to provide the complete grooming he needs. It's something you can easily manage at home.

BRUSHING

Smooth coated dogs like APBTs don't need more than a spit-and-polish when it comes to coat care. A healthy coat is not only attractive, it's the dog's first line of defense against injury. Fur lies in protective layers that shield skin from damage and provide insulation from temperature extremes.

Brushing feels good to the dog but serves as more than an all-body scratch session. Making a habit of touching your APBT all over on a regular basis doubles as an important health care check. During grooming, you can be sure that his skin remains clean and clear of sores or lumps and bumps. And if you find a potential problem, the early detection helps you get veterinary care quickly to head off more serious concerns.

Sebaceous glands at the base of each hair root secrete an oily substance called sebum. Brushing spreads sebum through the fur to waterproof and give the coat a healthy shine. Brushing removes dirt and loose hair and keeps it off your sofa and clothes.

Shedding

Shedding is normal. You may not see the drifts of undercoat that some breeds produce, but short hairs shed by a Pit Bull can be as aggravating and difficult to control.

Hair grows in cycles beginning with a period of rapid growth in the spring, followed by slower growth, and then ending in a resting stage. Mature hairs loosen in the follicles during this winter resting phase. In the spring, another cycle of hair growth begins, and new hair pushes the old, loose ones out, resulting in an all-over shed.

It's not the temperature that prompts shedding but the increased exposure to sun or artificial light. Dogs living in the northeastern United States who spend a lot of time outdoors tend to experience seasonal sheds, with the most fur lost in late spring for the several weeks during which daylight increases. But house pets under constant exposure to artificial light may shed all year long. You can't stop shedding, but regular brushing will reduce the amount of fur that ends up in your carpet or on your clothes.

How to Brush Your APBT

An American Pit Bull Terrier's smooth coat can be easily maintained simply with a bristle or curry brush and a chamois cloth.

It just takes some basic tools to groom your APBT.

- Establish a routine—same time, same place. A good example might be every Friday night during the evening news in front of the television. Have a small wastebasket handy to deposit loose fur.

- Begin with an all-over petting session, using the flats of your hands and fingers. Feel all over your dog, starting with his head and face. Run your hands down and around his neck and chest, and continue over his back and both sides. Don't forget each leg and his tail. Offer to rub his tummy so he'll give access to this area. Finger-combing and petting alert you to any lumps, sores, or bruises that need attention. Make a note of any favorite places he enjoys being touched, like his chest or base of the tail, and save those "sweet spots" for last.

- Once your dog is relaxed and ready, begin to gently brush in the direction the fur grows. Pay attention to what he "tells" you. Some dogs have tender skin in certain areas but relish a harder stroke in others. Start with

the head and neck area, and work your way lower down the body. Be most careful of too much pressure over bony areas, such as the backbone or the nipples.

- There is no rule that says you must brush your entire dog at one time—space it out over several days in ten-minute sessions if you or your APBT lose patience. Remember those favorite areas, and finish for the day with a brushing in those places. Follow each session with a treat or game so your dog identifies grooming with good things.

- To finish the grooming session, polish the coat with a chamois cloth. Alternately, slip your hand inside the foot end of an old pair of pantyhose and stroke the dog with that. It works just as well to polish the coat.

BATHING

In most cases, your dog won't need a bath more than once a month, unless he gets very grubby or is a show dog. A thorough brushing usually keeps an APBT looking great. Too many baths can strip the natural oils from his skin and dry out the coat. However, if he's a rough-

and-tumble canine with a tendency to get into smelly or otherwise objectionable messes, bathing is the answer.

It's a great idea to get your big dog used to bathing while he's young and more easily handled. Some dogs love baths and enjoy getting wet and splashing around. But if he has a bad experience one time, he'll remember, so make bath time fun for you both from the beginning. You really don't want to argue with a Pit Bull about getting into the tub! If it's a warm, sunny day, the garden hose in the backyard or patio may also work.

How to Bathe Your APBT

You'll need dog shampoo, mineral oil, cotton balls, a washcloth, and lots of towels.

- Assemble all the supplies you need beforehand. If he objects to baths, just seeing you prepare could get his tail in a twist, so wait until you're ready to let him in on the plan. Use shampoos approved for dogs, and avoid people products. Human scalp tends to be much oilier than dog skin, and even a baby shampoo can be harsh and cause allergic reactions in your APBT. Remember to wear a bathing suit or old clothes, because you will get wet! And according to your dog, that's only fair.

- When bathing indoors, the area should be warm and draft-free. Be sure to push shower curtains and any breakables that could spook your dog out of the way. If you're container-bathing, fill the tub with dog-temperature water (about 102°F [39°C]) before you bring in your pet.

- It's easier to bathe your dog when two hands are free. Bath tethers with a suction cup at one end are available, but to be useful, you'll need to train your Pit Bull to respect the leash and not pull. If you tether him directly

to the spigot, you may end up with a large plumbing bill, as a determined APBT can cause lots of damage should he panic and try to break away. Plus there's the chance that he could slip and hurt himself. A great way to avoid this is to make the experience so pleasant that he doesn't want to leave the tub. When bathing outdoors, tether the dog with a short lead to a fixed object, or better, have a friend help you.

Before beginning, place cotton in your dog's ears to keep out the water. A drop of mineral oil or artificial tears in each eye helps protect them from suds. Place the dog in the standing water. It doesn't need to cover him. Six or eight inches (15 or 20 cm) is more than enough and lets him stand above it if he prefers.

Dip water over your dog from the standing sudsy water, or use a hand-held sprayer. Many dogs are frightened by sprayed water, so use only a low force and keep it against the coat to soak the fur. Use a washcloth to clean and rinse the face. Once the fur is wet, apply a thin stream of pet shampoo along

Training Tidbit

When your dog objects to grooming, convince him there's a benefit by associating the activity with a favorite toy, treat, or special attention. Tether him to a stationary object for being wetted with the hose, and at the same time offer a rope tug-toy spiked with canine toothpaste. He can be chomping and cleaning his teeth while you bathe him.

Check your APBT's ears once a week.

the back—or lather the shampoo in your own hands and then apply—and suds your dog thoroughly, then rinse. Be sure to follow the directions on the label, especially if they call for diluting the product.

The rinse is the most important part, because left-over soap leaves the fur looking dingy and could cause an allergic skin reaction. Once you're sure the soap is gone, rinse one more time for good measure. Then allow your dog to shake as much as he wants. If his shaking doesn't fling out the cotton, then remove it from his ears.

Your APBT should air-dry very quickly. As much as dogs may dislike the bath, they often adore toweling off afterwards. Use an old towel, because he'll want a game of "tug" or keep-away with the fabric after the bath. Some dogs love chasing the water from the hose as a reward. Be sure the dog is dry to the skin before allowing him outside if it's a cold day.

EAR CARE

Healthy ears are pink. It's normal to see a small amount of amber wax, as it helps protect the ear canal. Any sort of discharge or bad smell can be an indication of infection or parasites. Check the ears at least once a week, while you're otherwise petting and rubbing or scratching your Pit Bull. Whether cropped or natural, the Pit Bull isn't known for ear problems but will benefit from a monthly cleaning.

How to Clean Your APBT's Ears

You'll need a commercial ear cleaning solution, which is available from veterinarians and pet stores, but a 50/50 vinegar and water solution is also fine for general cleaning. You'll also need cotton balls or a soft cloth.

- As with the bath, get your materials ready ahead of time, including a few tasty treats.

- Place a small amount of solution on a cotton ball or soft cloth. Show your dog the cleaning material (don't let him eat it!), and then ask him to sit or lie down and give him a treat.

- Gently grasp the outside portion of the ear (pinna) with one hand, and gently wipe out only the visible portions of the ear with the other. Praise him for holding still, and offer another treat. Repeat on the other ear.

- Never drip cleaner or put any instrument down into the ear canal unless instructed to do so by your veterinarian. You may inadvertently damage your dog's ear.

EYE CARE

Pit Bulls are not prone to everyday eye problems. However, like their owners, they can develop "eye boogers" in the corner of their eyes when tears spill out and dry. Normal eye secretions are clear, and dogs hold healthy eyes open with no squinting. Cloudy or excessive tears, or squinting, points to a problem that your veterinarian should address.

Tears can stain white fur, and allowing the discharge to dry on the skin can prompt irritation. If your Pit Bull has wrinkles around the eyes or muzzle that stay moist, clean these areas at the same time, as needed. That may be daily or weekly.

How to Clean Your APBT's Eyes

Necessary supplies include a cloth or cotton balls.

- Wipe out the skin folds regularly with a warm, wet cloth.

- Moisten a cotton ball or soft cloth with warm water or saline solution. Encourage your dog to close his eye, and wipe from the inner corner downward, toward his nose, to clean away soft discharge.

- When the discharge has crusted on the fur, hold a warm, wet cloth against the area to soften the secretions. Then wipe away.

- Stained fur is usually at the inside corners and below the dog's eyes; commercial products available from pet stores can help remove the stain from fur.

NAIL TRIMMING

For active dogs with access to running outside, frequent nail care may not be needed. But Pit Bulls who spend most of their time indoors require monthly trims, or more often. Nails grow nonstop and tend to curl, split, or become caught in bedding and carpet when too long. Dewclaws on the inside of the lower part of the leg need particular attention since they never contact the ground to wear down. Overgrown nails cause the foot to spread or

Multi-Dog Tip

Every dog in the family deserves special one-on-one grooming attention. To ensure that the dogs don't disrupt or distract each other, crate all the dogs individually. Then groom each one separately, one at a time, out of each other's sight.

Choose sharp nail trimmers you are comfortable using.

"grinders" available that some dogs may find more acceptable.

Many dogs have an aversion to having their paws handled or nails trimmed, even when they've never been injured. You can counter this by starting very early during puppyhood, making the paw-handling a happy, rewarding experience. This works with dogs of any age, too.

- With a pup or adult new to having nails trimmed, get him used to the idea first. Load up on a handful of his favorite treats. Handle each paw in turn, and when he accepts the touches, give a treat and say "good boy!" Do this once a day for a week.

- The second week, touch the trimmer to his nails in turn and work the clipper, but don't clip. Treat and praise as before. By the third week, you can begin actually snipping the nails.

- All the nails don't have to be done in the same session. If you're having difficulty getting the job done, finish the other toes later. It's helpful to have two pairs of hands during nail trimming, one pair to steady the paw and the other pair for handling the clippers.

- When the nails are white or clear, the pink quick that contains the blood vessels is visible and makes it easy to avoid the danger zone. Clip off the excess, and pay the dog with a treat, praising him for his patience. Once he's calm, clip the next one, and so on.

- Your dog's toenails may instead be dark or opaque, and the quick can't be seen. Clip off only the tips, the hooklike portion that turns down. This is especially important if the nail has been allowed to overgrow, because the quick will grow further down, too. Tipping the nails will prompt the quick to draw back

splay and can even curl and grow back into the dog's flesh. Nails at their longest should just clear the ground when the dog is standing. If you hear him "clicking" over the floor like a tap dancer, he needs a trim.

How to Trim Your APBT's Nails

A variety of commercial nail trimmers are available from your veterinarian, pet supply store, or mail-order catalog. They are typically either scissor-action or guillotine-type clippers designed to cut the dog's toenails at the proper angle without splitting or crushing the nail. The clippers you choose must be sharp, and you must be comfortable using them. There also are a few specialty Dremmel-type nail up, so you can trim a little each week until reaching the proper length. It's better to take off a tiny amount each week, than too much at once.

- If you cut too much, you'll "quick" the nail (cut into the living vessels that feed the nail bed) and cause it to bleed. If you do happen to quick a nail, use a styptic pencil or corn starch, and apply direct pressure to stop the bleeding. Or you can rake the claw through a bar of soap. Be sure to give your dog a double ration of treats if you happen to quick the nail, and engage him in a fun game. You want him to remember the good part of the experience, not the brief discomfort.

DENTAL CARE

Dogs inherit good teeth or potential problems. While some may keep shiny, white teeth and fresh-smelling breath all their life, others can develop dental problems. You'll notice bad breath and cruddy-looking teeth. Bacteria grow in left-behind food, mineralize, and form plaque. The bacteria also release enzymes that cause receding gums, loose teeth, and redness and swelling (gingivitis). Besides mouth and tooth problems, chewing pumps bacteria into the bloodstream and that affects your pet's heart, liver, and kidneys.

By the Numbers

Eighty percent of pets end up with periodontal disease (decayed teeth, sore gums, bleeding mouths) by the age of three.

Skunked!

Adult dogs often find ways to get themselves grubby, and nothing's worse than a skunk encounter. To remove the smell, combine one quart peroxide with one-fourth cup baking soda and two tablespoons dishwashing liquid. Sponge on the dog, allow it to bubble and foam for two or three minutes, and then rinse. Repeat as necessary, until the odor dissipates. This recipe, created by a chemist, neutralizes the odor but cannot be bottled in a closed container or it will explode.

The urge to eat keeps most pets munching even with a sore mouth. Dogs hide mouth pain very well. They often act depressed or irritable, though, and stop playing or even hide. You may think the behavior change simply reflects a pet's age when, in fact, a toothache makes him cringe and retreat from the world.

Once the evidence becomes obvious, your pet requires professional dentistry from your veterinarian. Dogs won't open wide and say "ah," so a teeth cleaning requires anesthesia. Most general practice veterinarians provide ultrasonic scaling, polishing, and sometimes antibiotics and pain medication, especially if teeth are pulled. Between veterinary visits and professional cleaning, provide home treatments to keep pungent breath under control.

- Dry dog food helps reduce the tendency of dental problems by only about 10 percent, according to veterinary dentists. There are therapeutic dental diets, however, that contain special enzymes or formulations that benefit dental health specifically. Look on the label for the Veterinary Oral Health look for dental rinse products from your veterinarian.

How to Brush Your APBT's Teeth

When your dog struggles with tooth problems, the best way to maintain dental health is to brush your Pit Bull's teeth. Use special meat-flavored toothpaste available from pet product stores or your veterinarian, which gives him incentive to have his teeth cleaned. Human toothpaste isn't good for dogs, as canines won't spit, and swallowed fluoride can be dangerous. A soft child's toothbrush works well, or simply wrap a damp cloth over your fingers and use that to scrub the outside of his teeth.

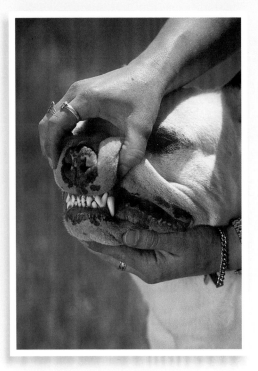

APBT's can hide mouth pain well, so check your dog's mouth regularly.

Council (VOHC) Seal of Acceptance, which endorses such products.

- Offer treats that pets must gnaw to encourage a natural scrubbing action that cleans teeth as they chew. Dogs relish raw veggies such as carrots and apples, and they also improve his breath.

- Most veterinary dentists dislike cow bones, pig hooves, and other hard chew objects that may break your dog's teeth. Sterilized bones designed for doggy dental care may be just what your Pit Bull needs.

- A wide range of commercial dental chews— like the ones Nylabone makes—are available for dogs and may also prevent doggy breath. Some are infused with special enzymes that kill bacteria and help prevent plaque. Also

- Encourage your dog to bite on a toy, to keep his mouth propped open for access to his teeth. Wrap your hand around his muzzle to close his jaws on the toy.

- Use the toothpaste-coated brush or cloth on your finger, and massage the outside of his teeth on both sides. His tongue cleans the inside so you won't have to worry about that.

- Brushing after every meal is recommended, but if that's not possible, a two- to three-times-weekly regimen is good.

GOING TO THE PROS

It's unlikely that your APBT will ever need a professional dog groomer. There may be times, though, when you don't have time to suds your dog or have his anal glands expressed. Or perhaps he's had a close encounter with a skunk, and you prefer having someone else clean him.

Ask for a reference from your veterinarian, friends, breeder, or other folks you trust. Some clinics have groomers on staff who can provide basic to high-end grooming services.

A trip to a professional groomer can keep your APBT looking and feeling good.

Should your APBT have issues with being handled by strangers and need this service, the veterinary staff also will be able to safely provide sedation, if necessary. Pet product stores also may have grooming services available.

Visit the grooming shop ahead of time. Ask how long they've been in business, and what training the groomers have had. See if they belong to any professional grooming association that provides training or accreditation, such as the National Dog Grooming Association of America (www.nationaldoggroomers.com) or the International Professional Groomers, Inc., (http://ipgcmg.org). Be cautious of non-veterinarian groomers who routinely recommend sedation, since giving drugs should be done only under a professional's guidance.

Check costs, and find out exactly what services are offered and what's included in the fee. Mobile groomers may be quite convenient by coming to your home, enabling you to have several pets bathed at once. But mobile groomers usually cost more.

Want to Know More?

For information about grooming a senior APBT, see Chapter 13: Care of Your American Pit Bull Terrier Senior.

CHAPTER 7

AMERICAN PIT BULL TERRIER NUTRITIONAL NEEDS

Your dog depends on good nutrition to stay healthy. Food goes beyond tasting good, or keeping his tummy from rumbling. Think of nutrition as what fuels the canine engine. Poor-quality fuel interferes with the inner workings the same way sand in the gears destroys your car. And while mediocre gas might move the wheels, you won't get the same fuel efficiency or quality performance. Your dog may not care what goes in the bowl, but you'll see the difference in his activity level, looks, and attitude when an optimum food is fed.

ESSENTIAL NUTRITION

Every dog requires good nutrition. American Pit Bull Terriers, however, are incredible athletes, very active, and need high-quality food to sustain the heavy muscling and strong bones that define the breed.

It's important that your dog like the food as well. After all, the best nutrition in the world remains worthless when it just sits in the bowl. The dog must actually eat the food to have any benefit. While you don't have to dig deep in your pocket to feed your Pit Bull, realize that the highest-quality ingredients cost more than second rate or poor products. However, you get to choose what to feed because your dog

doesn't have a wallet, or the opposable thumbs to get it open. You wouldn't allow your human child to eat junk food for every meal. While the occasional treat won't hurt, base your dog's nutrition on solid choices.

BUILDING BLOCKS

No matter what other dog owners—or your dog himself—may tell you, canines are not carnivores. Instead, your dog's body has evolved as an omnivore, a system able to eat and benefit from a wide variety of foods. While meat protein has great benefits, a diet limited to only meat is not healthy. Dogs require a combination of six different nutrients in the correct amount and ratio for ideal health.

Carbohydrates

Carbohydrates provide energy when digested, and the starches, sugars, and dietary fiber are turned into glucose. Carbs specifically fuel the neurological system and allow the muscles to work. Carbohydrates are obtained primarily from cereal grains and sugars like lactose (milk sugar). Fiber gives minimal energy but helps regulate the bowels, assists in normalizing the bacterial populations living in the gut, and may give a full feeling for obese dogs who are dieting. Too many carbohydrates will be turned to fat. Not enough carbohydrate may cause problems in whelping and interfere with the development of healthy puppies.

Fats

Fats make food taste good. They also provide energy more efficiently than carbs. Fats provide two-and-a-quarter times the available energy per unit of weight than carbohydrates or proteins, because up to 95 percent of dietary fats can be digested and used. Dogs who have high energy requirements, like working animals or pregnant bitches, benefit from higher fat content in their diet. But too much fat, as with excess carbs, can turn your dog into a pudgy pooch.

The American Pit Bull Terrier needs high-quality food to sustain the heavy muscling and strong bones that define the breed.

In addition, fats are essential for your dog to be able to process certain vitamins. Fats are the only source for linoleic acid, an essential fatty acid that helps in the absorption of fat-soluble vitamins. Dogs can use either animal- or vegetable-source fats. Fatty acids and fats promote healthy skin and fur. Not enough fat results in greasy fur, dandruff, weight loss, and poor healing of wounds.

Minerals

Minerals are present in relatively tiny amounts but are essential for nerve conduction, muscle contraction, acid/base balance, fluid stability inside the cells, and many other things. Necessary minerals include calcium, phosphorus, magnesium, potassium, sodium, chloride, sulfur, and the trace minerals copper, iodine, iron,

manganese, selenium, and zinc. Minerals work together, and the balance is as important as the amount. Too much can be as dangerous as too little. An imbalance can cause bone deformities, anemia, muscle weakness, heart or kidney disease, and countless other problems.

Proteins

Proteins are composed of 23 different chemical compounds called amino acids. Ten amino acids can't be produced by the dog's body in sufficient amounts. They're called "essential" since they must be provided in the diet. Dogs require dietary arginine, isoleucine, lysine, phenylalanine, histidine, leucine, methionine, threonine, tryptophan, and valine. Protein builds and maintains bone, blood, tissue, and even the immune system.

Proteins come from plant and animal (meat) sources. Other than eggs, proteins don't contain the correct balance of essential amino acids. So commercial dog foods combine two or more protein sources that complement each other by providing the amino acids the others lack. Signs of a protein deficiency may include loss of appetite, weight loss, poor coat, poor growth, and impaired reproductive performance.

Vitamins

Vitamins are used in biochemical processes inside the cells, and very small amounts are sufficient. Vitamins are divided into two groups. The fat-soluble vitamins A, D, E, and K are stored in the body. The B-complex vitamins are water-soluble, are not stored in the body, and must be replaced every day in the diet. B vitamins include thiamin, riboflavin, pyrodoxine, vitamin B12, folic acid, niacin, pantothenic acid, biotin, choline, and inositol. Unlike people, dogs don't require vitamin C in their diet, because their bodies produce adequate amounts of this vitamin.

Vitamins must be in proper combinations and amounts, or severe problems may result. Too much of a given vitamin can cause toxicity, while not enough results in dangerous diseases. Imbalances may result in problems that include

bone deformities like rickets, anemia, eye disease, anorexia, bleeding, and even death.

Water

Water is the most important nutrient. Sixty percent of a dog's body weight is water; the ratio is even higher in puppies. Water lubricates the tissues and helps electrolytes like salt to be distributed throughout the body. Moisture is used in digestion and elimination and helps regulate the body temperature. Even a 15 percent loss of body water results in death.

WHAT TO FEED YOUR APBT

Today, dog owners have more food choices than ever before. Every dog is different, and just because your friend's Pit Bull does well on a particular diet doesn't necessarily mean that's the best option for your dog. The most important factors in choosing what to feed have to do with matching the diet to your dog's life stage, activity level, and health status.

Pregnant females and those nursing a litter require much higher levels of energy than do most adult dogs. And because puppies need more protein, fat, and calcium than that of mature dogs, adults may gain too much weight if fed on a high-calorie puppy ration.

What kind of diet you choose depends on your own budget, expertise, time constraints, and access to information. Nutrition is a science. While you may be able to do it yourself, commercial pet food companies spend millions of dollars and decades of research to figure out the best formulations. They've done all the hard work for you.

Commercial Food

Commercial dog foods are manufactured by large companies and distributed across the

Multi-Dog Tip

Food bowls, meal locations, and bones/treats can incite dogs to wrangle over ownership. Any dog may feel possessive of these resources, but an APBT already on edge about other dogs can be particularly antsy. Feed dogs separately in their crates or in different rooms to prevent disputes.

Commercial dog food is a convenient choice.

country. You'll find these foods available in grocery stores and pet product outlets. They tend to be of a very consistent quality and reasonably priced, and they are required by law to abide by certain quality and labeling standards.

Reading the Label

The American Association of Feed Control Officials (AAFCO) provides guidelines for labeling pet foods based on regulations from the Food and Drug Administration (FDA), U.S. Department of Agriculture (USDA), and Federal Trade Commission (FTC). By reading labels, you can choose an appropriate commercial diet for your dog.

The label includes the *display panel*. That identifies the product by brand and/or product name, discloses the total amount of food in the package, and can also include a "complete and balanced" nutritional claim for a particular life stage.

The *information panel* contains a guaranteed analysis statement listing minimum levels of crude protein and fat and maximum levels of crude fiber and moisture. "Crude" refers to the amount measurable by laboratory equipment, not the amount that can be used by the pet. Look for the words "complete and balanced" on the label. Pet food manufacturers may label the food "nutritionally complete and balanced" only if it meets AAFCO standards. If this nutritional claim isn't on the display panel, it's on the informational panel.

Nutritional Claim

The nutritional claim can be proven in one of two ways. The first is by laboratory chemical analysis or calculation of nutritional values. Products tested this way will be labeled *"[Product name] is formulated to meet the nutritional levels established by the AAFCO Dog Food Nutrient Profiles for [life stage]."* Calculation methods cost less than feeding trials, so these foods usually are cheaper.

The second—and better—way to prove the nutritional claim is by feeding trials that determine whether pets benefit from the food. Products tested in this way will be labeled *"Animal feeding tests following AAFCO procedures substantiate that [product name] provides complete and balanced nutrition for [life stage]."* Feeding trials are the only good way to ensure that the nutrition is truly adequate, will be eaten, and is usable by the dog's body.

Life Stage

Choose a product that fits your dog's life stage. Commercial pet foods clearly label their products for growth and reproduction (pregnant or nursing mothers and puppies), maintenance (adult dogs), or all life stages (from puppyhood to motherhood and adult maintenance).

Ingredients

Next, look at the listed ingredients. They are required to be listed in descending order of the amount present. Therefore, look for a protein source to be in the first three ingredients listed. It should be a "whole" ingredient and will be listed as "meat," "beef," or "chicken"; the next best thing is "meat meal." Carbohydrates and fats fall farther down the list, and a variety of vitamins and minerals in small amounts are at the end. You'll also see preservatives to keep foods from becoming rancid, such as vitamin C (or ascorbic acid), vitamin E, or mixed tocopherals.

Pet food manufacturers aren't allowed to claim anything about the quality of ingredients, although some will try to say they use only "human grade" foods in their formulations. Much of this has to do with word play and marketing rather than any superiority of ingredients. The trend toward "breed-specific diets" appeals to owners who want a dog who looks like theirs on the product label but doesn't mean the formulation is particularly superior for that particular breed.

However, you will get what you pay for. Generic "store brand" products use less expensive ingredients and pass those cost savings on—and your Pit Bull may need to eat more volume of cheap foods to get enough nutrition. Premium and "performance" foods often include higher-quality ingredients and are more nutrient dense—they pack more calories into that cup of food. So even though they may be pricier, the dog can eat less volume of food and get adequate nutrition.

Dogs don't care what the food looks like, if it has gravy or peas and carrots, or if it smells awful. In fact, we know the sorts of disgusting things dogs willingly eat. Read past the glitz and marketing, and rely on commercial companies that have been in business for many years, with a proven track record of good research and sound product.

Commercial dog food companies are in the business of feeding our dogs well, and it's in their best interest to provide the highest-quality product and maintain good and trusting relationships with dog owners. The ultimate test of a dog food is how well your dog does from eating it.

Canned Food

The canning process for dog food is the same as for human products. The given formula placed in the cans gets cooked and sterilized in giant pressure cookers, sealed, then labeled and shipped. Canning preserves food without adding chemicals, so canned dog food remains fresh until opened.

It's difficult to can carbohydrate ingredients, so only small amounts are used in these

Choose a food that fits your dog's life stage.

products. Also, canned dog foods contain nearly 80 percent water, and while dogs love the flavor, they need to eat three times more canned product compared with dry food to fulfill the calories they need. It can be quite expensive to feed a Pit Bull an exclusive canned-food diet, but owners sometimes reserve canned products for special treats. Canned diets spoil quickly once opened, and leftovers must be refrigerated.

Dry Food (Kibble)

The ingredients for dry foods are mixed into a batter or dough and then cooked under extreme pressure for a short period of time. The still-hot ration is then pushed (extruded) through a die plate that gives the kibble its individual size and shape. The process of extrusion dries the kibble and gelatinizes the starches in the grain ingredients to make them more digestible for your APBT. Dry dog foods generally contain about 27 percent protein, up to 15 percent fat, about 6 to 10 percent water, and up to 50 percent carbohydrate.

Dry dog foods are cost effective and convenient because they can be purchased in large quantities, are easily stored, and do not require refrigeration after opening. You can fill the dog's bowl with food and allow him to eat at his convenience. Dry diets tend to be more energy dense than canned or soft-moist forms, which means your dog can eat less volume of the food while getting the same amount of energy.

Semi-Moist Food

This form of commercial food can be convenient for traveling. It can be stored without refrigeration and usually is packaged in single servings. Ingredients like corn syrup, which keeps the food moist and prevents it from drying out, tend to make the dog thirsty, but semi-moist foods are tasty and very appealing to most dogs. Because of the higher water content (15 to 30 percent), semi-moist foods are more expensive to feed, especially a big-appetite dog like a Pit Bull. Semi-moist foods contain about 16 to 25 percent protein, 5 to 10 percent fat, and 25 to 35 percent carbohydrate.

These foods often have the highest energy digestibility because the carbohydrate portion (composed of corn syrup) can be so quickly absorbed. They may be a poor choice for dogs with weight problems, though. Semi-moist foods, however, can make convenient "treat rewards" when used in moderation for training.

Noncommercial Foods

Noncommercial foods encompass any diet or formulation that you put together yourself. The "natural" pet care movement has encouraged owners to go this route, with the thought that being able to choose your own whole ingredients and preparing them at home is healthier for the dog. Internet sites and nutrition information put forth by self-proclaimed experts offers a host of advice and recipes. While home-prepared pet foods work

---

Want to Know More?

Your senior APBT has different nutritional needs from that of an adult. For more information about feeding a senior, see Chapter 13: Care of Your American Pit Bull Terrier Senior.

Some owners feed their APBTs a home-cooked diet in order to better control the ingredients.

xtremely well for many dogs, they can be angerous when not formulated correctly. It kes more than mixing up stew in the kitchen ⏵ meet the nutritional requirements for your PBT. Should you wish to pursue making ⊃ncommercial foods for your Pit Bull, it's best ⏵ consult with a veterinary nutritionist to get a ⏵ecific diet geared to your dog's needs.

ome-Cooked Diet

⊃me-cooked diets need to include the correct ⏵mbination of nutrients. As a very general ⥾ideline, a healthy dog does well on a diet ⏵mposed of equal parts protein, vegetables, ⥾d carbohydrates.

Any kind of meat provides both necessary ⊃tein and enough fat. Larger chunks

encourage the dog to chew rather than gulp, and that's better for his teeth. Cook the meat by either steaming it or zapping it for 30 seconds in the microwave, to kill harmful organisms, like Salmonella, that could make him sick.

Whole grains such as barley or brown rice, sweet corn, and potatoes offer an excellent source for carbohydrates. Dogs can't digest grains as easily as meats, so simmer the grains in a little broth until soft to unlock the nutrients and add flavor.

Vegetables provide the necessary vitamins, minerals, and some dietary fiber. You'll want to provide a variety to ensure that he gets all the nutrients needed. Puree the whole vegetable, like carrots, zucchini, broccoli, celery, parsley,

Picky Eater?

If your dog isn't eating enough, a veterinary exam can rule out possible health problems. A strong-smelling or flavored top dressing like warm chicken broth often prompts dogs to eat up to ten percent more of the food. However, a better choice for dogs with small appetites and big energy needs is a more energy-dense ration, like a complete and balanced super-premium food. Such diets provide more calories even if the dog eats less volume.

cucumber, alfalfa or bean sprouts, and beets, along with leafy greens like spinach and chard. The juice and peel include important nutrients. You'll also want to include a vitamin and mineral mix to make sure you've not overlooked anything important.

You can make your dog food in large batches and store in the refrigerator for up to three days or so. Try freezing it in meal-size portions to make it last longer. Treat home-prepared foods as you would canned diets—they'll spoil if left out indefinitely, so pick it up after about 20 minutes if your dog hasn't finished the food.

Raw Diet

A raw diet is exactly what you think—homemade but with raw meat ingredients. These diets can be just as good or as bad as you can imagine. Many dogs do incredibly well on raw formulas, and proponents believe they are closer to the archetypical food that wolves eat in the wild (although APBTs and other dogs are not wolves, of course). Those owners who are able to prepare a balanced raw diet certainly believe their animals benefit and that the

natural enzymes, bones, and other ingredients improve their dog's health.

Care must be taken, still, that the diet remains balanced. An improperly prepared raw diet can make your dog sick and risk causing you illness, too. While some people argue that dogs do not have the same susceptibility to the dangers of food-borne diseases such as Salmonella, people still do. Safe food handling is vital.

Commercially prepared and frozen raw food diets are available, if you wish to go this route but don't have the time to prepare food yourself or are concerned about doing it right. There also are commercial "dry mix" diets to which you may add your own raw meat. It's best to consult with your veterinarian about recommendations for the best choices.

Special Diets

Special diets go above and beyond the basics of nutrition. These foods are for dogs who need extra help to either maintain good health or to correct and/or support the body during a health challenge. In these cases, the special diet may be prescribed by the veterinarian just as prescription drugs would be recommended.

Therapeutic Diets

Therapeutic diets are available from all the major commercial pet food companies. Those that help control or treat health problems generally are available only through a veterinarian and should be used only as prescribed. Many are designed to relieve specific clinical signs of disease by manipulating nutrient profiles and are not appropriate for routine maintenance in healthy dogs.

For example, dogs suffering from food allergies may benefit from a diagnostic diet containing a single protein and single carbohydrate source. Should your Pit Bull develop heart disease, nutrition can be adjusted to relieve some of the symptoms and support his health. Diets are available that starve cancer but feed the treated dog; that dissolve urinary stones; that assist in weight loss; or even that reverse the signs of canine cognitive disorder. Your holistic veterinarian might even prescribe a specific recipe for a homemade diet as a treatment for a particular health concern.

Supplements

A food supplement is fed to the dog above and beyond an otherwise complete and balanced diet, as a benefit to his nutrition. When you're feeding a homemade diet, you'll need to supplement with an approved vitamin and mineral mix to ensure that your dog receives balanced nutrition. Many holistic veterinarians also recommend a number of dietary supplements, such as beneficial enzymes to aid digestion, or fish oil to improve the coat. But when your dog is eating a complete and balanced quality commercial food, adding vitamins or minerals can throw the nutrition out of balance.

For instance, too much dietary calcium can cause bone and cartilage deformities and interferes with absorption of phosphorus, iron, zinc, and copper, which may cause deficiencies of these minerals. Such deficiencies can result in skin disease, reproductive problems, nervous system dysfunction, and impaired immunity. Feeding too much raw liver can cause a calcium deficiency and possibly vitamin A toxicity, resulting in crippling bone disease, weight loss, anorexia, and even death.

Food supplements should not be considered benign—they are designed to cause an effect. So use them with caution and treat them as the medicine they are. Just because a product has been labeled "natural" doesn't mean it's safe, so follow your veterinarian's advice with such things. Some supplements could be beneficial when taken alone but may interact with other medications your dog takes and cause problems.

Treats

Treats are particularly tasty foods offered above and beyond the dog's balanced diet, which are given as a reward. A huge array of commercial dog treats is available, from soft and smelly to hard and crunchy. Some are formulated to be complete and balanced so they won't disrupt your dog's diet. But food from the owner's plate seems to have particularly high value to dogs.

Within reason, table scraps won't hurt as long as what you eat is healthy. Supplementing your APBT's diet with fresh carrots or a bit of

Training Tidbit

Mealtimes can be wonderful training opportunities. Once your dog knows how to sit and stay (see Chapter 9 for details on how to teach these cues), have him perform these behaviors before each meal. Hold his food dish off the floor and tell him to sit and stay. Then place the food dish on the floor. Wait a few seconds, then tell him "Okay." By having to wait politely for his meal, you not only avoid having him mow you down as he races to grab his grub, but you also teach him self-control.

lean steak is different from offering half a bag of French fries. Table scraps should make up no more than five to ten percent of the total amount of food your dog eats.

Treating your Pit Bull with an occasional healthy snack probably won't cause any problems. Dogs and owners seem to benefit most from the bonding experience of doing something "special" for the dog. A treat does not need to be huge. In fact, most commercial dog treats can be broken or cut into four or more pieces, so the dog believes he's getting four times the treats but without adding too many calories. Dogs can get into the habit of demanding treats, and that's often more about the attention than actual hunger.

Bones

Dogs love to chew. Bones seem to be the natural choice for giving your dog an outlet for his chewing. However, cooked bones splinter when gnawed by a powerful Pit Bull jaw. They can lodge in the dog's mouth, or swallowed broken pieces can block the intestinal tract and cause a life-threatening emergency.

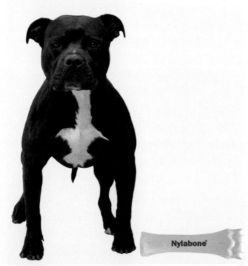

Pick a treat formulated with the best ingredients.

Raw bones splinter less often but are unsanitary and messy. Some dogs can actually break their teeth chewing on bones. Large beef bones that he can gnaw but not crunch may be a better choice. Chewing on a bone provides him with great exercise and helps keep teeth clean and healthy.

Pet product stores have available sterilized natural marrow bones, which still retain the scent and flavor your dog craves but without the nasty problems of being raw. Always supervise your dog during chewing. If he manages to break off pieces that could be swallowed, confiscate them.

WHEN TO FEED YOUR ADULT APBT

When and how often to feed your Pit Bull depends on your schedule and his individual needs. It is healthier to feed him two or three small measured meals each day, rather than one gigantic meal. For picky eaters, the dog may not be able to eat enough at one time to feel full for the rest of the day. That will result in him pestering you later.

A good time to feed your adult Pit Bull is in the morning during your breakfast and then again in the evening. Give him time to romp and empty his bladder and bowels in the morning, then offer his morning ration. Eating is a social event to dogs, and he'll be less likely to bother you during your meal if he has something in his own bowl. In the evening, be sure to feed him a couple hours before his last bathroom stop. That will give the meal time to process before everyone goes to bed.

OBESITY

About 40 to 50 percent of dogs older than five years are overweight. Obesity, defined as weight that exceeds the ideal by 20 to 25 percent, has serious health risks. An overweight dog has an increased risk for diabetes, cancer, skin disease, heart problems, and lameness from arthritis. Obesity also cuts short the dog's life. A 14-year study by Nestle Purina PetCare Company proved that keeping dogs lean extends their lifespan by 15 percent—nearly two years for the dogs in the study.

Why Do Dogs Get Fat?

Dogs get fat when they eat too much and don't exercise enough. Busy owners have less time to interact with pets, so we "love them to death" with extra food to show affection. When your APBT pesters you for attention, offering a treat can turn off the aggravation. We also want to feed our dogs the very best food possible and give them the equivalent of rocket fuel when they spend all their time sleeping on the sofa. Many dogs eat out of boredom, especially if free-fed from a never-empty bowl.

We often schedule our dog's spay or neuter at the point in development when growth begins to slow down. The surgery won't make your pet fat, but it will reduce the pet's activity level and lower the metabolism. Unless the amount fed and activity levels are adjusted, these pets often gain weight.

Few pets actually "work" for their food, and they aren't required to hunt for their meals as their ancestors did. The most exercise many dogs get is the trek from the sofa to the bowl. And the heavier your pet becomes, the less he'll want to exercise, setting up a vicious cycle of weight gain.

Slimming Down Your APBT

You may not realize that your APBT has become fat. You should be able to feel but not see the dog's ribs, and from the top and sides you should see a distinct tummy tuck or "dip" at the waist.

Most pet food companies offer therapeutic weight-loss diets, available by prescription only, and these are the safest choices for severely obese pets. Usually the target is to lose about one to one-and-a-half percent of starting weight per week.

Commercial over-the-counter "lite" pet foods provide 10 percent fewer calories than *that same brand's* regular food and may actually have *more* calories than a competitor's regular food. Free-feeding these diets won't work, because many pets simply make up for lost calories by eating more. Measured amounts fed in multiple meals works best so the dog doesn't feel deprived, and frequent meals speeds up the metabolism.

All dogs need a minimum of 20 minutes of aerobic exercise twice a day, but APBTs benefit from more—two hours a day isn't out of line. Walking or swimming is a low-impact exercise that works well. Start slow—perhaps ten minutes twice a day—and gradually build up the amount of time. Fill "treat balls," like the ones Nylabone makes, with one of the dog's meals, so he must work to shake the dry food out for breakfast. You can also place food bowls at the top of stairs or a ramp so your APBT must move his furry tail to reach the meal. Reward your furry friends with play and attention rather than treats, or reserve a portion of the regular ration and offer a kibble or two as a treat.

By the Numbers

Nearly 50 percent of dogs over the age of five are obese. Food must be adjusted to your dog's lifestyle and activity level. Keeping your APBT lean actually can extend your dog's life by as much as two years.

CHAPTER 8

AMERICAN PIT BULL TERRIER HEALTH AND WELLNESS

The greatest amount of veterinary care takes place during the first year of a puppy's life. So once your APBT reaches adulthood, routine care keeps him healthy. Although some dogs can be roughnecks and injure themselves by overdoing exercise and play so that they require veterinary treatment, the breed tends to be quite robust. Your Pit Bull shouldn't require more than standard preventive treatments throughout the year as well as an annual wellness examination by the veterinarian.

ANNUAL VET EXAM

Why should you take your dog each year for an examination? Pet dogs age much more quickly than people do, which means that 12 months between veterinary visits could be comparable to you seeing the doctor once every six or seven years. Much can happen in that time. And while owners can be the first line of defense in recognizing problems, some health issues remain hidden. Routine screening tests can reveal problems before they become dangerous, so that treatment can often cure or prevent worse difficulties.

Questions from the Vet

The doctor will first ask you about any changes in your dog's behavior, which can point to potential health issues. In particular, the vet wants to know about your dog's appetite and elimination habits. An increase in drinking water, accidents in the house, and an increase or loss of appetite tell the doctor to run further tests.

Physical Exam

The exam also includes a head-to-tail hands-on check. Your dog thinks he's just getting a nice massage or petting, but the veterinarian can feel for any lumps or bumps that might point to a tumor, as well as skin sores or inflammation that could reveal allergies or parasites.

Your dog will have his eyes checked to rule out any problems there. The inside of the ears are checked to be sure they're clean and free of discharge (possible infection), and his mouth opened to look at gum color and tooth status. Dogs often develop tartar buildup as early as two or three years of age, and catching and treating this early can prevent tooth loss and pain.

The inside of the dog can be evaluated by listening to his heart for abnormal sounds and to his lungs to ensure they're working well. A rectal thermometer measures his temperature to be sure it's within the normal range of 101° to 102.5°F (38° to 39°C), and a fecal (stool) sample is checked for the presence of intestinal parasites. A blood test checks for heartworm status.

Based on the results of these screening tests, your dog may be given medication to eliminate intestinal worms, a renewed prescription to continue preventing heartworms, and any other medications that may be necessary.

Vaccinations

The doctor also will give your dog needed vaccinations. Not all shots are required every year. What preventive vaccines your dog requires depends upon exposure, which has to do with whether he comes into contact with other dogs and in what part of the country you live. Rabies, required by law, may be given every year or every three years. Your veterinarian may choose to give your dog other vaccinations on an alternating every-other-year schedule, such as for parvovirus one year and distemper the next. If your dog is in contact with many dogs, he may need a kennel cough vaccination every year.

PARASITES

Parasites feed on other organisms, usually at the expense of that organism. Dogs are hosts to a wide range of both external and internal freeloaders. Fleas, ticks, and mites live on or in the pet's skin and can cause a wide range of skin disease. They may even cause systemic (whole body) illness when microscopic organisms are transmitted to the pet. Worms, protozoa, and bacteria form colonies in the intestines, blood, heart, or other organs. These can cause chronic to acute disease that may ultimately kill the pet. Most parasites can be easily prevented with proper treatment from your veterinarian.

Internal Parasites

Internal parasites that can affect your APBT include heartworms, hookworms, roundworms, tapeworms, and whipworms.

Heartworms

Heartworms are a kind of roundworm (filarid) that lives in the dog's pulmonary arteries and right heart chambers. Mosquitoes transmit the disease. All dogs can get the disease, but outdoor dogs with the greatest exposure to mosquitoes are at highest risk.

The heartworm life cycle takes six to seven months. Mosquitoes ingest baby heartworms (microfilariae) when they bite an already infected dog. After three weeks, the developing parasites migrate to the mouthparts of the insect. When the mosquito bites subsequent dogs, larvae deposited on the skin enter through the bite wound left by the mosquito and infect the new dog. The immature parasite eventually migrates to the heart and pulmonary arteries where it matures. Adult worms can reach 4 to 12 inches (10 to 30 cm) in length, and infected dogs typically carry dozens of worms. Adult worms live for up to five years. Females shed as many as 5,000 microfilariae each day into the dog's bloodstream.

Want to Know More?

For more information on vaccines, go to Chapter 3: Care of Your American Pit Bull Terrier Puppy.

Early signs include coughing, shortness of breath, and reluctance to exercise, with some dogs fainting after exertion. Infected dogs become weak and listless, lose weight, and may cough up blood. Late-stage disease results in congestive heart failure, sudden collapse, and death. Diagnosis relies on signs of disease, blood-screening tests, X-rays, and echocardiography. Treatment involves drugs to poison the adult worms in the heart while restricting the dog's activity to prevent embolism caused by dead worms moving and blocking the arteries.

It is much easier and less expensive to prevent heartworm disease than to diagnose, treat, and cure it once infection is present. A variety of effective and safe preventative medications from your veterinarian can be given daily or monthly and often also prevent other parasites.

Hookworms

Hookworm (Ancylostoma), a thin tiny parasite, grows to less than half an inch (1 cm) long. They suck blood from the wall of the dog's small intestine. All dogs are susceptible, but puppies are at highest risk.

The adult hookworms mate inside the intestine, and females lay eggs, which are passed with the dog's stool. The eggs hatch in about a week, then develop further in the environment into infective larvae that may live for two months. They prefer sandy soil, but may crawl onto grass seeking a host. The highest incidence is in the south where higher humidity and temperature conditions provide an ideal environment for the parasite.

Puppies become infected from nursing infected milk or before birth while in the uterus. Adult dogs swallow larvae from the environment, eat an infected mouse

Training Tidbit

During routine checks, your APBT will be required to have a blood sample taken for heartworm. Teach him to "shake" on command, as it also involves extending a foreleg from which blood can be drawn. Dogs naturally offer a paw as a submission gesture. Watch for the spontaneous "shake" posture, and mark the behavior with a clicker, then treat to reward.

or cockroach, or become infected when larvae penetrate the footpads. Called pododermatitis, infested feet become painful, swell, feel hot, and become soft and spongy.

The most common sign in pups is bloody to black tarlike diarrhea, resulting in anemia that can lead to sudden collapse and death. This is an emergency situation, which may require hospitalization, a blood transfusion, and supportive care. Adult dogs more typically develop chronic disease characterized by mild diarrhea or vomiting.

Hookworms are diagnosed by finding eggs during microscopic examination of the stool. Repeated tests may be required, since eggs won't appear for two to three weeks after the initial infection. Several dewormers effectively treat hookworms and generally should be repeated every one to two weeks to ensure that maturing worms are also killed.

Prevent hookworms by promptly picking up waste, keeping kennel areas clean and dry, and washing down concrete runs with

Moms can infect nursing puppies with hookworms through infected milk.

single day, which pass with the dog's stool and live in the environment for months to years. Eggs hatch into infective larvae, completing the cycle.

Roundworms interfere with absorption of food, resulting in a potbellied appearance, a dull coat, diarrhea, or mucus in the stool. Roundworms rarely cause serious problems, but massive infestations damage intestines, block the bowel, and potentially cause ruptures. Seeing the worms coiled in the feces or vomit is diagnostic. Eggs identified by your veterinarian's microscopic examination of a stool sample confirm that worms are present.

Children may be at risk for infection from accidentally ingesting infective stages from a contaminated environment (most often by eating dirt). Because of this human risk, the Centers for Disease Control (CDC) recommends that all puppies and their mothers undergo deworming treatments, whether diagnosed with the parasite or not.

Liquid oral medication given at the age of two weeks (before eggs can be passed into and contaminate the environment), then four, six, and eight weeks is the current CDC recommendation. Many current heartworm preventatives also protect against roundworms.

a one percent solution of bleach. Have your dog checked and dewormed as needed. Several heartworm medications also prevent hookworms.

Roundworms

Roundworms (Ascarids) are intestinal parasites found in almost all puppies at birth. When passed in the stool or vomited, these seven-inch (18-cm) parasites resemble masses of spaghetti. Puppies may be infected before birth when immature worms in the mother migrate to the uterus, or from nursing infected milk. The parasite can also be contracted when a dog swallows infective larvae found in the environment or by eating an infected host like a mouse or bird.

The eggs turn into larvae in the intestines, migrate to the liver and lungs, and can be coughed up and swallowed again to mature once they return to the intestines. Mature females lay 200,000 hard-shelled eggs in a

Tapeworm

Tapeworms (cestodes) are ribbonlike intestinal flatworms. Immature worms must spend developmental time inside a flea before being able to infest your dog. Tapeworm eggs are eaten by the flea larvae, which then develops as the flea itself matures. When a dog nibbles to relieve that itch, he often swallows the flea and infects himself with tapeworm.

The head of the tapeworm, called the scolex or holdfast, anchors itself to the wall of the small intestine with hooks and suckers. Nutrients from what the dog eats are absorbed through the segmented body, linked together like a chain. Each segment (proglottid) is added as the worm continually grows, with potentially hundreds of segments attaining two feet (61 cm) or more in length. Each proglottid contains both male and female reproductive organs and can produce up to 200 eggs. Once "ripe," they are shed from the worm's body and pass in the dog's feces. They move independently like tiny inchworms, but when dry, they look like grains of rice. Infested dogs typically have segments stuck to the hair surrounding the anal area or in their bedding. Eventually, the segments dry and rupture, releasing the eggs they contain into the dog's environment. The life cycle is complete in two to four weeks. It's considered diagnostic to find the segments on the pet.

Tapeworms are usually considered an unpleasant annoyance. Without treatment, however, massive tapeworm infestations potentially interfere with digestion and/or elimination. Puppies may suffer intestinal blockage should too many worms become suspended the length of the intestinal tract. Also, the hooks of the holdfast can damage the intestinal wall. Diarrhea with mucus and occasionally blood may be signs of tapeworm infestation. Long-term infestation can result in an unkempt, dry-looking coat and a generally unhealthy appearance and reduced energy.

There are several safe and highly effective treatments for tapeworms, which may be administered either as a pill or injection. Unless a dog is constantly exposed to reinfestation by fleas, a one-dose treatment will eliminate the tapeworms. Controlling fleas is the best way to prevent tapeworm infestation.

Controlling fleas is the best way to prevent tapeworm infestation.

Whipworm

Whipworms (*Trichuris vulpis*) are thin, two- to three-inch-long threadlike worms that are narrow at one end, like a whip. All dogs are at risk, but puppies may be more profoundly affected.

Dogs contract the parasite by ingesting eggs found in the soil. The parasite feeds on blood by burrowing into the wall of the intestine. In small numbers, whipworms cause few problems, but a heavy worm load may cause diarrhea, vomiting, anemia, and weight loss, and such dogs typically have a rough coat or "unthrifty" appearance.

Diagnosis is made by finding eggs during microscopic examination of the stool. Effective medications are available, but once whipworms are in the environment, infestations can be hard to contain, since dogs are often reinfected from egg-contaminated soil. Treatment for three months or longer may be necessary to totally eliminate the infestation.

Good hygiene is the only way to reduce the chance of your dog contracting whipworms. Pick up the yard after your dog at least weekly. Some monthly heartworm preventatives can control whipworms as well.

External Parasites

External parasites that can affect your APBT are fleas, mites, ringworm, and ticks.

Fleas

Fleas are wingless insects adapted to pierce the skin and drink blood. The biting adults remain on your dog unless killed or mechanically removed but represent only five percent of the total bug count. Eggs, larvae, and pupae (cocoon) remain in the environment. The life cycle lasts 14 to 21 days, but newly emerged flea larvae can survive two weeks without a blood meal, and the cocoon stage can survive six months without feeding. Ten adult females can create nearly a quarter million different life stages in 30 days.

Diagnosis is made by seeing fleas. The presence of tapeworms, which are transmitted by fleas, is also diagnostic. Some dogs won't be bothered, while others develop severe allergic reactions to flea bites. Skin becomes inflamed and itchy, particularly on the rear half of the dog above his tail. In addition to scratching and chewing, you'll see black specks on the skin (flea excrement) that turns red when moistened. Very young puppies with large infestations could develop anemia from blood loss.

A wide variety of commercial flea products is available. Some kill fleas or sterilize them when they bite, and so reduce the bug population, but dogs that are allergic need products that keep fleas off entirely. Shampoos kill fleas on the pet but won't repel new bugs, and collars aren't as effective as newer spot-on products that last a month or more.

The safest products affect insects but not mammals. Flea treatments may incorporate combinations of insecticides for quick flea kill, insect growth regulators that prevent immature life stages from maturing, or

Multi-Dog Tip

Contagious skin disorders include ringworm, ear mites, and sarcoptic mange (canine scabies). When one dog develops a contagious illness, it often means you must treat the entire gang. At times, you may be able to separate the dogs to prevent exposure.

Sarcoptic mange is transmitted by direct contact between dogs.

hemicals that attack the insect's nervous ystem. Avoid combining different products collar with a spot-on product, for instance) r you could potentially poison your APBT. ead and follow the product directions to be ure the dosage is suitable for the age and size f your dog.

Mites

Mites infest the skin and are related and look milar to spiders. Several types of skin mites ffect dogs, and all can cause skin irritation nd disease.

Ear mites (*Otodectes cynotis*) live on the urface of the skin of the ear and ear canal and at debris and suck lymph. The life cycle lasts hree weeks from egg to adult. The crawling ites inside the ear create intense itching

and discomfort. Dogs shake their ears and scratch, and you'll usually see brown waxy debris or crust inside the ear. While not life-threatening, ear mites are the most common cause of otitis (ear inflammation), which can lead to infection. Excessive scratching and head shaking also can cause a kind of blood blister, called a hematoma of the ear flap. Ear mites are extremely contagious between pets, so if one dog has them, all must be treated. Diagnosis is made by seeing the mite while examining ear debris under a microscope. Treatment consists of flushing out the debris and applying insecticide to kill the mites. Bland oil, like mineral oil, squirted into the ear canal, followed by gentle massage, helps flush out the crumbly material. Because of the three-week lifespan of the mites, more than confirms the disease. Treatment consists of repeated baths in a benzoyl peroxide shampoo, followed by six consecutive weekly dips with a two to four percent lime-sulfur product. However, this product has a bad smell and stains white fur. Your veterinarian may instead treat with oral ivermectin or with one of several heartworm preventive products labeled for treating scabies.

Ringworm

Ringworm isn't actually a worm; it's a fungal infection caused by *Microsporum canis* that grows on the hair shaft and causes skin disease. In people, ringworm infections spread outward from a central spot, and as the inside central sore heals, the "ring" of reddened skin surrounding the area gives it a characteristic look and name.

Dog sores also expand but not in rings, and they leave a stubby patchwork fur pattern, with mild to severe crusty sores. Some pets become itchy, others do not. In some cases, infected hairs glow lime green when exposed to a specialized light called a Wood's Lamp. For a definitive diagnosis, the veterinarian plucks suspect hairs from the pet and cultures them in a special medium that changes color when positive. A healthy adult immune system usually prevents infections, but very young or old animals are susceptible.

Once a pet becomes infected, spores contaminate the environment and can remain infective for months. Even if only one pet has ringworm, you must treat *all* pets. In a single-pet home, treatment may be needed for three to eight weeks but probably will be longer in multipet households. Treatment consists of oral medication, topical treatment, and dealing with the environment.

The spores are nearly indestructible, so treating the environment involves removing

Ticks thrive in long grass, so limit your dog's access to those areas.

one treatment may be necessary to kill the mites as they hatch.

Sarcoptic mange, also referred to as canine scabies, is caused by a circular, short-legged mite that burrows under the dog's skin. It's transmitted by direct contact between dogs and from contaminated grooming equipment or kennels. The mite causes intense itching, skin sores, and hair loss, especially on the thinly furred parts of the body. Canine scabies is diagnosed by seeing these signs, and finding the mite in skin scrapings examined under a microscope reservoirs such as carpet, drapes, and pet bedding and repeatedly bleaching all surfaces with a one-to-ten bleach and water solution. Vacuum repeatedly, but remember to toss out the bag every time or you'll simply spread the spores. Disinfect the vacuum, too, with the bleach and water spray. Sunlight also kills ringworm spores. Anything that can't be thrown away or bleached can be left outside in the bright sun for a couple of weeks.

Ticks

Ticks are spiderlike parasites that suck blood during their larvae, six-legged nymph, and eight-legged adult stages. Adult ticks usually must feed before mating, can remain dormant for months, and then lay 4,000 eggs. Finding the tick diagnoses the problem. The parasite buries its head beneath the dog's skin, often around the ears and neck, and the leathery-tohard body inflates with blood.

Besides local irritation that can become infected, various tick species transmit several devastating diseases that affect both dogs and people, including Lyme disease, Ehrlichiosis, and Rocky Mountain Spotted Fever. Ticks thrive in long grass or forest habitats, so keeping grass short and limiting your dog's access to those areas reduces exposure. Several effective flea treatments also address tick prevention.

BREED-SPECIFIC HEALTH ISSUES

The APBT is generally a very healthy breed. However, like all breeds, there are a few health issues that can affect them.

Congenital Heart Disease

Dogs can be affected by a variety of heart problems, and the APBT occasionally suffers from congenital heart defects, present from birth. These may be inherited, and responsible breeders should know if their particular dogs have a potential for passing on the problem. A defective heart can't effectively pump blood throughout the body. Affected dogs quickly become exhausted from exercise or play or act weak or lethargic. They also may have a bluish tinge to the skin from lack of oxygen. The veterinarian usually hears abnormal heart sounds. Diagnosis requires X-rays, ultrasound, and electrocardiograms, which pick up irregular heart rhythms or sounds.

Patent Ductus Arteriosus

The most common congenital heart disease, patent ductus arteriosus (PDA), may or may not be inherited. Normally, the ductus arteriosus, a short blood vessel, allows blood to bypass the lungs of an unborn puppy. If the duct fails to close after the puppy's birth, blood leaks back into the heart through the opening, leading to left heart failure. Surgery can cure the problem when performed early. A thoracotomy opens up the entire chest wall to offer access to the heart, and then the hole is repaired.

Giving Your Dog a Pill

To give a pill, you can try hiding it in something tasty, like peanut butter or a hunk of cheese. Dogs will open their mouth if you gently press their lips against the sides of their teeth, or press a finger against the roof of their mouth. Once the mouth opens, push the pill to the back of the pet's tongue. Then close the mouth and stroke his throat until you see him swallow. Watch for him to lick his nose—that generally means he's swallowed.

Severe hip dysplasia may be seen as early as four months of age but usually develops in 9- to 12-month-old pets.

Pulmonic Stenosis

Another congenital heart problem, called pulmonic stenosis, consists of a narrowing of the connection between the right ventricle (lower heart chamber) and the pulmonary artery that leads to the lungs. This congenital defect makes the heart work harder to push blood through the narrow opening. Heart muscles sometimes compensate by growing stronger, but many times the heart defect becomes life-threatening. Large-breed dogs also can be born with aortic stenosis, a narrowing of the connection between the left ventricle and the aorta, the large artery that carries blood out of the heart.

Generalized Demodectic Mange

The American Pit Bull Terrier appears to have an inherited predisposition to the generalized form of demodectic mange. Localized spots spread into massive patchy or generalized hair loss and skin inflammation, often complicated by bacterial infection that may cause the feet to swell. The skin looks red, crusty, and warm and has many pustules. It bleeds easily, becomes very tender, and has a strong "mousy" odor due to bacterial infection on the skin. The condition can ultimately kill the dog, and generalized demodicosis requires aggressive therapy.

Treatment

Treatment involves shaving the dog to offer better access to the skin, and weekly or every-other-week whole-body dips with a miticidal preparation. Mitaban (amitraz), though quite effective against the mite, has some contraindications. Use this product only with veterinary supervision. Antibiotic therapy fights secondary infections. Exfoliating shampoos such as those containing benzoyl peroxide are helpful.

Unfortunately, APBTs suffering from generalized demodicosis have a guarded prognosis and may never achieve a cure. Because of the potential heritable components involved in this disease, dogs who have suffered generalized demodicosis should not be bred.

Hip Dysplasia

The dog's pelvis cups the head of the femur (thigh bone) in a socket of bone that forms the hip. If the alignment isn't perfect, a progressive degenerative joint disease called hip dysplasia (HD) develops. The misalignment causes wear and tear on the joint, which promotes arthritis. Hip dysplasia is the most common cause of rear-end lameness in dogs, especially large dogs like APBTs.

Although very common, a relatively small percentage of dogs suffer the severest, most crippling form of the disease. Some dogs may never show problems at all. Medical treatment can lessen the symptoms, but you can't cure the disease by treating with medicine or surgery.

Genetics accounts for about 25 percent of a dog's chance for developing hip dysplasia, and even dogs with normal parents can develop the condition. But the genetic component of HD can be influenced by lifestyle, nutrition, weight, and activity level. Severe disease may be seen as early as four months of age but usually develops in 9- to 12-month-old pets. These dogs have trouble getting up, difficulty jumping, limp after exercise, or display a classic wavery or bunny-hop gait. Dogs with HD should not be bred, to avoid passing on the trait to offspring.

Diagnosing Hip Dysplasia

Outward signs may point to a problem, but for a conclusive diagnosis, X-rays are performed. While some vets will take the X-rays without sedating your dog, others may insist on sedation. The dog is placed onto his back, and the veterinarian takes the X-ray and then looks at the film for the typical arthritic changes and subluxation (laxness) of the bone fit. Some changes won't be seen early on, because as the dog grows, changes take place.

The Orthopedic Foundation for Animals (OFA) provides a consulting service for purebred dog owners and breeders. The OFA reviews hip X-rays provided by an owner to evaluate the dog's conformation and sends a certificate stating their findings. If abnormal, they send a letter explaining why the dog didn't pass. Dogs must be two years old to be certified. You may ask for the X-rays to be returned to you (for a small fee). It's a good idea in case of future injuries or debilitation. It takes training to take correct OFA X-rays but can be done by experienced general practitioners. Ask around at local dog clubs to find a vet practiced in taking OFA films. If done incorrectly, the test can give false readings.

The PennHip technique tests puppies as early as four months old and reveals joint laxness even before arthritic changes take place. This method takes three X-rays and requires anesthesia. It positions the pet onto his back but uses a form to position the dog's knees into a froglike posture to mimic what happens when he stands.

The genetic component of HD can be influenced by lifestyle, nutrition, weight, and activity level.

Dogs can be certified free of hip dysplasia by sending appropriate X-rays to either the OFA registry or the PennHip registry. The OFA costs less because there's only one X-ray taken, which is evaluated by three radiologists who score the hips fair, good, or excellent. PennHip evaluation uses computer analysis to compare the three X-rays to all the other dogs of that breed in the registry.

Management and Treatment

Most dogs do well with medical management to control discomfort. Weight control and moderate exercise help keep these dogs flexible. Cartilage-enhancing medications like chondroitin sulfate and glucosamineglycan, used at a very high dose early on, and then a maintenance dose for the rest of the APBT's life, can slow the development of hip dysplasia. But cartilage never heals once it's damaged. Restricting the growth rate of pups during the first year delays the development and severity of the condition. Foods that promote a moderate growth rate are particularly important.

When hip dysplasia can be diagnosed before arthritis develops, surgery can rebuild the hip joint. A triple pelvic osteotomy (TPO) is best performed at 7 to 12 months of age. The procedure cuts the pelvis in three places to rotate the socket to a more correct angle. Wire and a plate hold the pelvis in position, so the pet can bear weight during the six weeks needed for the fractures to heal. This expensive surgery prevents arthritis from developing, and after a 24- to 48-hour hospitalization, the dog can walk out the door. Most surgeons perform TPO on one hip at a time, with a four- to five-week period between procedures to allow for healing and rehab.

Once arthritis develops, a total hip replacement surgery (similar to that done

Elbow Dysplasia

Some APBTs suffer joint pain in the elbow as they grow, due to elbow dysplasia, and end up having arthritis in the elbow. The Orthopedic Foundation for Animals (OFA) evaluates elbow dysplasia in dogs.

The elbow joint consists of three bones in a complex hinge joint, making it difficult to develop workable artificial joints for replacement surgery. When "floating" fragments of bone or cartilage result, surgery to remove them can relieve the pain. In most cases, though, treatment relies on pain medications. As a last resort, athrodesis—freezing the joint—can be an option. The motion of bone rubbing on bone as cartilage deteriorates causes the pain. Making the joint stationary causes a loss of some function but eliminates the pain.

for humans) offers the best prognosis. A prosthetic joint replaces the damaged joint. A third surgery, the least expensive, can benefit dogs who weigh less than 40 pounds (18 kg). The femoral head ostectomy (FHO) removes the femoral head, or "ball" of the joint, and prompts the APBT's body to create a new "false" joint from fibrous scar tissue.

GENERAL CANINE HEALTH ISSUES

APBT's are also at risk from problems that can affect any breed, including allergies, cancer, and ear and eye problems.

Allergies

An allergy is an overreaction of the immune

system when protective cells mis-recognize harmless substances as dangerous. The response to these substances (allergens) results in the symptoms your dog suffers. Dogs develop allergies to the same things as people do. But rather than sneeze attacks or runny noses, allergic dogs itch.

Flea Allergy

Flea allergy, the most common dog allergy, results from the reaction to a protein in flea saliva. Dogs display extreme itchiness on their rear half, especially above the tail. The worst reactions happen during the summer months, but fleas can live in the house year-round and drive your dog crazy. Treatment consists of administration of flea products that repel and kill the parasite on the dog and eliminate them in his environment.

Inhalant Allergy

Inhalant allergy (atopy), the second most common allergy, also can be seasonal. Dogs react to pollen, mold, fungi, or other inhaled allergens. Most signs first develop when a dog reaches one to three years old. Signs include front-half itchiness, including ear infections and foot licking. To diagnose and treat this type of allergy, skin tests identify the specific allergens. Suspect allergens injected into the shaved skin of the sedated dog develop redness or swelling if positive. Dogs may react to a single allergen or multiple culprits, and since allergens exist naturally in the environment and can't be avoided, allergy shots help some dogs by helping his body tolerate exposure. Your veterinarian also

Some allergies may be seasonal, as a reaction to pollen or other inhaled allergens.

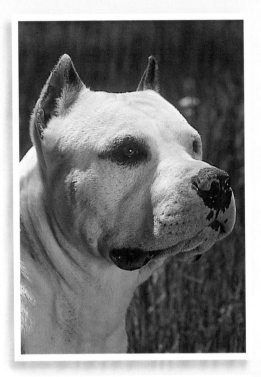

Eye infections may be the result of an injury.

one, over a period of several weeks, common proteins are added to the diet to see which cause a reaction. Once problem proteins are identified, they can be avoided in the diet.

Cancer

Cancer strikes dogs at any age but primarily affects old pets aged ten and above. The cells of the body constantly die and are replaced, but for unknown reasons, sometimes the new cells mutate into abnormal fast-growing cells (cancer) that crowd out healthy ones. Dogs suffer from more kinds of cancer than any other domestic animal. But according to veterinary specialists, cancer is the most treatable—and curable!—of any chronic pet disease. Common kinds of cancers include skin cancer (the most common), followed by breast cancer, lymphoma, mouth tumors, bone cancers, and testicular cancer.

Signs of cancer vary, depending on location and the type of tumor. Common symptoms include abnormal swelling, sores that won't heal, weight loss, bleeding or discharge from any body opening, weight loss, bad odor, difficulty eating or swallowing, reluctance to exercise, persistent lameness, and difficulty breathing or eliminating.

Diagnosis requires taking sample cells with a needle, when possible, and examining them under the microscope to determine the kind of cancer. An ultrasound, X-ray, or other imaging technique can find tumors on the inside of the body. Benign tumors isolated to one spot tend to be very treatable, while malignant cancers can be challenging because they spread throughout the body.

Treatment

Standard treatments of surgery, chemotherapy, and radiation may be used alone or in combination to treat cancer, depending on the

often prescribes drugs to help reduce the itching. You can reduce exposure by rinsing dust and pollen off your pet with regular baths and getting rid of reservoirs like carpeting and fuzzy dog beds that attract and capture allergenic substances. High Efficiency Particulate Air (HEPA) filter systems can be helpful, too.

Food Allergy

Food allergy results from a sensitivity to one or more proteins in the diet, including beef, milk, corn, wheat, or eggs. Dogs must have been previously exposed to the protein to become allergic to it. Affected dogs itch all over, all year round, but rarely vomit. To diagnose food allergies, dogs are fed an elimination diet, starting with one protein he's never before eaten (and so will not react to). One by type of tumor. However, dogs rarely feel sick or lose their hair during treatment.

Other treatment options include cryosurgery (freezing the tumor) or heat therapy (hyperthermia), which "cooks" the cancer to kill it, using sound waves. There are therapeutic "cancer" diets for dogs, which prove helpful. Genetically engineered tumor vaccines also are being used to treat canine cancers. A veterinary oncologist offers advanced options and provides the best chance of successful treatment.

Ear Infections

Canine ear infections are common because dog ear canals are shaped like an "L" and tend to trap moisture that creates a perfect environment for bacteria, fungus, and parasites like ear mites. Clean, dry ears stay healthy, but water, soap, excess wax, or foreign objects can lead to infections.

Ear infections prompt head shaking and scratching and often arise from allergy or ear mites. Any kind of discharge, from goopy and sweet-smelling to greenish-yellow or dark and bloody with pus needs immediate treatment. Ears may smell rancid, fruity, or doggy, and a head tilt or loss of balance indicates a deep infection. The wrong medication could make the problem worse or even cause deafness.

Treatment

Your veterinarian will evaluate the discharge and prescribe medicated drops or salve based on the type of infection—whether it's yeast, a specific kind of bacterium, or mites. Some types of infection may be tough to cure and require twice-daily treatment for several weeks.

Eye Infections

Eye infections develop when something scratches the eye and introduces bacteria.

The eyelids swell and/or a green to yellow discharge develops. Dogs paw at the eye or squint from pain, and infected eyes often mat shut.

Infection that develops from an injury usually affects only one eye, but it can spread to the other if not treated. When both eyes look nasty, the infection probably comes from a virus such as tracheobronchitis, which causes kennel cough.

Treatment

Eye infections can lead to blindness if not treated right away, especially when due to an injury. The veterinarian may need to culture the eye secretions to choose the right medicine to fight the infection. When infection is due to an injury like an ulcer, pain medicine may also be prescribed.

ALTERNATIVE THERAPIES

Also called holistic, alternative therapies offer a range of treatment options said to be more "natural" than traditional Western medicine. Alternative therapies work particularly well for chronic conditions and often are termed "complementary therapies" because they may be used in conjunction with (not instead of) traditional medicine.

mechanism, conventional medicine recognizes that stimulation of acupoints works. Acupuncture is particularly helpful to dogs for the relief of arthritis pain. The American Academy of Veterinary Acupuncture (AAVA) offers training and certification for veterinary acupuncturists.

Chiropractic

Chiropractic manipulation adjusts the bones of the spine and the joints to keep them in healthy alignment and in normal communication with the nervous system. Chiropractic care relieves pain and sometimes even paralysis. Canine athletes, in particular, benefit from regular chiropractic adjustment.

Veterinarians must acquire chiropractic training, or chiropractors receive veterinary training, to become accredited to work on animals. The American Veterinary Chiropractic Association (AVCA) can assist you in finding qualified help.

Herbal Therapy

Herbal therapy uses plants (bark, seeds, roots, leaves) as medicine. A large percentage of modern drugs originally came from herbs—for instance, willow bark contains a chemical similar to aspirin. Those who use herbs believe they can be as effective but cause fewer side effects than purified drug forms. Herbal therapies often are combined with conventional medicine for the best effect.

Healing herbs come in many forms, from dried and concentrated to packed in capsules or extracted into liquids and tinctures. Effectiveness and potency varies depending on when harvested, how packaged, and how preserved.

Herbs are potent medicine and are not benign, and they can have dangerous interactions with other medications. Herbs should be prescribed by a knowledgeable veterinarian. The Veterinary Botanical Medicin

Alternative therapies can work in conjunction with traditional medicine.

Acupuncture

An ancient medical practice called acupuncture holds that the body has the ability to heal itself. Acupoints throughout the skin are said to correspond to and be connected with various body systems through invisible energy pathways (meridians). Practitioners believe that sickness arises when these meridians are blocked.

Acupuncture treatment consists of inserting needles into the appropriate acupoint to stimulate and unblock the pathway, thus allowing the body to heal itself. Acupuncture has been used for at least 3,000 years in China.

To scientists, meridians sound like nonsense. But even though we don't understand the

Association (VBMA) is a group of veterinarians and herbalists dedicated to developing responsible herbal practice.

Homeopathy

Homeopathic treatment gives the sick dog a microscopic amount of a substance which, in larger amounts, would prompt the same symptoms of disease. This serves to "wake up" the dog's immune system and kick it into protection mode to treat the illness. There are more than 2,000 homeopathic remedies said to work just as well in dogs as in people.

Homeopathy works differently than conventional medicine because the doses are diluted to such an extent that no measurable amount of the substance remains. The more dilute, the "greater" becomes the potency—which doesn't seem to make any sense. Although experts can't say how it works, studies comparing homeopathy to placebo (sugar pills) proved that the method does work in a percentage of cases. Over-the-counter homeopathic medicines are safe, but the most effective treatments for your dog come from a veterinarian. You can find a homeopathic veterinarian through the Academy of Veterinary Homeopathy (AVH).

Physical Therapy/TTouch

Physical therapy (PT) includes various forms of bodywork, including massage. Used to relieve stress, improve range of motion, and strengthen and rehabilitate injury, manipulative therapies focus on the proper functioning of the joints and related muscles, including the spine. PT usually requires a specialist in canine physiology. Techniques vary from hands-on manipulation to electro-stimulation of muscles and swim therapy.

Massage therapy concentrates on the soft tissues of the body—the muscles and tendons, rather than bones and joints. Massage uses the fingers and hands to stroke and knead tissues with varying pressure to relieve the effects of injury. Massage increases blood circulation to the area, which helps nourish the tissue, relieve pain, and promote healing. Massage can also help release scar tissue, loosen tight muscles and tendons, and increase flexibility to improve mobility. Gentle massage can be performed by owners, but deeper therapeutic massage, especially when the dog is sore, should be left to professionals.

According to founder Linda Tellington-Jones, TTouch therapy addresses problem pet behaviors by changing the way the brain operates and learns. TTouch particularly helps with fear. The technique can be performed by owners and uses

Knowledge of first aid can help save your American Pit Bull Terrier's life.

First aid offers immediate treatment until you are able to get to the vet.

a series of circular touches, pushing the skin in a clockwise direction, done all over the body.

FIRST AID

First aid is exactly that—the emergency medical care given before seeking professional veterinary help. Some situations, such as stopped breathing, require first aid, because your dog would die before you could get him to the veterinarian. First aid does not replace medical care, though; it simply offers immediate treatment until you're able to reach a medical professional.

Shock

Any sudden trauma, from a bite, broken bone, bleeding, or other injury, can cause shock. Due to decrease in blood volume or a collapse of the vessels, the heart can't adequately move the blood, and the tissues of the body become starved for oxygen. The body attempts to compensate by shutting down normal blood flow to nonvital areas. But as the organs become more and more oxygen starved, they start to fail. This creates a vicious cycle that intensifies the shock. Left untreated, the dog will die. He acts dizzy, seems unaware of his surroundings, and has pale gums. Shock happens very quickly and requires vet help within 10 to 20 minutes or the dog will die. Keeping the dog warm by wrapping in a blanket can slow the process and buy more time to get help. If he's conscious, offer some honey or Karo syrup rubbed on his gums.

Rescue Breathing

Injuries from animal bites, being hit by a car, falls, heatstroke, poisoning, drowning, and more can cause your dog to stop breathing. You have minutes to save your APBT's life. If your dog has stopped breathing and is unconscious, give artificial resuscitation.

- Close the dog's mouth with your hands and place your lips over his nose.

- Give three quick breaths.

- If that doesn't start him breathing again, you'll need to blow into his lungs once every three to five seconds.

- Watch for his chest to rise, then remove your lips and let the air escape.

- Continue rescue breathing until you reach help—have another person drive you to the clinic.

Injuries

Bites

APBTs sometimes get bitten by wild animals but more often suffer bites from other pets. Bites are always more serious than they look, especially from other dogs. The pointed canine teeth leave superficial-looking punctures but rip the muscle underneath.

The pressure of bites can tear internal organs, bruise the lungs or heart, or break bones. Bites require veterinary attention, but serious wounds need first aid to control bleeding, shock, or breathing problems until you can get your dog to the veterinarian. Apply pressure to control bleeding, keep the dog warm to counter shock, and if he stops breathing, administer rescue breathing.

Bleeding

Bleeding arises from cuts, scrapes, bites, or other injuries. Bleeding can help clean wounds, and clotting starts in about 90 seconds to seal the injury. Most bleeding looks worse than it is, and shallow cuts or abrasions may not need a vet's attention. But a cut artery or vein and gaping wounds can result in life-threatening blood loss. Internal bleeding may be hidden, or blood can appear in the vomit, urine, or stool. Bleeding from the rectum or other body opening could be caused by disease, poison, or trauma. All can result in shock. Severe bleeding requires emergency first aid and immediate veterinary help.

- Rinsing with water makes severe wounds bleed worse. Instead, apply a clean soft cloth or sanitary napkin to the wound with direct pressure for up to ten minutes to stop the bleeding.

- If the pad bleeds through, place a second pad on top of the first and continue pressure.

- Elevating the injured area helps slow bleeding, but don't force this if it makes your dog uncomfortable.

- Should the wound continue to spurt blood

Even the most gentle dog can bite when in pain—a muzzle will allow you to give first aid without injury to yourself.

In hot weather, watch your APBT closely for signs that he's getting overheated.

from a leg or tail despite efforts to stop the bleeding, a tourniquet may be necessary.

- Use pantyhose, a necktie, roll gauze, or other one-inch (3-cm) strip of soft material that won't cut, loop around the limb two inches (5 cm) from the wound (toward the body), and tie once. Knot a rigid pencil or similar object on top, and gently twist until bleeding slows (but doesn't stop). Fasten in place with more cloth so it doesn't move, and get to the veterinarian quickly, as the tourniquet shouldn't be in place longer than 15 or 20 minutes or it risks damage to the limb.

Broken Bones

Fractures don't kill dogs, but they're very painful. Broken bones happen from trauma, such as being hit by a car. Injuries that cause breaks could be life threatening. Dogs favor the injured area, so a dog with a broken leg or pelvis refuses to stand. With a broken jaw, he may refuse food. Broken ribs make breathing painful. When the bone stays inside the tissue (closed fracture), you might see the leg held at an odd angle. But an open fracture pokes bone through the skin, complicating the injury with bleeding and possibly dangerous infection. Watch for and treat your dog for shock.

- Even friendly dogs lash out when injured. As long as he's able to breathe, a muzzle allows you to give first aid without yourself being injured. Use a scarf, leash, or other long strand; wrap it around and tie a knot on top of his muzzle; and then pull the ends under the jaw and tie a second knot. Finish with the ends tied behind the base of the neck.

- Get help to carefully move your dog (shoulders and hips at the same time) onto a stiff surface like an ironing board to transport. You want to move the dog's spine as little as possible in case there's injury of the back.

- Cover him with a blanket, and tape him to the board over his body behind the front legs and in front of rear legs to keep him immobile.

- If you don't have an ironing board, place him on a blanket and use it like a stretcher.

- For open fractures, you'll see blood-clotted fur whether the bone still protrudes or not. Leave the fracture in place, and just cover the area with sterile gauze or clean cloth.

- Treat to stop any bleeding.

- If you are more than 30 minutes from the vet, stabilize leg fractures with a temporary splint. Wrap a towel around the leg, then wrap with bubble wrap and secure with self-sticking plastic wrap to hold it together until you reach the vet.

Frostbite

Tissue is 90 percent water, and freezing causes cells to rupture when the water expands, just like ice cubes overflowing the tray. The resulting damage can be painful and severe and is referred to as frostbite.

Pets conserve heat in cold weather by diverting blood circulation from the extremities to protect the organs in the central part of the body. But reduced circulation leaves the ear tips, toes, scrotum, and tail unprotected, and these areas most commonly suffer from frostbite.

Your APBT may limp from frozen toes; frozen ear tips tend to droop, and the skin will be very cold, hard, and nonpliable. Redness, blisters, and serious infection develops days later. Severe frostbite causes the tissue to become leathery and insensitive to sensation, and if not removed surgically, the damaged tissue falls off. First aid may save the tissue.

• Thaw frozen areas with lukewarm water.

• For areas hard to dunk, hold (don't rub) a warm wet towel against affected skin and exchange for a fresh towel every few minutes.

• Tissue that's completely frozen may take up to 20 minutes to thaw. Less deeply frozen areas immediately turn very red as they rewarm, and the skin becomes softer, warmer, and more pliable.

• Apply an antibiotic ointment to the oozing area to help protect against infection until your veterinarian can treat your pet.

Mild, first-degree frostbite usually resolves within a week or so. Bandages protect the area, minimize pain, and encourage healing.

Antibiotics, pain medication, or even surgery to removed damaged or dead tissue may be necessary. It may take several weeks for the damage to completely heal.

Heatstroke

APBTs don't sweat. To cool off, they pant with mouth open and tongue lolling so the moisture evaporates off the tongue. But for panting to work, the outside air must be a lower temperature than the dog's normal body temperature (101° to 102.5°F [38° to 39°C]). If self-cooling fails, heatstroke kills in less than 15 minutes.

Signs of mild heatstroke include rapid panting, bright red tongue and gums, sticky saliva, and body temperature of 104° to 106°F (40° to 41°C). Most rectal thermometers register only up to 108°F (42°C), though, and severe cases of heatstroke may go off the scale—110°F (43°C) or higher.

• For mild heatstroke, offer ice cubes in cold water or a sports drink, and wrap the dog in cold, wet towels.

• Bring him into an air-conditioned space and turn on a fan so he breathes air that's cooler than his body. That helps panting bring down his internal temperature naturally.

Poisonous Foods

Adult dogs become quite inventive begging for or even swiping tasty treats, but some of these can be poisonous. Chocolate contains theobromine, a stimulant related to caffeine, and shouldn't be fed; and cocoa bean mulch causes the same problems. Grapes, raisins, and macadamia nuts also are toxic to dogs.

- For severe heatstroke (body temperatures over 106°F [41°C]), douse the pet with cold water from the hose, or dunk him in the bathtub or sink.

- Ice packs placed in the "armpits" or groin (near major blood vessels) help chill the blood so it cools the pet during circulation.

- Have someone drive to the emergency clinic while you administer to the pet in the back seat.

Poisoning

Dogs tend to be affected either by swallowing poison such as candy-coated people medicine or by absorbing it through their skin (the wrong flea treatment). Dogs can have toxins spilled on them or walk through poisons (motor oil), or they can swallow sweet-tasting substances (chocolate or antifreeze).

Poisons cause a huge range of symptoms that develop from within minutes to days later. Signs of flea product toxicity include excessive salivation, watering eyes, urination, defecation, and labored breathing and develop within about 20 minutes. Warfarin poisoning (rat bait) makes the dog bleed from the mouth, nose, ears, or rectum. Antifreeze poisoning initially causes drunken behavior but ultimately causes kidney failure (the pet stops urinating) and death. Poison can also cause seizures and vomiting. Be prepared to treat for shock or to perform rescue breathing for your dog.

Poisoning needs immediate medical attention, and first aid can save the dog's life by either getting rid of the poison, neutralizing it, or diluting it to give you time to seek help.

- When the poison arises from skin contact, give your dog a bath. Use a degreasing shampoo or dishwashing liquid. Rinse, rinse, and rinse again!

- If you've seen the dog swallow the poison and he's conscious, feed him half a meal to dilute the poison. Milk can help coat the stomach.

- Make him vomit up to an hour after ingestion. Use a syringe or turkey baster to give household hydrogen peroxide, one teaspoon for every 10 to 15 pounds (5 to 7 kg) he weighs.

- Be sure to bring a sample of the poison (or the vomit), including the package, to the veterinarian for analysis so the proper treatment or antidote can be given.

DISASTER PREPAREDNESS

When Mother Nature throws a tantrum, you have no time to waste. Keeping your human and furry family safe can prove daunting unless you've made advanced preparations.

Watch weather reports. When weather turns iffy, bring your dog inside so you won't have to search for him. Create a "safe room" in the house to safely confine him until the all-clear signal. If you must evacuate, take your pets along. It may be days before authorities allow you to return home.

Find out before a disaster whether shelters accept pets. Even those that do may have a size or number limit, and a Pit Bull likely won't be allowed unless he's a certified service dog. Stack the deck in your dog's favor by putting together

> ### Disaster Services Program
>
> For more about the Humane Society of the United States Disaster Services Program, visit www.hsus.org/disaster, e-mail disaster@hsus.org, or write for their disaster preparedness brochures.

a credential packet with his obedience titles, Canine Good Citizen credentials, health records, and anything else that documents what a great dog he is.

The following list can help you prepare for evacuation.

- Find a hotel, friend, or other accommodation in advance that will let you bring your APBT. You can find information on pet-friendly hotels at www.petswelcome.com. Hotels that normally refuse pets may make exceptions during disasters.

- Each dog should wear a collar with tags containing current identification and your contact information. Attach the phone number and address of your temporary shelter, if you know it, to the pet's collar tags. You can buy temporary tags or put adhesive tape on the back of your APBT's ID tag, adding information with an indelible pen. Write directly on a flat nylon collar or halter to make it easy for a stranger to read the information. If you have nothing else handy, use a permanent felt-tip marker and write your cell phone number and name on the collar and on your dog's abdomen.

- Prepare a "pet kit" ready to take along that contains a three-day supply of all your pets' essentials. If easily packed, take an extra towel or blanket for each pet. Don't forget sturdy leashes, harnesses, or crates for safe confinement.

- Include a favorite comfort toy or treat, and the pets' food. Have plenty of plastic bags and newspapers as well as containers and cleaning supplies to help deal with pet waste. Puppy training pads work well in such cases.

- Prepare for the unthinkable, too. Include current photos of your pets in case they get lost, and bring a first-aid kit to care for possible injuries. Include disposable latex gloves, sterile dressings, antibiotic towelettes and ointment, eyewash, thermometer, and any prescription medications your pets need.

- Your evacuation kit should also include a cell phone, flashlight, extra batteries, battery powered radio, map of the area, whistle/air horn to signal for help, and matches in a waterproof container. Keep a list of emergency numbers with your phone, including a pet emergency clinic number and shelters that may temporarily house animals. Keep your car tank filled with at least half a tank at all times.

The Humane Society of the United States (HSUS) has been recognized by both the American Red Cross and FEMA as a source of expertise and partner in disaster relief for animals.

Allow your dog to cool off on hot days.

CHAPTER 9

AMERICAN PIT BULL TERRIER TRAINING

We don't appreciate rude behavior from human relatives, and canine family members are no different. While you can explain "no elbows on the table" and "use a napkin" to your nephew, it takes creative thinking to teach your Pit Bull to refrain from crotch-sniffing visitors or knocking people down as he dashes through the door. Ideally, your dog must know his manners at home and beyond. He is an example of his breed—for good or for ill—and to keep everyone happy and safe, train your APBT to ensure that he makes a good impression wherever he goes.

INTERMEDIATE OBEDIENCE

American Pit Bull Terriers not only are intelligent, they're incredibly powerful animals. A smart dog quickly learns he can out-pull, out-run, and out-clown humans into getting his way. Since people physically can't out-maneuver canine athletes, training intermediate obedience commands requires thinking outside the bully-brain. A good training class plus lots of practice can help you instill better manners in a month's time.

Work your dog at least twice a day. Dogs learn better with several short practice times throughout the day rather than one long session. Choose a training area with few distractions, such as the basement. Once he's mastered the commands in a calm setting like the living room, you can add distractions such as other family members being present, or doing exercises in the backyard, and progress to new places like the neighborhood park.

An APBT becomes reliable only with practice in much the same way a child hones musical

By the Numbers

Dogs of any age can learn obedience commands. While puppies can be taught more quickly, adult dogs have longer attention spans. Because adult APBTs already have an extensive vocabulary simply from living longer with humans, you can build on this knowledge.

A proper "heel" is necessary if you are showing your APBT.

skill by playing piano scales. Think of these intermediate commands as "doggy piano scales" that with practice allow your dog to eventually play the canine Carnegie Hall.

INTERMEDIATE COMMANDS

If you are a novice trainer, don't be afraid to seek out the help of a professional trainer who can help guide you and show you proper techniques for obedience training.

Heel

Your APBT will be required to leave your home upon occasion, if only to visit the veterinarian for routine care. Once out of the safe confines of a fenced yard, dogs can be injured or killed by running across a busy highway.

Even friendly dogs can become frightened. A scared Pit Bull won't think rationally—he'll react. Just imagine (from your dog's viewpoint) walking through a crowd of strange people, all taller than you with reaching hands and loud voices—that's overwhelming to nearly all dogs. Your Pit Bull doesn't want or need to be in charge and feels comforted when a trusted human guides him through new or scary situations. A leash provides safety and a feeling of security for the dog and control for the person. Leash laws may require you to keep your dog leashed.

But dogs won't automatically know how to politely walk on leash. When you pull, the dog instinctively counters by pulling back—and trust me, he's stronger than you are. When he "wins" the tug-of-war, that's like having four-year-old child directing traffic. "Heel" is an obedience command performed in competitions, and it means your dog walks calmly, without pulling, at knee level on your left side.

- Your APBT should wear a flat nylon or leather collar with a metal buckle that you can fit two fingers beneath. The collar should have attached any identification and vaccination tags. If he's mastered walking nicely on leash, you can clip the leash to his collar, but for first-time adult dogs, use a no-pull harness.

- Let the dog sniff the collar and leash. Don't let him chew or mouth it. These are not toys. They are tools that your dog should soon associate with fun games and freedom to explore.

- Make sure you have favorite smelly soft treats or a toy handy to use as a combination lure and reward. Stand to position your dog correctly, at knee level on your left side. Hold the leash in your right hand at your belly button, capturing the slack so it doesn't drag but keeping the leash loose.

- Show him your reward held in your left hand. Let him sniff or taste, but don't yet give it to him. Hold the reward right in front of his nose and say "heel" as you begin to walk forward with your left foot taking the first step. If you've been using a "let's go" verbal cue, you'll simply replace this with the "heel" command.

- Your goal is for him to walk nicely by your

Want to Know More?

For a refresher on clicker training, see Chapter 4: Training Your American Pit Bull Terrier Puppy.

No-Pull Harness

No-pull harnesses are training tools that can work for leash-training powerful dogs like the APBT, to prevent him from pulling you around. The leash hooks to a clip on the front of the dog's chest, so that when he pulls, the harness turns him back toward the person holding the leash. In order to move forward, he must walk with a loose leash. Effectively, the dog trains himself not to pull. Most dogs eventually can be transitioned to a collar and leash alone, but some may always need the reminder of a no-pull harness.

side on a loose (not tight) leash. If he pulls, stop and don't allow him to go any further, and don't give him the treat.

6. Set up and begin again, saying "heel" as you step out with your left foot and keep your left hand with treat in front of his nose. If he's jumping up to reach the treat, you're holding it too high.

7. After a few paces, stop and ask for a "sit." Reward him with the treat or toy.

8. Repeat the leash-walk exercise with the lure. Stop every few steps and place your dog in a sit each time.

9. He'll quickly understand that "heel" means to walk at your side—and you will pay him with a treat when he sits as you stop. After several exercises, your dog won't need to be lured but will want to know you have treats available. You can increase his attention and anticipation by eventually offering the reward intermittently. Rather than every time, pay him every second, third, or fourth time. This teaches your dog that he should

always obey, since he never knows when a treat will be produced.

10. Once you notice he listens for your "heel" command and begins to anticipate the "sit" when you stop, increase the several paces to a dozen or more of the "heel" exercise. Try heeling your dog around the entire perimeter of the yard, or do laps outside the house.

11. Vary the pace. You want your dog to maintain the pace at your side, whether you walk, trot, or run. Be sure to also practice changing directions. When your dog walks on the left, a turn to your right or an about-face to the right should be relatively easy for the dog to follow. Turning to the left may require luring with the reward, at least initially.

12. Once he's mastered "heel" without distractions in the backyard, begin practicing the exercise in the front yard during morning rush hour or when your

◎ Training Tidbit

Although the training methods mentioned in this chapter will work for a majority of dogs, some APBTs are so high drive that food/ toy rewards make them lose focus on the training exercise. Know your dog and find the appropriate reward that works best for him. A simple "good," "yes," or other praise word in a happy voice along with a quick pat may be more than enough to motivate your dog and communicate that he is doing the correct thing.

spouse tosses a ball on the other side of the room.

Stay (Wait)

Dogs easily get into trouble, and the "stay" command can save you aggravation. It can also save your dog's life if a worker accidentally leaves the gate open and you can't catch the dog before he dashes out after the teasing squirrel. What if the neighbor calls a friendly greeting from across the street and your dog races through traffic to reach him? Any open door, inside or out, invites a race to be first— do you enjoy being a human bowling pin knocked down in your dog's wake? The "stay" command stops your APBT before he leaps through the gate, scatters groceries from your arms, or becomes a hit-by-car statistic.

"Stay" means different things to different people. For those training for obedience contests, the command means that your dog doesn't move from his position once he's given the command. In other words, if he's seated, then the "stay" means he remains seated. If standing, the "stay" means he doesn't move from that pose.

Others use the command with more flexibility. I like the "wait" command, which basically means "don't move forward" or "delay action." For instance, command the dog at the door to "wait," so that he pauses and allows you to go out first. He's able to stand, sit, or down—or even back up—as long as he does not cross that invisible boundary. Or ask him to "wait" until the food bowl touches the floor before being allowed to approach and eat.

You'll teach these behaviors the same way and simply name them appropriately with the proper cue word. Whatever cue word is used, begin with "wait" and practice/refine to a full "stay."

If your dog already understands the "wait" command, you can use that to transition him to the "stay" command.

1. One of the quickest and most effective ways to teach "wait" is at the door. There's no need for a treat or toy reward, either, because allowing your dog to go through the opening serves as the reward. Simply approach the doorway as you normally would. When the dog comes with you, tell him "wait."

2. Start to open the door. Before he can muscle through, say "uh-oh!" (or some other cue that means he blew it) and close the door in his face.

3. Wait a few moments until he's again looking at you. Tell him "wait." Reach for the door—if he moves forward, pull your hand away until he's again calm. Start to open the door as you again say "wait." Continue to open it as long as he contains himself and doesn't move forward.

4. If he moves forward, "uh-oh" and shut the door. It may take half a dozen or more repeats for the light bulb to go off, so that he realizes the door will only open if he remains still.

5. Reward him for even a short "wait" of three to five seconds by giving him a release command—"okay!" (or something similar)—in a high pitched happy voice so that he can bound through the door. Be consistent using your release word as well as the "wait" command.

6. Once he has mastered a five-second wait, you'll know that your APBT understands the concept. Extend the time to 10 seconds, 15, and so on.

7. Practice at a variety of doors in the house so that he understands that the command applies no matter where it's given.

Sit-Stay

Every dog should have a solid "sit" command to use the same way humans use "please and thank you" to receive what they want. When a polite dog sits to gain access to all-good-things (a toy, a treat, dinner, playtime outside), he's also practicing control. Just the body position of a "sit" can help calm the exuberant canine.

Smart dogs know how to work the system, though, and may plant their nether regions when told to sit but then immediately bounce back up. Many dogs know how to sit when told to do so in the car, but want to fly out the door as soon as it opens or pace from window to window whenever the car stops. The longer he keeps still, the less trouble your dog can find.

A "sit-stay" simply extends the length of the butt-on-floor time. Should you decide to compete with your dog in obedience, the "sit-stay" command is required; the novice dog must hold a "sit-stay" for one minute in the presence of other dogs, while you stand across the ring from him.

But holding a "sit-stay" goes beyond winning kudos in the ring. Teach your APBT that the longer his tail remains planted, the more privileges he gains. He'll look for more and more ways to demonstrate what a good dog he is. Once he knows how to sit, you simply begin to reward him for staying in place. This will be incremental increases of time. If your dog already understands the "wait" command, you can use that to transition him to the "stay" (don't move at all) command. Here's how.

1. Have some very high-value treats handy, cut into tiny amounts. Also make sure you have a secondary, lesser-value reward handy. Plan to train in a place that has as few distractions as possible, like the living room. Make sure he's not just eaten a meal, so that he's eager for treats but not starving.

2. Show your dog the treats and reward, but don't give them to him. You want him to know good stuff could be his, but he must pay attention.

3. Tell him "sit."

4. As soon as his tail touches down, say "stay" and feed him the first tidbit.

5. Continue to give him tiny treat after treat as long as he holds the "sit." Aim for a reasonable ten-second "stay" to set him up for success. Release him with the "okay!" cue word and a "click" if using the clicker.

6. Give him a lesser-value reward (perhaps a toy), and throw him a praise party ("Good boy, what a smart doggy!") as

you release him from the "sit-stay." You want him to look forward to the high-value rewards for the "stay," rather than for breaking the "sit."

7. If he breaks the "sit-stay" before you've released him, stop the treats. Say "uh-oh, you blew it!" and turn your back with the treat/rewards for another ten seconds. This gives him time to connect the dots—that when he "sit-stays," the treats keep coming, but they go away if he moves.

8. Repeat the exercise. Say "sit-stay" and treat treat-treat for ten seconds, and release with "okay" and throw a praise party.

9. Practice this exercise several times, and try increasing the "stay" by two to five seconds, continuing to treat the whole time.

10. Once he's managing to hold the "stay" for 15 to 20 seconds at a time while treating constantly, begin to slightly delay the treats. He should continue to "sit-

Multi-Dog Tip

If your dogs get along well, you can turn dog-training exercises into a competition. Ask all your dogs to "sit" but give a huge bonus-treat only to the one who does so first. Do your dogs drag their feet when you call them inside? Call the dogs to "come," but only the first to respond gets the reward, and the rest stay outside. Your dogs will pay closer attention to commands, compete with each other to obey first, and all will improve their response time.

APBTs able to "down-stay" on command can offer great peace of mind to their owners as well as strangers they meet.

stay" for two to four seconds at a time between treats.

11. If he's successful in the last step 80 percent of the time, then increase the time between treats by another two or three seconds in the next training session—and so on.

12. Work toward reducing the numbers of tiny tidbit rewards to a taste every five to ten seconds, and beyond. If he holds a one-minute "stay," for example, give him several treats instead of one. Dogs quickly understand the bonus concept of higher value for better performance.

13. Once your APBT understands the concept of "sit-stay," practice hones the skill. Ask him to "sit-stay" in other places in the house. Why not make the "sit-stay" part of his dinnertime routine, with the full bowl being the ultimate reward.

14. Train for duration and length of the "sit-stay" before adding distance. Working close to your dog gives you greater control in teaching the concept. Be sure he's solid and can sit-stay for a minute or longer with you within touching range, before stepping back and practicing at increasing distances.

15. Ultimately, you want your dog to sit-stay even when he sees no treat or reward. Accomplish this by phasing out the treat-every-time to intermittent rewards. That way, he knows rewards are always a possibility and becomes more likely to remain faithful.

Down-Stay

Dogs communicate as much with body language as they do with whines, barks, or growls. You may have heard of "calming signals" that dogs use to diffuse tension in themselves and other creatures. These include yawns, averting their eyes, and licking the nose—and also assuming a "down" position.

Lying down not only tells other dogs that he's no threat, it also helps relieve his own stress and tension, relaxes him, and helps him think. The "down-stay" simply adds duration to the length of time he holds the position. In an obedience trial novice class, the dog must hold a "down-stay" for three minutes in the presence of other dogs, while you are some distance away.

More than that, an APBT able to "down-stay" on command offers great peace of mind to his owners as well as strangers he meets. He's less likely to aggress in this position. You may know he's a big teddy bear of a pooch—but others may be suspicious, and a "down-stay" posture diffuses suspicion.

1. As with the "sit-stay," prepare high-value rewards and a secondary award. Train in a low-distraction area.

Training Tidbit

Once your dog knows basic commands, you can "chain" them into more-complex behaviors or wow-factor tricks. Look for opportunities to reward (and name) natural behaviors. For instance, when he flops onto his side and rolls onto his back, tell him "stay." Couple the command with a hand signal of you "shooting a gun," and you've turned his spontaneous action into a play-dead trick.

2. Give the command "down," and lure him into position with the treat, but don't give it. His nose should contact the treat as he lowers himself into position.

3. As soon as he's in position, command "stay," and give him one, two, three, several treats in a row—treat, treat, treat—to keep him in place. Aim for five seconds, then give the release word ("okay!") and throw him a praise-party as you offer the secondary reward (a toy, for example). Remember, you want your dog to associate the unending treats with "stay" and not with the "okay" release, so be sure there's a big difference to the dog between primary and secondary rewards.

4. Continue to practice the "down-stay," just as you did with the "sit-stay" exercise. If he breaks the "down-stay" before you release him, tell him, "uh-oh, you blew it!" and turn your back and hide the treats for a ten-count. Then try again, but be sure this time you adjust the timing to a shorter "stay" duration so he can be successful. The key is to reward success and reduce the chance of failure.

5. Gradually increase the duration of the "down-stay" by two seconds at a time. Keep track of his performance, so that you can up the challenge when he's 80 percent successful on a previous session.

6. Aim to reduce the stream of rewards to a taste every few seconds. Remember to stay in close proximity until he reliably performs a "down-stay" for a minute or more at a time, without a treat.

7. Once he's reliable in close work, challenge your dog with "down-stays" at a distance. Give the command, then back away one step as you hold the treat. If he breaks the "stay" (sits up, stands, follows you), say "uh-oh, you blew it!"

and turn your back with the treat. Give him a minute for the consequences to make an impression before trying again.

8. When he's reliable with a "down-stay" and with you taking one step away, next take two steps—and so on.

9. As with the other commands, gradually phase out rewards until he receives treats for successful "down-stays" only intermittently. But instead of multiple tiny treats, he should get a boatload bonus every once in a while, unexpectedly. If he never knows when he'll be blessed with goodies, your dog comes closer to performing each time in the hope that he'll hit the jackpot.

Stand

Should you want to show your dog, he'll be expected to stand for a hands-on examination by the judge—a stranger he's never met. But the "stand" command proves useful every day. Your veterinarian will appreciate him knowing the command. And you'll also appreciate the "stand" command whenever you want your APBT to hold still during grooming.

1. Place your dog in a "sit."

2. Offer a treat at nose level for him to sniff. Bring it forward in a straight line away from his nose.

3. The dog should naturally go into a "stand" to follow the treat.

4. Let him go only a step or two to reach the "stand" position. Then treat and praise, and release.

5. Alternately, have treats and your clicker ready. Watch your dog and anticipate when he'll stand on his own.

6. When he moves into the proper position, immediately "click" and give the reward. Waiting for him to make the move on his own, and then capturing it with the clicker, can be a powerful way to teach your dog. He'll likely be confused about what prompted the click and treat and begin offering you various behaviors.

7. Avoid offering treats or clicks for anything *except* when he stands still.

8. If he sits or downs, and then stands, give a click and a huge bonus treat—and throw a praise party! It takes several times for the light bulb to go off, but once it does, and he realizes that standing turns on the human treat machine, that's a lesson he'll not soon forget.

9. Repeat the lesson frequently to keep him sharp.

Show dogs need to learn to "stand" for examination.

CHAPTER 10

AMERICAN PIT BULL TERRIER PROBLEM BEHAVIORS

Has your Pit Bull Terrier turned into a Pit Bull "Terror?" By reading this chapter, you deserve a (click-treat!) reward. Whether you have an existing issue or simply wish to prepare just in case, please take a deep breath and read this next sentence out loud—as often as needed:

All dog owners experience problem behaviors—and responsible people seek help.

There's no shame in identifying and seeking to resolve objectionable doggy behaviors. However, the vast majority of issues that owners have with their pets actually arise from misunderstood normal behaviors.

Our pets don't come preprogrammed to know what humans want or expect. For instance, aggression is normal—and justified—in some circumstances but is rarely acceptable behavior to humans. The urges to bark, chew, jump up, leash-pull, and nip come naturally and do not make him a bad dog, just a canine in need of human guidance.

Most people don't speak "dog" and may make behaviors worse if they react inappropriately, especially if what they do is also misunderstood by the dog. It takes time for you and your APBT to get acquainted, understand each other's needs, and adjust

to each other. After all, puppies are clueless infants, dogs adopted as adults could have bad habits, and rescued pets often have emotional problems from losing their home.

The good news is that most problem behaviors can be helped, especially when a determined owner acts out of love and commitment to provide a forever-home to a special American Pit Bull Terrier.

FINDING HELP FOR PROBLEM BEHAVIORS

Many irksome behavior issues can be solved with common sense. For example, if you don't want the dog to tear up the toilet paper, keep the bathroom door closed. Other issues such as leash-pulling can be turned around with help from a competent and savvy dog-training professional or class. But some behaviors could actually be signs of a health issue.

You know your dog best, and any change in behavior can signal a health problem. Aggressive behavior might indicate that the dog is suffering from a painful injury, or bathroom indiscretions could be due to your old dog's diabetes. Always consult a veterinarian about changes in behavior, to rule out physical causes.

Many clinics can refer you to a local trainer or class. But your veterinarian may not have the time, and not every trainer has the ability to address more challenging issues. Some problems you see could be due to chemical imbalances in the brain that prompt actions of aggression, fear, or obsessive/compulsive behaviors. Serious problems require professional help that may include prescription medication as well as plans to help your dog react in more positive, acceptable ways.

Anyone can claim to be a behavior expert. Following poor advice can make your dog problems worse, so verify credentials. You can find behavior help through the following resources:

- **The American College of Veterinary Behaviorists** (ACVB) consists of veterinarian behavior specialists ("diplomates" or DACVB). They are also able to diagnose concurrent health conditions and prescribe drug therapies that may be helpful. There are currently about 50 board-certified veterinary behaviorists in the United States and Canada. Find a listing of members at www.dacvb.org.

- **The Animal Behavior Society** (ABS) certifies qualified individuals as Applied or Associate Applied Animal Behaviorists, with the title Certified Applied Animal Behaviorist (CAAB). These may or may not be veterinarians and hold doctorate-level animal behavior education. There are currently about 50 members. Find more information at www.animalbehavior.org/ABSAppliedBehavior/caab-directory.

- **The International Association of Animal Behavior Consultants, Inc.** (IAABC) is a professional organization that accredits and qualifies members as Certified Animal Behavior Consultants (CABC) or Certified

Dog Behavior Consultants (CDBC). These experts may or may not hold graduate-level degrees and often work in partnership with local veterinarians. Learn more about the organization at www.iaabc.org/about.htm.

- **The National Association of Dog Obedience Instructors, Inc.** (NADOI), founded in 1965, promotes modern, humane training methods and endorses members who pass written tests and have accumulated demonstrable experience in training and canine behavior. To find a trainer endorsed by NADOI, see www.NADOI.org.

Some behaviors could be signs of a health issue.

The Association of Pet Dog Trainers (APDT) boasts 5,000 members worldwide and certifies dog trainers as Certified Pet Dog Trainer (CPDT). Members are qualified to help you with a wide variety of canine training issues, and some also have expertise in general dog behavior problems. For more information and list of member trainers, see www.apdt.com.

> ## Understand Your APBT
> Your Pit Bull doesn't act "bad" out of vindictiveness or because he's dumb. Dogs always have a reason for their behavior. It's up to humans to understand why dogs act out and provide better ways for them to deal with their environment and their beloved owners.

AGGRESSION

While there are exceptions, APBTs are known to be dog-aggressive. With proper direction, usually they can learn to be more tolerant. Dog-to-human aggression in American Pit Bull Terriers is rare, despite what you might hear from the media.

Pit Bulls do not have "locking jaws" or bite pressure greater than that of other dogs of similar size. However, they have been selectively bred as a "catch dog," which means once they decide to bite, they don't let go. All dogs, including the APBT, have exquisite control of their bite. A growling, snapping dog doesn't "miss" because you jerked your hand away in time; that dog missed on purpose—exercising great control to deliver a nonbloody warning to back off, instead of a bite. In fact, you *want* your dog to give a growled warning, not simply attack out of the blue. Then you can take the proper steps to address the issue before it's too late.

Poorly socialized dogs, and those with little training, lack the experience or skills to properly react. They don't know how to pull punches and may bite with little provocation. Each episode of aggression allows a dog to practice bad behavior and increases the probability of a repeat offense. One dog fight predicts the next, usually within 24 to 48 hours and in the same vicinity.

Because of the APBT's reputation in the public eye, as a Pit Bull owner you must take aggression very seriously. Even a warning growl could get you and your dog into trouble. So anticipate high-risk situations, and avoid them. **Serious cases of aggression require professional help.**

Dog-to-Human Aggression

Canine aggression can be categorized in different ways, based on a combination of the dog's target and the underlying trigger. Dog bites of humans usually result from *fear aggression* when a dog can't escape a perceived threat, *predatory aggression* when play turns rough, or *territorial aggression* if the dog tries to protect his yard from a visiting stranger.

- **Fear aggression** happens when the dog must choose between fight-or-flight. Dogs chained or tethered outside become defensive and cannot escape, so are forced to fight if approached. Some municipalities now forbid chaining or tethering of dogs for this reason. Provide a fenced enclosure in which your dog can keep a safe distance from approaching humans and you'll greatly reduce the potential for fear-aggression.

- **Predatory aggression** includes stalking, chasing, catching, biting, killing, and eating. Dogs target quickly moving animals, people (joggers), and objects (bikes, cars). The squeals of excitement/distress from a human child or adult also can trigger aggression. Identify triggers, and teach an alternative behavior. For example, when your dog eyes the jogger, ask him to find a favorite toy or to go for a walk.

- **Territorial aggression** happens when your dog believes he must defend his house, yard, street, or even the neighborhood. Defensive displays most often take place in doorways, gates, or hallways and along fences. Kitchens (food source) and bedrooms (sleeping territory) are prime guarding locations. Ask your dog to "sit-wait" so a human doesn't have to compete to get through doorways. Dogs often growl at people outside the fence and are rewarded when the mailman leaves. Instead, ask the mailman to toss treats as he nears, and when the dog stops growling to pick up the treat, the stranger says "good dog" and leaves. Dogs that think about treats forget to growl.

Multi-Dog Tip

A new adult dog introduced into a household of resident dogs often takes time to reveal his normal personality. He may have been stressed or uncertain while in the shelter, or less confident as the new guy in your home. After one or two months of initial calm, these dogs may become more confident and begin challenging the others for social standing. Proper introductions and prompt separation so they don't practice aggression helps enormously.

Dog-on-Dog Aggression

Interdog aggression (also called status-related) most often occurs between same-sex canines (usually males) and often consists of a junior dog trying to move up through the ranks. Neutering decreases the problem in the boys. But female-female fights usually result in more serious injury, and spaying these females can actually make the aggression worse.

Dogs challenge with stares, shoves from hips or shoulders, mounting behavior, or blocking access to food, play, or attention. Less secure dogs bark, growl, snarl, and try to bite, while dogs confident in their position already know their status and won't waste time starting a ruckus—but they will finish it.

Well-adjusted canines can "play fight" and roughhouse without causing injury, and the altercations sound horrific but mostly include lots of neck wrestling, open-mouth biting, and raised hackles. One or both dogs may get nicked with a tooth through an ear or lip. This can be bloody but is rarely serious.

Fights become dangerous when you resort to physical punishment and/or inadvertently encourage and support the wannabe dog over the true top canine. Preventing the high-ranking dog from putting the wannabe in his place, and/or giving the lower-ranking dog preferential treatment, or treating both dogs equally encourages squabbles to continue.

Preventing Dog-on-Dog Aggression

1. Know your dog. Figure out if he's dog-tolerant or reactive around other canines. Protect him by avoiding situations that set him up for potential failure. You can't control badly behaved owners/other dogs at a dog park, for example, so make educated choices.
2. When you live with more than one dog, identify (with your veterinarian's help)

Well-adjusted canines can roughhouse without causing injury.

which is the higher-ranking canine, and support that position. In 95 percent of the time, the older dog holding the longest residence is in charge. If they've squabbled, the key to calming them down means explaining to the wannabe that he doesn't want to be in charge.

To help establish and support the top dog, feed him first, greet him first, hand him toys first, and let him be allowed to go through doors first (even if you must crate the other dog). In all things, the top dog should receive highest privilege.

The wannabe dog should see this and be aware that the top dog gets preferential treatment. If you keep the dogs always separated, they will never learn. Allow supervised encounters but with both dogs wearing training leads for safe control.

If an altercation takes place, one person should have control of one dog's line, and a second person has the other. Tie them to immovable fence posts for safety sake but out of reach of each other. Let them howl and snarl and flail at each other from the distance away, until they quit.

6. Once the sound and fury passes, crate the underdog. And within sight of the underdog, make a big fuss and praise the top dog, making it very clear which dog "won" that round. Dogs truly understand body language, and the lesson will be powerful.

7. Leave the wannabe crated for 20 minutes before trying again—with both dogs still on leads. If they go at it again, you repeat the lesson.

8. Treatment won't always be this simple. Some dogs will never get along and will always need to be managed.

9. Separate Pit Bulls (even friendly dogs) any time you can't watch them, in different rooms or kennels. Keep a drag-line (leash) attached to the dogs so you can control interactions more easily by stepping on it or picking it up.

Dogs can be the best of friends but still may someday have an argument. When you're home, you often can quickly stop a small spat with a loud noise. But if you're not home, the same disagreement can escalate into a fight and injury to one or more dogs. Avoid this by getting the dogs used to being separated in a crate, in various rooms, or on a tie-down, first while you're home and then while you're away. You can rotate dogs so one is out while the other is contained.

Stopping Fights

1. To stop a fight, be safe and avoid getting bitten yourself. When your Pit Bull hasn't yet gotten a firm hold on the other dog, you may be able to stop the fight without bloodshed.
2. A loud, firm "wait!" or other command may interrupt the dog's concentration and focus.
3. Dumping a bucket of water, or even spraying with a fire extinguisher, may stop or at least interrupt them long enough for you to separate the dogs.
4. Setting a kitchen chair over top of the dogs or a baby gate between them also can work.
5. Once you've broken up the fight, if there's been no bloodshed, tie up or crate the "wannabe" troublemaker. Then make a huge fuss over the top dog again and again in front of the other dog, demonstrating it's just not worth it to the "wannabe."
6. If your dog has an established grip, he'll not let go without persuasion. A smooth, wedge shaped "break stick" can induce the dog to release his tenacious hold. Never use a break stick on other breeds, as they'd simply turn their teeth on you. Ask for a demonstration from an experienced APBT professional breeder to learn the proper way to use it. Do not attempt to use this piece of equipment without speaking to an expert first.
7. Once apart, crate separately and seek veterinary care when needed for the wounds.

BARKING

Barking communicates during play and defense to greet, warn, and garner attention. Think of your dog's bark as a shout-out or a fire alarm—he barks to alert his family to anything unusual. Dogs in general, and Pit Bulls in particular, are such social creatures that being left alone in the fenced yard can prompt barking from loneliness and frustration.

If you yell for him to shut up, he'll assume you're joining the bark-fest and redouble his efforts. Even negative reactions like scolding can reward a barking dog by giving the attention he wanted.

Curbing Problem Barking

You'll never totally eliminate barking. After all, your dog loves you and wants to protect and warn his family. So instead of trying to stop it, teach barking limits.

1. Problem barking that stems from boredom can be addressed by offering him something better to do with his mouth. He can't bark when he's munching a chew toy stuffed with peanut butter.
2. Dogs also want an audience and company. Thank him for barking (in a calm voice—don't bark back!), and then say "quiet" after two or three barks. If he keeps barking, tur

your back and leave. He'll learn that the audience goes away if he's noisy and returns only when he's quiet.

3. Block scary sounds that inspire barking. White noise machines are available, or simply turn the radio to a normal volume and tune it to static.

4. Pay attention to the circumstances. Barking at the mailman or other delivery folks teaches dogs to repeat the behavior, because your dog believes barking drove the person away. Enlist your mail carrier's help. Ask the person to toss your dog a treat after he's bark-announced the delivery. He can't chew and bark at the same time, and the food changes the association so the dog identifies the delivery person as a good thing—not something to fear or become defensive about.

5. Pay as much attention to him when he's being quiet as you do to shush. Catch him in the act of being a good dog, and tell him so.

6. Special head-halter training tools can work wonders. Pulling on the lead gently presses the dog's mouth shut for the few seconds of pressure, signaling him to be quiet, and you don't have to say a word. The halters are available from pet product stores and veterinarians.

7. Tone collars have a built-in microphone that emits a loud, short tone at the first "woof." That's often enough to make a dog stop and search for what caused the tone, and eliminates boredom and the barking, often within minutes. However, the collar must be adjusted properly or can "punish" the wrong dog if a canine friend barks nearby.

8. Researchers at Cornell University in New York found citronella collars to be much more effective in bark training than shock collars. Citronella collars give a warning tone first; additional barking prompts a

Try teaching the "quiet" command to reduce problem barking.

squirt of scent that stops the barking. Some of these collars have remote control activators.

Not all techniques work for every dog. If you haven't seen improvement in three to five days using one of the anti-bark techniques, try a different approach, or enlist the help of an experienced trainer. Just please, for the love of your APBT, stay away from shock collars. (See Training Tidbit sidebar for more information.)

CHEWING

Chewing is a normal behavior for dogs. They chew to manipulate objects, relieve boredom, and because it feels good. Puppies test their world the same way human infants do, but they don't have hands to grab things, so everything goes into the mouth. Teething youngsters chew objects to relieve the discomfort, but adult dogs rarely outgrow the habit.

Don't be surprised if your Pit Bull targets shoes or other items that smell like you. He's not doing it out of spite but chooses objects that remind him of a favorite person, because the smell comforts him. It's actually a canine compliment.

But chewing not only damages property, it can break teeth or result in dangerous swallowed objects or deadly electrocution should your dog target the computer wire.

Preventing Chewing

Don't blame the pet for doing what comes naturally. Instead, prevent problems by reducing opportunities to make mistakes.

1. Dog-proof the house by picking up tempting forbidden objects like shoes.
2. Avoid offering toys to your APBT that might confuse him or be dangerous. He may not understand why new shoes are forbidden but an old slipper is legal, or that it's okay to fetch the tree limb but he's not allowed to chew it.
3. Confine your Pit Bull to a safe zone when you can't supervise, so he doesn't chew off the arm of the chair. That may be a small room in the house or a crate when you go out, cook dinner, talk on the phone, or otherwise can't eyeball him.
4. Apply smelly or bad-tasting products such as menthol or Bitter Apple on objects you can't remove, such as baseboards or dangerous items like electric cords. (Some dogs like the taste of some of these products, so don't rely on this tip until you're sure it works.)
5. Avoid chasing after your dog when he makes a mistake, because playing keep-away with the illegal object is great fun and rewards the canine thief. Instead, run the other way. When he chases you in response,

Training Tidbit

Electrical stimulation (shock) collars for curbing barking can be inhumane. Dogs sometimes refuse to interact at all after being shocked, cease barking only while wearing the collar, and can be "punished" if other barking dogs or other loud noises set off the shock. Multiple controlled studies have shown that these types of shock-punishment tools do more harm than good, potentially causing both physical and emotional injury to the dog and damaging the bond you share.

Exercise can help prevent some problem behaviors, such as digging.

make a big deal over him with a trade of a legal chew-object for your wallet that he's stolen.

6. Commercial chew objects from pet product stores come in various sizes and flavors. Teething objects made from rawhide, rope, rubber, or sturdy canvas, some with squeakers, provide pups with lots of options. The best products, like the ones Nylabone makes, are nearly indestructible and can be filled with kibble or soft treats like peanut butter that makes them irresistible to your dog.

7. While the toy may be fine for teething youngsters, even "Pit Bull indestructible" toys could be eaten by a determined dog. Supervise your dog's chewing routine until you know what to expect, and leave him alone only with items you consider to be safe.

8. Provide at least three to five "legal" options for your chew-happy hound, and rotate a couple of times a week. That keeps your pet

happy, his teeth clean and healthy, and your walls and other precious belongings safe.

DIGGING

Terriers were bred to dig to capture critters, but American Pit Bull Terriers take after their bulldog heritage and don't tend to be problem diggers. However, any bored dog may indulge in dirt-kicking to escape under a fence, for example. Dogs feeling protective of toys or chew items may "plant" them in holes. In hot weather, dogs scoop out holes to cool their tummies against the damp soil. In the winter, dirt offers great insulation, and a hole offers a warm place to rest. Understanding why pets dig can help you figure out ways to stem the excavation.

1. Dogs who dig out of boredom need more one-on-one attention from the humans they love. Exercise tires out pets and reduces digging—a tired APBT is generally a much better behaved APBT. A minimum 20 to 30 minutes of aerobic exercise twice a day

is a good starting point, but APBTs do better with twice that amount. Break up the exercise into two or three periods, and make sure both you and your pet don't over-heat when playing fetch.

2. Interrupt your dog's digging habit with an air horn, handclap, or short, emphatic no! Then praise when he stops digging, and offer a toy or treat to replace the forbidden activity.

3. Spayed and neutered dogs have much less incentive to escape a fenced yard in search of company. Provide interactive chew-toys filled with treats to keep the dog entertained inside the yard.

4. For hard-case dogs, build a sand box for legal digging pleasure. A shaded area about three feet (1 m) wide, six feet (2 m) long, and two feet (.5 m) deep will satisfy most dogs. Let him see you bury one or two of his toys (very shallowly), and then encourage him to dig them up.

JUMPING UP

Jumping dogs aggravate and even terrorize people, and being tackled by a Pit Bull can be unpleasant or even dangerous. It's also rude, unacceptable behavior from the human's point of view. But the dog actually thinks he's being polite.

> ## *Cool Off*
> In hot weather, give your APBT plenty of shaded, cool damp places to rest, with lots of available water whenever he's in the yard.

> ## *Want to Know More?*
> For a refresher on teaching the "come" and "sit" commands, see Chapter 4: Training Your American Pit Bull Terrier Puppy.

Dogs lick each other's faces as a greeting display, and a submissive dog aims attention at a dominant individual's eyes and mouth. Therefore, licking the owner's face is a polite canine "howdy!"—a way for him to acknowledge you are the boss and to solicit attention. Since your Pit Bull can't stand eye-to-eye with you, he'll leap high to compensate for his shorter stature. And what's cute when he's a puppy becomes a safety issue once he reaches adult size, especially around children or elderly folks easily knocked down.

Preventing and Solving Jumping Up

Teach your dog that his behavior offends you, and he'll be happy to learn a more appropriate way to greet.

1. Causing pain by stepping on a dog's toes or kneeing him in the chest as he leaps trains him to avoid you altogether and in some dogs may prompt aggression. But petting, playing, yelling, or pushing him away rewards him with attention—remember, even negative attention is better than no attention at all.

2. Instead, teach your dog a contradictory behavior as a greeting. In other words, he should learn that jumping up gets him nothing, but a polite sit (for instance) garners the attention he desires. Ask a family member or friend to help train this concept.

3. Stage an arrival at the front door. As the person enters, he should stop, remain still, and greet the dog with, "[Name], come!" followed by "[Name], sit!"

4. When your APBT sits as requested, the visitor should offer his hand for a sniff as the reward, since this is a vital part of canine greetings.

5. Once the dog finishes sniffing, the visitor can stroke his cheek or neck and praise his calm behavior.

6. When a dog insists on jumping up, step backward so his feet miss, and at the same time, turn away. That interrupts the canine "howdy," because a dog can't properly greet a person's back.

7. Once the dog's feet hit the floor, again give the "sit" command and repeat the exercise. Only after this social greeting has been exchanged should your visitor walk into the house and take a seat. The dog will likely follow. Have other family members waiting in the room to reinforce his behavior with "good dog!"

8. Practice this over and over until sitting during greeting prompts more attention for him than jumping up ever did.

9. If you don't mind a doggy kiss on your face, you can kneel down on your dog's level so he doesn't have to leap. There's also nothing wrong with training your extremely well-behaved dog to jump up. But only on your command.

Jumping up is your APBT's way of saying "hi!"— you'll have to teach him a more polite way of greeting people.

LEASH PULLING

American Pit Bull Terriers easily pull owners around, if you let them. Bottom line, your dog has more muscle than you do. He'll win any contest of strength. So don't play that game. Each time you try to correct a behavior and then let the dog win, you reinforce his belief that 1) your commands don't matter and 2) he can do whatever he wants. Your dog, like a two-year-old human toddler, needs limits. So it's important that your training establishes fair boundaries that you humanely enforce.

Preventing and Solving Leash Pulling

1. The retractable leashes that spool out line actually teach dogs to pull. Very long leashes that allow your dog to range too far from you give little control. To eliminate leash pulling, choose a standard leash no more than six feet (2 m) long.

2. Training collars such as slip (choke) chains or metal prong collars look tempting but can injure your dog unless you've been properly trained to use them. The

APBT often has quite a high tolerance for discomfort, and you'd need to be inhumane with some dogs to get an effect. The flat buckle collar can still work to teach your dog.

3. Clip the leash to the collar, slip a handful of high-value treats into your pocket, and say, "Let's go" or "Heel."

4. If he surges ahead, stop dead in your tracks. Say nothing. Don't pull on the leash, simply become an immovable object. If necessary, train next to a fence, tree, or pole, and loop the leash around so your dog cannot move forward or pull you off your feet.

5. When your dog releases the tension in the leash, offer him a treat, and say, "Let's go" to again move forward. If he pulls forward, stop. Be patient. Pit Bulls are smart and stubborn, and he'll try to wear you down, so prepare yourself for a long session of starts and stops. When you're consistent, he'll soon realize that to move, he must keep the leash slack.

6. Once you get him moving, he'll still forget from time to time and pull. When that happens, instead of stopping, simply do an about-face without warning, and walk in the opposite direction. If he pulls, again about-face. Rather than trying to stop him from moving, it's easier to maneuver a strong dog into moving forward but in a tight circle (around and around and around!) until he's dizzy with frustration. Move in a straight line only once he chooses not to pull—and it does have to be his choice. Once he makes that correct choice, reward with a treat as well as forward progress.

7. For hard-case dogs, I recommend you invest in a no-pull training harness. Rather than clipping the leash to his

A leash-trained APBT is a joy to walk.

collar, it's attached to a ring at the front of the chest. If he surges ahead, the halter tightens and turns him back toward you, so he must stay by your side if he wishes to go forward. You will still need to train your APBT when using this training aid, using the same commands and rewards as with the collar and leash training. Once he's learned he cannot pull with the harness, leave it on, but clip the leash to his collar. He should transition, with time, to proper leash manners whether he wears the halter or not. Some dogs simply do better with a harness than a collar, and if you never intend to compete, there's nothing wrong with using a no-pull harness for safe leash walks.

NIPPING

Dogs use their mouths the way people use hands. As puppies, they learn to "inhibit" their bite so it causes no damage during play, for example. Mom-dogs and siblings yelp and nip back if the youngster chomps down too hard, and so he learns limits.

Pups who don't have the opportunity to learn these lessons, or dogs who become overly excited, can overdo mouthing even when they mean no harm. Some puppies, like children, become more agitated when tired, and uncontrollable rough play may be a cue he needs a nap.

Dogs also can learn to use nipping to get their own way, especially when they don't want to do something. For instance, a dog who objects to having his nails trimmed might nip at your hands. Herding-type dogs more commonly nip, because they've been bred to drive livestock this way. American Pit Bull Terriers, bred to be catch dogs, are more likely to grip and hold on. They'll target pant legs, gloves, and skirts and turn them into tug-o-war toys. This breed is a "gripping" breed, and you won't stop the behavior, but you can point the dog to better targets. What's cute as a pup could become dangerous as an adult, so it's best to teach polite behavior as early as possible.

1. Yelling or physical punishment makes the biting worse. Instead, when the mouthing becomes uncomfortable, say "ooooooooooh" in a gentle tone of voice, and then whimper, "*I* don't like that, you hurt me" with as much emotion as possible. This works especially well with tough dogs. Most dogs look shocked, but they stop.

2. If the mouthing hurts, *yelp* just like another pup. As soon as you yelp, give the dog a time out of 30 to 60 seconds (confine in a small room out of sight).

3. Let him out of the room, and give him another chance to play nice. Make sure you have a legal tug toy available, and direct him to that. But immediately repeat the yelp and time out if he bites too hard again. He must learn that hard bites make the fun stop.

4. It may take several repetitions before he understands that *he* controls whether or not the fun continues.

5. Bite inhibition doesn't mean stopping mouthing behavior altogether. That would be equivalent to tying your hands behind your back. Bite inhibition simply explains to the dog that his teeth can hurt, and since he doesn't want to hurt you, he pulls punches.

Any dog may bite if provoked—that's simply self-preservation. But a dog with good inhibition that bites will *cause no harm*. Translation: no medical bills or lawsuits. And that's a comfort zone owners owe to themselves and to their dogs.

By the Numbers

While most APBT puppies accept other dogs, adult dogs more typically develop some degree of dog aggression—usually around one year old. Socialization and training can help turn dog-aggressive dogs into dog-selective or dog-tolerant pets, but supervision will *always* be necessary. Avoid situations that place your dog at risk. Never leave your APBT alone, unsupervised, with other dogs no matter how friendly you believe them to be.

CHAPTER 11

AMERICAN PIT BULL TERRIER SPORTS AND ACTIVITIES

The APBT as a breed can do nearly anything. Including your dog in activities and canine sports enriches your bond and promotes both physical and mental health for you both. It's also dog-gone fun!

ACTIVITIES

Dogs love to simply spend time with their owners. If you've chosen an APBT, chances are you admire the breed in part for their high energy because you also enjoy outdoor activities. Your dog does not need to be a highly trained competition dog to enjoy and do well with outdoor activities.

It's important that you and your dog be physically sound before leaping into a new activity, so discuss your plans with your veterinarian. Some may be fine for dogs of all ages, while others require conditioning to do safely. Different canine personalities also fit better in some activities than others. Your breeder can offer guidance about reasonable expectations for your particular Pit Bull.

Bicycling

Many American Pit Bull Terriers enjoy running alongside a bicycle. Special extensions that attach to the bike hold the bike-leash, designed just for the purpose. Practice in a private area with your dog, and be sure you're both ready before attempting this on public streets. You'll need to take care that the dog's pads don't burn on hot pavement and that he doesn't overheat in summer weather.

Camping

Dogs love the idea of exploring new smells, sounds, and sights. Before planning your trip, be sure that the campsite allows dogs—and APBTs in particular. Many state and national parks prohibit dogs, but those that allow canines have rules for you to follow, such as cleaning up after your dog's waste or keeping him leashed. Try to choose a site that has adequate shade for your dog, along with privacy so you don't infringe on others—and they don't bother you.

Any dog taken out in public must have impeccable manners around strange adults, children, and other dogs. If the location allows pets, you can be sure your APBT won't be the only dog there. He must have the basics of obedience and be under your control (voice and/or leash) at all times to earn the right to go camping. No excuses.

Any dog taken out in public must have impeccable manners around strange adults, children, and other dogs.

microchipped for identification.

Bring along his crate. You'll need it to safely transport the dog anyway, and you may need it for safe confinement or to double as his bed during your trip. It's dangerous to leave him unattended outside, and the crate can be your safety option.

Don't forget his regular food, and pick it up promptly so it doesn't attract bugs or wildlife. Water for both of you from home works best, but it may be difficult to keep your dog from playing in and drinking from streams, lakes, or puddles he encounters. Pay attention to adverse weather conditions, too, and protect your dog from overdoing in the heat or becoming too cold.

Walking/Jogging

Walking or jogging with your dog can be a fun activity for you both. He'll need to have good leash manners, of course, or will end up dragging you along the way. When you know your APBT enjoys meeting strangers, a public walking path or track at a park can be a good option.

Jogging and running also offer good exercise for you both. There are hands-free leashes available that you can clip to your belt that work for experienced runners to exercise with their dogs. But don't expect that a leisurely walk—or even a power walk—will be sufficient exercise for an energetic APBT. Jogging for several miles comes closer to meeting his exercise needs.

Be sure your dog's vaccinations are up to date, and obtain a health certificate from the veterinarian and carry it with you. This may be required for some camping areas, and it's simply good sense to have your veterinarian's contact information and dog's records and any medications on hand in case of an emergency. Depending on the region, a Lyme disease vaccination may be recommended, as well as standard flea and tick preventive treatments. Along with one for yourself, pack a doggy first-aid kit, and have the name of a local vet handy. If you haven't done so before, get your dog

CANINE GOOD CITIZEN TEST

The American Kennel Club (AKC) created the Canine Good Citizen (CGC) program as a way to encourage owners to provide basic "manners" training for dogs, at home and particularly when out in public. Your dog must master these skills before participating in activities and sports.

Any age dog, from puppy to senior, is eligible (even dogs not registered with the AKC), and the program often is the first training that youngsters receive. Evaluations take place at AKC shows and events that may require minimum ages, but a CGC Evaluator can test your dog outside of these venues as well, as long as it is not on your property. Because puppies need continued reinforcement, and temperament can change as dogs mature, youngsters that pass the CGC should be retested as adults, with adults also being reevaluated every couple of years.

The first part of the program teaches the skills, and the second part tests dogs and certifies that those who pass are under good control and pose no danger to other dogs or people. Dogs are judged individually on their on-leash performance. It is not a competition between dogs—the CGC is an award to be proud of.

In the test, a series of ten common situations that owners and their dogs encounter are staged, and dogs should react in a calm and nonthreatening manner in each situation, such as:

- Remaining calm when the owner interacts/ speaks with a stranger

- Sitting politely and accepting a friendly stranger's petting

- Allowing a stranger to touch/groom with a familiar brush

- Walking on a loose lead, including through a crowd of at least three people

Walking with your dog can be a fun activity for both of you.

- Basic obedience—sit, down, stay, come when called
- Calm reaction to the presence of another dog
- Calm reaction to visual and audible distractions such as dropped chair or jogger running past

Eliminating (urinating or defecating) during the test will be a cause for failure. Any sign of aggression (growl, bite, snap) from the dog causes failure. Harsh corrections from the handler also results in dismissal, and food rewards are not allowed.

SPORTS

Some canine sports require more specific or advanced training than others. Individual dogs often have greater aptitude for certain activities than others. But APBTs are people-pleasing athletes and have the desire, the brains, and the physical ability to excel at nearly any canine sport. Those that allow your dog to capitalize on the breed's working heritage and inborn instincts offer a great outlet for your APBT to enjoy being himself.

Some sports require lots of preparation, especially if you plan to seriously compete. Competitions involve entry fees, investment in specialized equipment, travel to competitions, training classes, and time. Dogs not properly conditioned won't do well and could even injure themselves by overdoing.

Those who simply wish to participate for the fun also can enjoy these sports. Take care to match your dog's ability with realistic expectations. Your dog wants to please you and doesn't particularly care about winning a prize. After all, it must be fun for the dog and owner, or what's the point? Trophies and bragging rights are gravy for owners, but if your dog falls short, take joy in the fact that he did his best because you asked. All your dog cares about is going home with you.

Agility

Agility tests a dog's ability to race over and around obstacles. He's judged on both speed and accuracy as he navigates weave poles, jumps, tunnels, and ramps at the direction of his handler. Think of agility as the canine equivalent of horse-jumping contests, and in fact, the sport got its inspiration from equestrian competitions.

Spending time at trials allows you to connect with savvy folks in the sport who can direct you to appropriate classes. Equipment such as jumps, tunnels, teeters, and weave poles are needed for training and competition and may be available from classes and clubs.

Several sponsoring organizations offer agility trials, including Canine Performance Events (CPE), North American Dog Agility Council (NADAC), United Kennel Club (UKC), and United States Dog Agility Association (USDAA). The difficulty and layout of the course varies between organizations, from more simple entry-level layouts to complex setups for the highest level. Winning times often come down to fractions of seconds.

By the Numbers

Before your APBT can compete in agility, he'll need to have finished growing—he'll need to be at least 9 to 12 months of age before he can safely practice the jumps, or he could damage his legs.

American Kennel Club Canine Partners

The American Kennel Club (AKC) has amended the obedience, rally, and agility regulations to allow mixed-breed dogs to compete in the same classes and earn the same titles as purebreds. Starting April 1, 2010, dogs with an *AKC Canine Partners* listing number will be eligible to participate in AKC agility, obedience, and rally trials accepting mixed-breed entries. *The Canine Partners* listing is available to spayed and neutered dogs who are not currently eligible for AKC registration, AKC Foundation Stock Service (FSS) enrollment, or an AKC Purebred Alternative Listing (PAL). Find out more about the AKC Canine Partners program at www.akccaninepartners.org

Handlers get to walk the course first without the dog and then run alongside to direct the dog through the course with verbal and/or hand signals. Dogs run the course off leash one at a time but compete against others of similar weight, with jumps adjusted accordingly.

APBTs can do well in agility and enjoy the experience, but typically the herding dogs take top honors in the sport. You can take your time getting started, and teach other skills first before attempting agility with your dog. Agility can be a fun sport for your dog well into middle age, as long as he remains healthy.

Canine Freestyle

If you and your dog love music, canine freestyle may be for you. Also known as dancing with dogs, the sport encompasses off-leash rhythmical, choreographed movements of dogs and their owners, to preselected music. Performances are judged on technical and artistic grounds, including difficulty and precision of movement, attitude of the dog, choreography and interpretation of the music, and synchronization of dog, handler, and music. Dogs must be able to follow commands, and any breed (or mix) is welcome to compete. The key to success in this sport is the close bond shared between the dog and owner, and their responsiveness to each other. Titles are given in some organizations.

Several sponsoring organizations offer events that may include costuming of the owners (or the dogs), or not. These include the Canine Freestyle Federation (CFF), Musical Dog Sports Association (MDSA), and World Canine Freestyle Organization (WCFO). Attend an event and learn how you and your APBT can get involved. Before you decide on a routine, find out the competition requirements of the sponsoring organization.

Top training skills are necessary to reach competitive levels, and certain skills are required, such as being able to heel on both sides of the handler, walking backward, pivot, and side-step. A dog must enjoy performing to be successful.

Conformation (Showing)

Most people think of a dog show as a "beauty pageant" competition. Conformation shows compare individual purebred dogs to the "ideal" described in the written standard. The purpose of a conformation show, aside from winning ribbons and bragging rights, is to determine the best examples of the breed, with an eye toward breeding those dogs. Therefore, only intact dogs can participate in conformation shows.

Conformation shows compare individual purebred dogs to the "ideal" described in the written standard.

Not all dogs will be good candidates for a conformation show, as different sponsoring bodies may restrict certain colors or have slightly different standards. The American Pit Bull Terrier can be registered and shown with the American Dog Breeders Association (ADBA), American Rare Breed Association (ARBA), All American Dog Registry (AADR), International All Breed Canine Association (IABCA), and the United Kennel Club (UKC). Only dogs registered in a sponsoring organization may be shown in that particular sanctioned conformation competition.

Conformation competition includes all-breed shows, specialty shows that are restricted to a specific breed, and group shows that feature dogs within a certain identified group (such as terriers). A show dog needs special skills to compete, and you'll need training to learn how to show him off to best advantage. Dogs must gait (walk and run around the ring), stack (stand in a posed position), and be handled by the judge, including inside the mouth and on the testicles. They also will be in contact with many other dogs and people and must have a sound temperament for this, with no aggression exhibited whatsoever.

You won't need special equipment, other than a slip chain and a light show lead (or martingale-type collar and lead) designed to be "invisible" to keep the focus on the dog. Join a breed club to learn more about showing in conformation. Your breeder, or an experienced club member, can be incredibly helpful as a mentor.

Obedience

Competition obedience measures how well a dog has been trained to execute various formalized tasks on command. These range from the basics of loose walking on leash (heel), sit, stay, and recall (come), to high-level trials that test scent discrimination and retrieving through obstacles. You'll need a flat buckle or other collar approved by the judge, and a fabric or leather leash to get started. Dumbbells, jumps, and gloves for scenting will be needed for more-advanced competitions.

Even if your APBT isn't the best candidate for conformation, he can excel at obedience trials. Dogs must be registered with the sponsoring organization, such as the UKC, in order to participate. Each level of competition (Novice, Open, and Utility) increases in difficulty, with a specific group of skills mastered before "graduating" to the next level.

The American Pit Bull Terrier can be an outstanding obedience dog. Skills can be taught beginning as soon as the puppy arrives home. Dogs must be able to respond with quick precision to verbal and hand signals, perform scent discrimination, and sit, heel, stay, fetch, and jump on command.

Weight Pull

No other dog can out-pull an American Pit Bull Terrier—he is tops in this sport. The competition involves harnessing the dog to a sled or cart loaded with weights to see how far, how quickly, and how much weight can be moved in a specified amount of time. They're also judged on the proportion of their body weight compared with the amount pulled.

Dogs pull several times, with weights added after a successful leg/round and a short rest period between pulls. They must pull each load about 16 feet (5 m) within 60 seconds for that effort to count. The surface varies and can be grass, dirt, carpeting, rail tracks, or snow, depending on the sponsoring association.

Sleds are used for snow surfaces, and wheeled carts for all others. They must be capable of holding at least 4,000 pounds (1,814 kg). Special harnesses are designed to spread the weight evenly as the dog pulls, to keep the neck free of pressure for easy breathing and to prevent injury.

There are eight weight classes, and dogs compete against dogs of their own general weight. The dogs must be properly conditioned, just as a weight lifter might be built up, so that they don't hurt themselves.

High-level obedience trials include scent discrimination.

Special harnesses are designed to spread the weight evenly as the dog pulls, to keep the neck free of pressure for easy breathing and to prevent injury.

The most successful dogs not only have strength and endurance, they follow commands, want to pull (baiting with treats isn't allowed), and won't give up. All are positive attributes of the APBT.

The UKC sanctions weight-pulling events for purebred dogs aged 1 to 12 years who are registered with the UKC. The International Weight Pull Association (IWPA) requires dogs to be a member of the association to earn points and is open to any breed or mixed-breed animal. Dogs may compete only within their own geographic region.

Check with a weight-pull club in your area to learn more about the sport.

THERAPY WORK

The people-loving American Pit Bull Terrier has the perfect disposition for therapy work. A therapy dog visits people of all ages in a variety of hospitals, nursing and rehab facilities, and schools. They provide a nonjudgmental presence, wagging encouragement, and feeling of normalcy to those living in abnormal and/or stressful situations.

Animal Assisted Therapy (AAT) uses dogs or other companion animals as a part of the patient's therapy. A treatment plan designed by a health care professional incorporates interactions with the dog as a way to improve the patient's physical or emotional function. For instance, tossing a ball for the dog to fetch encourages a child to repeat hand-eye rehabilitation coordination exercises.

Animal Assisted Activities (AAA) therapy seeks to help withdrawn people become more willing to open communication by allowing them to relax in the presence of a friendly animal. No formal treatment plan includes the animal, and a trained professional does not need to direct the activity. Neither AAT nor AAA dogs are considered service animals by federal law, which by definition are dogs who actively help people with disabilities.

Dogs must be people-friendly, quiet, and calm in all kinds of environments. They should enjoy being touched by strangers, especially children, and know how to take treats nicely. Older dogs often make the best therapy animals, as they are less excitable and know basic obedience. Handlers also should be friendly and good listeners. Dogs of all sizes do well in therapy, with smaller ones snuggling on a bed or lap and larger dogs standing beside the chair or bed for interaction.

A leash and collar, treats, and a grooming brush can be handy tools. People whom your dog meets may wish to brush him, feed treats for obeying trick commands, or even walk him around the hospital room.

While you can informally make arrangements with some open-minded institutions to visit with your dog, it's best to undergo formal training. Delta Society (www.deltasociety.org) provides services for people by providing positive interactions with trained animal-handler teams. Even dogs with disabilities themselves are welcome. Attend a workshop to learn more, or look into the home-study course. Dogs must be deemed healthy by a veterinarian, including being up

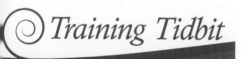

Weight Pull Association

The United National Weight Pull Association (UNWPA) www.unitednationalweightpullassociation.com is a coalition of clubs and individuals dedicated to the sport of weight pull.

to date on vaccinations, and will be tested on basic obedience and conditions that you might encounter on a visit.

Therapy Dogs International (TDI, www.tdi-dog.org) also tests and registers therapy dogs. This volunteer group requires that the dog be at least a year old, pass the AKC's Canine Good Citizen test, and then be assessed by a TDI evaluator for temperament and suitability for the job.

TRAVEL

All dogs must travel at some point in their lives, if only to visit the veterinarian for wellness checks. If you wish to compete in dog sports and activities, good manners traveling by car or plane and staying overnight become important. You need to know what to expect and how to plan ahead so that the experience is fun for you and your APBT.

By Car

Some dogs love car rides so much they get too excited, while others fear or dread car rides because of unpleasant past experiences. They'll pace, drool, cry, climb over the driver—some even get sick. An unrestrained dog in the car is an accident waiting to happen. And you can't strap your dog on the roof of the car like luggage to get him out of your hair. Teach the dog to appreciate car travel and abide by car etiquette, and traveling will be effortless.

Training Tidbit

The American Kennel Club's Canine Good Citizen program offers an excellent training start if you are interested in getting involved in competition obedience.

An unrestrained dog in the car is an accident waiting to happen.

Safety

Most dogs welcome the security and familiarity of a crate. It smells like home and can be a comfort to them when they are in the strange confines of a car. Seat belts designed for dogs work quite well to not only restrain dogs but keep them safe. A harness fits on the dog and has a loop that you run the seat belt through. Another option is car barriers that divide the human seats from the dog area. A variety of styles and sizes for different vehicles are available, from netting material to nylon screens or metal wire grills. Barriers give dogs a bit more freedom and space of their own to move around in, and the dog is prevented from diving out the door if you need to open it.

Bathroom Breaks

You can't explain to a dog that he needs to "hold it" another ten minutes for a pit stop.

So give dogs ample opportunity to do their business about half an hour before you hit the road, and provide adequate pit stops along the way, about every three or four hours. Puppies need more-frequent bathroom breaks, so adjust accordingly. When the dog knows a command for eliminating, you'll save much time while on the road, especially when he'll "produce" while on leash. It also prevents dogs from doing their duty in the wrong place. Don't forget to pick up after your dog.

Food and Water

A change in food can upset digestion and result in vomiting or diarrhea. Maintain the dog's feeding schedule as much as possible, and take along enough food to last until you can buy more at your destination. If you can drink the restaurant water without problems, so can your dog. A baggy full of ice cubes works great to quench the dog's thirst while in the car and won't be as messy as a jug of water.

Teaching Your APBT to Love the Car

What if your American Pit Bull Terrier, so strong and brave, turns into a whimpering weenie at thought of a car ride? It's not his fault. Dogs can't imagine something that's never happened to them before—instead, they remember past experiences and believe the same thing will happen again. If he had a bad experience at the veterinarian, for instance, he may associate the car with that. Rather than trying to comfort the whining dog, which reinforces his idea that a car ride is horrible, help him learn positive and fun associations with the car.

- Make mealtime car time. Feed all his meals in the car for a week. In between times, throw treats in the open car door for him to find, and play fun games near the car.

- Get in the front seat behind the steering wheel while he's munching kibble in the back. Just sit there for a while—no big deal—then get out, so the dog understands nothing scary happens when you're in the car with him.

- The next day, start the car, then turn off the motor and get out without going anywhere. Do this three or four times during the day until the dog takes it as a matter of course.

- Finally, start the car and drive to the end of the driveway and back, then let the dog out. Repeat several times in a row.

- Continue increasing the dog's car time by increments—a trip around the block and then home; then a trip to the nearest fun place, like getting French fries at a drive through, before returning home. Make every car trip upbeat and positive, so the experience makes the dog look forward to the next trip.

By Plane

Dogs love new sights and smells, so a plane trip can be doggy nirvana—especially for dogs allowed in the cabin with their owners. However, the American Pit Bull Terrier does not fit under the seat as carry on luggage and must travel in a crate in the belly of the plane (unless certified as a service dog). This creates extra issues if you want to fly with your APBT.

- Airline-approved shipping carriers are available in molded hard plastic. Get him used to it well before your trip so that he accepts it as a happy, safe retreat. Most dogs learn to sleep during crate time and become perfect travelers.

- Avoid sedatives, as these can act differently at high altitudes and be dangerous for your dog. For the same reason, never use a muzzle.

- Be sure all your contact information is on the carrier and on the dog.

- Flying with a dog has always required health clearances, additional fees, and certain restrictions if you want to ship the dog as "extra baggage" (preferred) or as "cargo." Recently, fees have grown to embarrassing

Want to Know More?

Training basic commands is easier than you think! Check out Chapter 4: Training Your American Pit Bull Terrier Puppy, for step-by-step instructions.

Some airlines won't fly "snub-nosed dogs" in warm weather because of health risks.

proportions—double or even triple the cost of flying the human.

- Rules for flying your pets vary from airline to airline. Some carriers, such as Southwest and Jet Blue, accept pets only as carry on, which would exclude adult APBTs. Continental will not allow American Pit Bull Terriers older than six months to fly due to the perception they are dangerous. Others may prohibit "snub-nosed dogs" (which includes Pit Bulls) because of the health risk during warm weather that reaches 70°F (21°C) or more.

Do your homework before planning a trip that includes the dog. You can find specific "pet travel" regulations for various carriers at this AKC link: www.akc.org/pdfs/canine_legislation/airline_chart.pdf

Lodging

Dogs love adventure, and APBTs are no exception. Most have a wonderful time at hotels, but nobody else will enjoy the visit if your dog waters the potted palm in the lobby or jumps up to make friends with everyone he meets. Dogs don't mean to be rude when they lap ice cream off a strange child's face, but they can be downright scary to people who don't know them. Before traveling with your APBT, make sure he's got his basic manners down pat.

Don't just show up at a hotel or motel expecting that your dog will be welcome. Not all hotels accept big dogs, or they may charge extra, so research good options in advance. The website www.petswelcome.com offers a good listing.

Room Etiquette

Some dogs make a fuss when you leave them alone in a strange room—these tend to be the same dogs that get upset when you go to work and leave them at the house. They feel abandoned, so they howl and cry to call you back home again, or they scratch the door or pull down drapes trying to follow you.

A crate or carrier teaches dogs they can't be with you all the time but that you do always come back. And dogs that use crates as beds identify them as a familiar and comforting island in a strange place. Most hoteliers prefer your dog be crated when he must be left alone in the room, because kenneling dogs virtually eliminates the chance of room damage and also reassures the housekeeping folks who may be afraid of dogs.

Strange sights, smells, and sounds are exciting and will keep dogs occupied for quite a while. But once the new wears off, dogs tend to get bored pretty easily,

Do your research before showing up at a hotel with your dog.

Walks

The best time to walk dogs at hotels is very early in the morning, before 7 a.m., to avoid running into other hotel guests who may not care for dogs. Most business travelers have meetings during the day, but try to avoid busy lunch and dinner hours when traffic in the hotel increases. Ask about using the service elevator to avoid contact with other guests or pets.

especially when left alone with nothing to do. Leave him a legal chew toy, especially something from home that he already loves. Leave on the radio or television. The sounds are not only soothing and distract dogs from being bored, they can also mute outside noises like doors slamming, which tend to raise canine blood pressure. Put a *do not disturb* sign on the door when dogs are left alone in the room to keep housekeeping from entering when you're not there.

Duplicate the dog's home bedtime plan. Bring his blanket, bed, or crate. If your APBT usually sleeps with you, spread a blanket or towels over top of the bedspread to protect it from the dog's shedding. The sheets should be washed anyway, and if you don't mind and the dog is clean, snuggle away.

LEAVING HIM HOME

Many times, dogs simply aren't welcome on trips. The expense, having multiple dogs, or work-related travel could prevent him from accompanying you. One option is to leave him at a facility that takes care of your dog when you can't.

Boarding Kennels and Doggy Daycare

Boarding kennels offer good options, particularly for well-adjusted canines. These tend to provide individual dog runs, either indoor or outdoor or a combination, with staff that attends to the dog's needs. They tend to book up around the major holidays, so you'll need to make reservations in advance.

Doggy daycare also can be helpful and costs a bit more for added service. These facilities may have options such as larger kennel runs, extra "playtime perks" with the staff or friendly dogs, and even swimming facilities. A few provide cameras that owners can dial up from computers to view their dog's vacation experience.

Look for boarding kennels and doggy daycare facilities listed in the yellow pages. Visit the establishment yourself, ask for recommendations from other clients or veterinarians, and satisfy yourself that your dog will be happy and that any special needs can be met. For instance, if he needs a particular food, or medication at certain times of the day, ensure that the staff is aware and can manage this. You'll be required to

Multi-Dog Tip

When you must leave your dogs behind, ask the pet sitter about discounts. They'll often be willing to cut the cost since they can care for several dogs with only one trip to the house. Boarding kennels also sometimes offer discount rates for more than one dog.

A pet sitter is a great option to look after your APDT when you are away.

provide proof of vaccinations, and it's best if you provide the dog's regular food.

Pet Sitters

Leaving home won't be a good option for some dogs. If your APBT has dog-aggression issues, he may not be welcome at a boarding facility. Elderly pets and those needing special medical care do best when the normal routine can be maintained in the home. A pet sitter may be the perfect answer.

A pet sitter comes to your house at predetermined times to provide the one-on-one attention and care your pets need while you are away. It's important that both you and your pets feel comfortable with the pet sitter. Plan at least one visit with the pet sitter to meet your furry crew before you depart, and see how everyone gets along. Always ask for references, and be sure they are bonded. Provide details about the dog's routine, so that the pet sitter can follow the schedule. Be sure the pet sitter has the phone numbers to contact you during your trip. Leave emergency information and authorization for veterinary care, if the need should arise.

There are two professional "pet sitter" organizations. National Association of Professional Pet Sitters, Inc. (NAPPS) maintains a website at www.petsitters. org with a database of members, so you can find a referral in your area. Pet Sitters International (PSI) maintains a website at www.petsit.com with a referral service. Both the NAPPS and PSI websites have great tips regarding what to ask the pet sitter and how to prepare for the service.

PART III

SENIOR YEARS

CHAPTER 12

FINDING YOUR AMERICAN PIT BULL TERRIER SENIOR

Why adopt a senior dog? These golden oldies have many special advantages and may be a perfect fit for you and your family. Old age can be defined as the last 25 percent of life. If you can expect a healthy APBT to live to age 12, old age would begin at about 9 years old.

THE BENEFITS OF A MATURE DOG

Beyond the benefits to you, a senior American Pit Bull Terrier has few options for adoption. Taking one of these loving old guys into your home can save a life. It's also incredibly rewarding to know that you've provided a happy, safe, and loving environment for the last years of a dog's life. They often seem to act gratefully, as if they know that you are their last chance at happiness.

Mature dogs have already been housetrained, spayed, and neutered. They should be up to date on vaccinations. They also are a known quantity, with fewer surprises than a younger dog. In most cases, the adopting agency or rescue organization will have a history of the dog's previous owners and the dog's temperament, training, and health status. You'll know in advance of any ongoing health challenges that need attention. You'll know if they get along with other pets and travel well—or not.

They Are More Sedate

A senior dog has grown out of the crazy puppy antics and hard-headed adolescent hijinks. Old dogs are more sedate than younger APBTs and could be the ideal choice for a first-time APBT owner. Senior dogs won't be as likely to pull and drag owners off their feet or barge through doors after critters. You'll learn all about the foibles of the breed with a dog who's already had much of the hard work done.

Good for Children

Adopting a mature pet can be a great choice for children. A senior dog who's kid savvy can be a stabilizing influence, teaching responsibility and empathy for other living creatures and even acting as a bridge toward making friends.

Want to Know More?

If adopting an adult is more your speed, see Chapter 5: Finding Your American Pit Bull Terrier Adult.

Adopting a mature pet can be a great choice for children.

reason many senior dogs lose their homes, when their owners died and no relatives could take them in.

A Rewarding Life

Over time, we learn to anticipate the senior pet's needs, likes, and dislikes and enjoy a comfortable companionship together. The last several years of a dog's life can be extraordinarily rewarding. An American Pit Bull Terrier senior citizen dog can pack a lifetime of love into even limited time together. And the more time you share, the greater your affection grows. Our compassion, love, and empathy for each other reach a depth that has no parallel in human existence.

Extra years together mean that the bond we share becomes even stronger. The universal slowing of physical and mental processes commonly results in behavior changes. We want to support dogs during their golden years even when behaviors prove challenging.

People seek the same things for their pets as they do for themselves—to enjoy a healthy vigor, preserve a youthful outlook, age with grace, remain vital and connected to the world around them, and enjoy quality of life until they leave this world for the next.

A dog friend can bolster the shy child's confidence to help him come out of his shell.

Good for Retired Couples and Singles

But old dogs do particularly well with retired couples or singles. The unmarried professional won't need to rush home for the puppy's potty break when a senior dog knows how to manage potty duty. And people who are senior citizens themselves may not feel equipped to deal with puppy antics. A senior dog has already learned all the rules. He'll know to tell you when he has to "go" and won't be inclined to steal the television remote. The old dog will be more content to sit on the sofa with you each evening rather than demanding hours of outdoor exercise.

When older people have concerns about outliving a young pet, a senior canine could be the perfect option. In fact, that can be the

THE DISADVANTAGES OF A MATURE DOG

While older dogs can be extraordinarily rewarding pets, they also bring challenges with them. The greatest health care costs take place during puppyhood and old age, and age-related behavior changes may also be common. Being prepared helps owners keep these golden oldies happy and healthy.

Patience

Older dogs can take longer to adjust to new situations and environments. Patience will be eeded to integrate them into the home. Older animals who have lost homes and loved ones may take days, weeks, or even months to trust and love again. But most pets adopted from shelters eventually bond with new owners who show them patience and kindness. These pets thrive on routine and benefit from a stable home. A senior dog can become the most loving companion of all.

eparation Anxiety

bout 14 percent of pet dogs suffer from eparation anxiety, with senior dogs and ogs adopted from shelters most commonly ffected. They become overattached to their uman, and if left alone, they cry, forget ousetraining, try to escape, and destroy roperty to relieve tension. The worst behavior appens in the first 20 to 30 minutes after wners leave, so distracting the dog during

this time works wonders. Pick up the car keys 50 times a day and then set them down. Put on your coat or open the front door dozens of times, but don't go outside. Repetition will make these cues lose their power, so your dog will stop identifying them as your departure cues and stay calmer when you do leave.

They Are More Fragile

While they can do quite well with children, older dogs are more fragile both physically and emotionally. Kids must be taught to act gently with a senior dog and to respect his privacy and space. There can be a benefit to the old pet too—playing and interacting with children keeps the pet's mind and body active and youthful.

Diseases

Senior dogs do eventually require special care. Old-dog diseases tend to be chronic conditions that may demand a special diet, regular medication, or environmental accommodations when the old APBT loses sight or hearing. Even healthy senior dogs without special health demands may need some extra help to ensure that they continue to enjoy their last years.

Aging problems of dogs mirror those of aging humans. These problems can appear in

Patience will be needed to integrate an older dog into the home.

combination, make other conditions worse, and sometimes masquerade as something else. Rather than looking to cure or extend their life span, medical treatments for aging pets seek to control and manage disease and provide quality of life. Nonmedical accommodations simply allow dogs to feel happy and content and continue to enjoy their life with you.

What if arthritis makes leaps up onto the sofa or bed painful? Maybe navigating stairs or getting into or out of the car proves to be a challenge. Move boxes or chairs close to these places for a helpful step up. Elevated food bowls accommodate the stiff neck and shoulders that no longer easily bend. Your dog will want to continue enjoying the activities that made him happy during his prime and can become frustrated when creaky joints get in the

way. Allow your pet to continue to participate in the things he loves most.

If your dog adores playing fetch, indulge him. Keep the toy near the ground so he won't have to jump. Treat your competition dog by going through some obedience drills so he still feels like a winner. Take your dog hunting for the pure joy of being together again in the field.

Old dogs know that they feel good and are happy only in *this moment*. They don't worry about tomorrow. So keeping them comfortable as long as possible is the goal. In fact, the healthiest pets seem to stay well right up to the end of their lives. Instead of lingering with a debilitating disease, many instead decline very quickly—which perhaps can be a blessing.

Vision-impaired dogs rely on memory to get around safely.

Pet-Proofing

Pet-proof your home for your dog's comfort and safety. Enriching your pet's environment and stimulating him mentally acts like the fountain of youth for the brain. There also are safety considerations for aging pets that you'll need to address.

Blind pets rely on memory to safely navigate, so avoid rearranging the furniture. Place baby gates to prevent tumbles down stairs, and announce your presence when you enter a room to avoid startling the pet. Vision-impaired dogs rely on memory of certain landmarks to get around safely. Scent-mark pathways with a dab of vanilla extract to help guide blind pets to the pet door into the yard. Products designed for child safety can be adapted for use with blind pets.

Potty Breaks

Old dogs won't have the same capacity to wait all day long for a potty break. Schedule extra bathroom outings for your dog. Come home from work at lunch to accommodate his needs, or add a pet door for convenience. If you can't make extra trips home, reduce cleanup by confining your dog to linoleum areas, or protect carpet with sheets of plastic lined with Depend Undergarments to catch any accidents. Your old dog doesn't have accidents on purpose, and he'll feel less stress when he is able to take care of business in an appropriate and acceptable manner that you've provided for him.

Training Tidbit

Senior dogs are more prone to develop separation anxiety. Desensitizing them to your departure signals helps reduce their anxiety. Avoid trying to soothe the whining, as that only rewards the anxious behavior.

CHAPTER 13

CARE OF YOUR AMERICAN PIT BULL TERRIER SENIOR

B etter medical care over a lifetime means that dogs live longer than ever before. Today's dog lovers also care nough to accommodate the special needs f their aging dogs. This aging population onstitutes more than 50 percent of patients en by veterinarians. Older pets, though, ean age-related challenges. Senior pets get ck quicker, heal more slowly, and, like ed humans, may lose their sense of umor about such things. However, old age not a disease. In fact, many old pets stay retty healthy throughout their golden ars and won't require more than routine edical care.

WHEN IS THE APBT A ENIOR?

ongevity is influenced by a combination of netics, environment, and health care over a etime. With an average potential life span of out 12 to 15 years, onset of old age—when APBT becomes "senior"—would be about e 9 to 11.

Aging is a natural process. Throughout life, e body constantly creates new tissue and heals uries as new cells are created, function for a short time, die, and are replaced. Aging causes the body to lose its ability to self-repair and protect itself.

Signs of Aging

Aging pets tire more easily and become less active as a result of slowed body functions. The agility champ no longer clears hurdles with his previous precision. Even though the will to compete remains, aging joints and muscles become less flexible and impair his performance.

Physical Changes

Dogs go through some of the same changes as people. Gray hair on the ear rims or muzzle won't bother pets the way it does people, but other changes impact the way dogs react to the world around them.

Problem Behaviors

Problem behaviors may become more apparent when age-related health challenges lower this threshold. A dog who's been tolerant of a housemate dog and never been aggressive may bite when pain from arthritis or dental disease causes unexpected discomfort.

Aging pets tire more easily and become less active as a result of slowed body functions.

More Bathroom Breaks

Older dogs typically need more-frequent bathroom breaks. Sometimes they have less capacity to "hold it," and other times pets have trouble remembering to ask to go out in a timely fashion.

Lessened Senses

It's also common for pet senses to dim. Deaf dogs startle easily when touched or are unresponsive when called. Failing vision leaves pets nervous or fearful in unfamiliar territory. Fading scent and taste sense can prompt pets to snub even favorite foods.

Aging Eyes

Another typical change turns the eyes bluish or hazy, because the lens loses flexibility. That's the same condition that makes people need glasses when they turn 40 or so. Pets don't see up close anyway, so they don't even notice this normal change. Glaucoma is another eye problem more typical of older pets and can result in blindness. It is extremely painful, and pets squint or paw at the affected eye. Blind dogs compensate very well, because the rely on other senses to get around. You may not notice your dog's vision loss unless you rearrange the furniture or the pet is taken to a unfamiliar place.

Aging Ears

With age, the delicate structures within the ear begin to lose sensitivity to vibrations. Age-related hearing loss, termed presbycusis, shows up in any animal if it lives long enoug

Dogs compensate by becoming more visually attentive and paying attention to vibrations—your footsteps on the floor, for instance. Deaf pets startle more easily and may seem to ignore the doorbell or other cues.

Aging Taste

Dog taste is so similar to that of humans that it's used as a research model for people. Therefore, we suspect flavor perception for pets also changes with age, just as it does with aging humans, but pets can't tell us for sure. In people, bitter sensations seem most affected, and dogs pay little attention to those flavors anyway. If your dog suddenly snubs a favorite food, though, he may have had a change of taste.

Aging Nose

Dogs do lose smelling sense the older they get, but nobody knows how much. Studies have shown that dogs drop off in scenting ability at about age ten. Scent partners with taste and lack of smell can change food flavors, affecting appetite. Pets with compromised sniffers may stop eating altogether or decide that they prefer a different food.

Other Aging Changes

Other aging changes, such as how well the kidneys work, are detectable only with specialized veterinary tests. Dogs age about seven times faster than people do. A pet's emotional health is also important to his quality of life. Recognizing your pet's changing needs will keep him comfortable and happy during his golden years.

FEEDING

The senior dog can become a more reluctant eater for several reasons. Changes in ability to smell and taste food can make even favorite treats unappetizing. Loss of teeth, common in aged canines, makes hard kibble more difficult to chew. And when activity level decreases, your dog simply doesn't need as much fuel as he did in his youth. Canned foods are easier to chew and may be preferred by older dogs who have dental challenges or no teeth. You'll also find products labeled specifically for "senior" dogs, which manufacturers often define as older than age seven.

Calorie Intake

Once dogs become aged, most of them naturally eat fewer calories anyway. The dog's metabolism slows until his caloric requirements decrease by 20 to 25 percent during the last third of his life. Yet old dogs require about 50 percent more protein than young adult dogs to maintain healthy muscle mass. When dietary protein intake is insufficient, the body responds by burning muscle mass for fuel, and that results in muscle wasting so commonly seen in old dogs. In otherwise healthy animals, even mild

Recognizing your pet's changing needs will keep him comfortable and happy during his golden years.

Impaired Pets

Deaf and hearing-impaired pets may bite out of reflex if startled, so take care not to sneak up on them. Stomp a foot, wave your hand, or use other visual signals to gain your dog's attention before petting. Use hand signals, a flashlight beam, or a remote vibrating collar to communicate with deaf pets.

protein deficiency can significantly impair immune function.

In addition, calorie intake affects the need for dietary protein. With lower calorie intake, the percent of calories from protein must increase to maintain the same protein intake. Most commercial foods for geriatric pets contain a reduced concentration of dietary fat and calories. Some have dietary fiber added to further reduce the caloric density. These products may be appropriate for the large number of pets who are overweight or likely to get that way. Pets who become overweight have an increased risk for associated health problems, including arthritis and diabetes. Commercially formulated "senior" dog foods adjust the calories and protein levels and may include additional substances that address joint health, for example.

Underweight Dogs

Not all older animals are overweight or less active. In fact, while "middle-aged" animals tend to be overweight, a greater proportion of dogs over 12 years of age are underweight compared with other age groups.

Diets for older dogs should contain a higher percentage of dietary protein, or an increased protein to calorie ratio, to meet their needs. Diets containing at least 25 percent of calories from good-quality, highly digestible protein should meet the protein needs of most healthy senior dogs.

Diseases

A number of diseases common to older dogs may benefit from nutritional modification. In most cases, these changes are designed to compensate for the metabolic effects of the disease or its complications. This isn't a cure or prevention but simply a means to help relieve the signs of disease and keep dogs more comfortable for as long as possible. Dogs with kidney, heart, liver, intestinal, arthritis, cancer, and other medical problems may be helped with these specially formulated foods. Several pet food companies make therapeutic diets, available from your veterinarian, for these conditions. If your pet snubs one brand, don't hesitate to ask about trying another. Your pet must eat the food for it to help him.

Soft Foods

Aging pets often prefer softer foods. Warming up food in the microwave increases the scent

You might want to consider a "senior" dog food for your APBT.

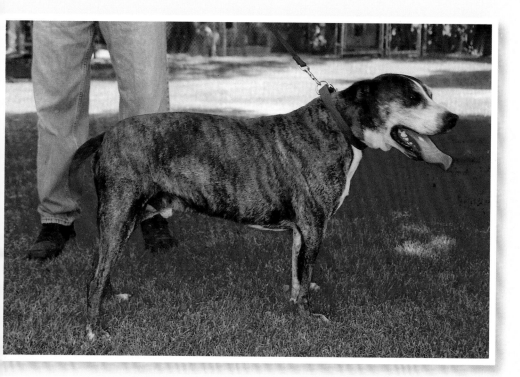

Be aware of any baseline changes in your senior APBT.

nd can stimulate flagging appetites. You can
so add warm water to dry kibble and run it in
e blender for a familiar-tasting but easier-to-
t meal.

wice-Daily Feedings

ost adult dogs, including seniors, do best
n twice-daily feedings. But if your older dog
n't able or willing to eat enough in those
vo meals, add a third feeding. Eating is a
cial occasion for dogs, and they'll be much
ore likely to munch when you're present.
im for a morning meal and another in the
rly afternoon. This will allow the dog's
dy time to process the nutrition and have
needed potty break before everyone retires
r the night.

GROOMING

Your APBT doesn't demand a great deal of
grooming. A daily going-over with a rubber
curry works well to pull off loose, shed fur. It
also doubles as a massage, which older dogs in
particular relish.

Old or sick dogs can be stressed by bathing,
so check with your veterinarian if you feel
the need for a dunking on one of these guys.
There are "dry shampoos" available that can
be sponged on and brushed off that may be a
better option.

When the senior dog doesn't exercise as
much to wear down the nails, more claw trims
may be necessary. Dogs appreciate routine, so
find a time every day that's convenient for you
and comfortable for your dog. Perhaps that's
sitting on the floor with your dog or sharing

the sofa during the evening news. Choose one nail to trim each day—just a tiny bit is more than enough. Then "pay" your APBT with attention, perhaps a treat, and the massage/grooming curry. This can become a special time that you both look forward to each day.

As far as dental care is concerned, your pet may require a professional dental cleaning from your veterinarian, which requires anesthesia. There are drugs available that can be used to keep geriatric pets safe, so ask your veterinarian. Most general practice veterinarians provide ultrasonic scaling, polishing, and sometimes antibiotics and pain medication, especially if teeth are pulled. Between veterinary visits and professional cleaning, provide home treatments to keep pungent breath under control.

HEALTH CARE

As in humans, aging is very individual. "Geriatric" screening should be considered as a preventive medicine service, conducted to identify diseases in their early stages or to head off preventable conditions.

Regular Checkups

Regular checkups, each year or more frequently, are helpful. Remember that dogs age much more quickly than humans do, so 12 months between exams can be the equivalent of seven or more years in human terms. A lot can change during that time. The older your dog becomes, the more frequently he should be seen by the veterinarian—usually twice a year.

Listening to the dog's heart and lungs, checking the eyes and ears, and examining the skin and hair coat offer many clues to your dog's health status. Thin, brittle hair or flaky skin can have any number of causes—for example, nutritional deficiency. The veterinarian will also take blood and urine

samples. Changes in blood or urine values may provide evidence of obvious or even hidden problems that can be addressed only once they are diagnosed. Some of the most common old dog illnesses can be managed quite well.

You are a partner with your veterinarian in your old dog's good health.

Baseline Changes

Because you live with him, you will notice any changes long before the doctor has a chance to suspect a problem. Early detection increases the chance of being able to treat and manage the problem and keep your dog comfortable should his health begin to fail. So keep track of all his normal behaviors and body functions so that any deviation alerts you to get him to the clinic for a checkup.

Start with a baseline of normal behaviors and body functions. Then once every two weeks (oftener if your pet is ill), update your list with current information to track any change. Use these examples to get you started:
- appetite (finicky; glutton)
- breathing (regular; easy; strained; bad breath)
- elimination (frequency; amount of feces and urine)
- eyes, ears, nose (clean; no discharge; clear)
- favorite games (fetch; tug games; being groomed)
- gait/movement (limps; races around; avoids stairs)
- skin, fur, nails
- sleep schedule (naps all day; sleeps through night)
- vocabulary (words he knows)
- water intake
- weight loss/gain

SENIOR ILLNESSES

Many of the most common old dog conditions don't happen suddenly. They sneak up on owners and develop very gradually, over a long period of time. The sooner they can be diagnosed and treated, the better the outcome will be. Chronic old dog illnesses rarely can be cured, but with treatment the dog often can maintain a high quality of life and continue to enjoy spending time with his favorite humans.

Arthritis

The cartilage cushioning the joints wears thinner and becomes more brittle over time until it hurts to move. Dogs limp or hold up a paw. Heavier pets suffer more, and obesity increases the risk for arthritis. If your APBT has any degree of hip dysplasia, arthritic signs can include reluctance or difficulty getting up, especially after a nap. Once the dog has moved around for a while, the joints tend to warm up so that he moves more easily. Controlling the pet's food intake to reduce excess weight or to keep him lean, and increasing exercise is the two-pronged treatment of choice. A variety of commercial therapeutic reducing diets are available.

There also are "joint health" diets available that include ingredients to help relieve the joint inflammation or slow down the degeneration of the cartilage. Omega-3 fatty acids can also help with arthritis pain. Products that contain green-lipped mussels (perna mussel) are helpful because they slow the degeneration of cartilage in the joints. The newest diets that address canine arthritis employ neutrogenic principles and may actually reverse some of the joint damage. Compounds such as chondroitin and glucosamine also have anti-inflammatory properties. They don't prevent arthritis, but they may slow the progression and ease discomfort.

Treatment

Dogs can develop dangerous problems if given over-the-counter human pain medicines. But canine-specific arthritis prescriptions such as carprofen and etodolac are mainstays for arthritis treatment. Rimadyl and Etogesic can help, and human products such as Celebrex and Vioxx may be useful in certain cases, too, when prescribed by the veterinarian. Acupuncture provides effective safe pain relief for many arthritic dogs.

When joints ache, dogs compensate and put strain on other muscles. Massage helps relieve sore muscles, and arthritic dogs love it. Older dogs thrive on routine, so set aside the same time each day. Use the flat of your hands to gently and firmly stroke in the direction the fur grows. Dogs will moan and tell you where they like to be touched. Heat also relieves arthritic stiffness and pain. A soft bed heated by the sun or a warm lamp prompts moans of delight. An arthritic APBT would love a heating pad slipped under a blanket for comfortable napping.

Dogs who have always been athletes likely still enjoy exercise. Continuing to move keeps

By the Numbers

It's not unusual for senior dogs to become more anxious. About 14 percent of pet dogs suffer from separation anxiety. Use a pheromone product to reduce the fear. A puzzle toy stuffed with a tasty treat can also help keep the dog occupied. Harp music has a natural sedative effect, so distraught dogs can sleep during their owner's absence.

joints lubricated and relieves stiffness and pain. It also helps keep older pets fit and more engaged in life. Go for walks with your dog. Swimming works very well for arthritic dogs.

Canine Cognitive Disorder (CCD)

A certain percentage of dogs over the age of ten develop behavioral changes that mimic those of Alzheimer's patients. These pets forget housetraining, fail to recognize familiar people and places, have confused awake/sleep cycles, and may develop separation anxiety.

Treatment

Cognitive dysfunction—senility—is heartbreaking for owners when beloved pets no longer remember them. The drug Anipryl reverses signs of cognitive dysfunction for a while in a percentage of dogs within two to eight weeks. According to studies, about one-third of dogs show great improvement, another one-third have moderate improvement, and the final third do not show any significant improvement. Drug therapy, even when it works, is not a cure. It simply buys you and your dog some time, but the signs of cognitive dysfunction will inevitably return.

Dietary therapy also proves temporarily effective with many dogs. Therapeutic diets formulated using nutrigenomic principles contain antioxidants that can also reverse the signs of CCD. Choline and phosphatidylcholine, natural components of some foods, help brain cells send and receive nerve impulses more efficiently. The dietary supplement Cholodin, which contains these components, seems to help some pets. This helps preserve the loving relationship you've shared over the years.

In addition, enriching your pet's environment and stimulating him mentally acts like the fountain of youth for the brain. Studies by Dr.

Continue practicing obedience exercises with your senior APBT—it will help improve his cognitive function.

Norton William Milgram at the University of Toronto proved that enrichment—puzzles, training games, and making the dog think—improved cognitive function.

So encourage your APBT to practice obedience exercises. If he participated in weight-pull competitions, get out the harness and put him through his paces—but with less weight than in his prime, of course. Even if he's not able to perform to the same level as in his youth, the fun and challenge of doing a job and using his brain can keep him healthy and connected to life.

Congestive Heart Failure (CHF)

Valvular heart disease affects about a third of all dogs over the age of 12, when the heart valves simply start to wear out. Blood carries nutrients and oxygen throughout the dog's body via the heart and circulatory system. The right side of the heart pumps blood to the lungs to gather oxygen, and the left side of the heart pumps the oxygenated blood to the rest of the body.

When the heart can't contract as well as it used to, it can't get adequate blood to the rest of the dog's body. As a result, fluid builds up in different organs. The most common type of congestive heart failure in dogs involves the left side of the heart, causing blood to back up into the lungs. The lungs become congested with fluid (pleural effusion), leading to panting, coughing, or difficulty breathing. Dogs typically sit with an "elbows-out" posture to relieve pressure on the chest and help themselves breathe.

When the right side of the heart fails, fluid collects and swells the abdomen (ascites), and accumulates beneath the skin (edema—the legs may swell). Fluids collect when the body tries to compensate for reduced heart efficiency. Sodium and fluid are retained to increase blood volume, and blood vessels are constricted to increase blood pressure. Dogs suffering from congestive heart failure will have a heart murmur. Many times, right heart failure develops as a result of the strain from existing left heart failure. Fatigue, loss of appetite, and general ill health can be associated with either type of heart failure in dogs.

To diagnose, the veterinarian will listen to your dog's heart for abnormal sounds. Additional tests, such as an X-ray, electrocardiogram, or echocardiogram (ultrasound), can help determine the extent of the heart damage.

Treatment

Once diagnosed, treatment for CHF usually consists of medications that decrease the amount of work the heart needs to do or that increases the strength of its contraction. Drug therapies also can reduce the fluid retention to relieve breathing difficulties. Some of the same heart medicines that people use are prescribed for dogs, such as Digitalis and calcium channel blockers, or beta blockers.

Your vet may also prescribe a special diet for your dog that is low in salt. Holistic veterinarians say that hawthorn helps make the heart muscle stronger. The nutritional supplement coenzyme Q10 also has benefits for the heart. With proper medical management, many seniors with heart disease can live months to years.

Cataracts

Dogs suffer from cataracts more than any other species. A normal dog's visual acuity is about 20/50 to 20/80. Cataracts gradually impede the pet's vision until he becomes blind.

The clear lens directly behind the pupil in the eye works like the lens of a camera. A cataract turns the lens cloudy, and vision loses sharp focus. The severity of the problem varies, from a tiny spot of white to total blockage. Essentially, the lens changes in the same way a clear raw egg white becomes opaque as it cooks.

You may not notice any change until severe vision loss occurs. Dogs are very good at making accommodations and hiding impairment. Your APBT can still easily get around the house and yard or any familiar setting using memory and scent. But rearranging the furniture can cause confusion, and the sight-impaired dog loses confidence and bangs into walls or furniture when he can't see.

Treatment

The same surgical techniques used in people can restore the vision of dogs. In the past, pets with cataracts often weren't treated until they had suffered a significant amount of vision loss. These "mature" cataracts still have about an 85 percent success rate with surgery, but there's a 95 percent success rate when the cataract is immature.

A special hollow needle breaks up the lens and removes it using ultrasonic sound waves (phacoemulsification). The instrument acts like a tiny jackhammer, using ultrasound in thousands of cycles per second. Then the pieces are sucked out through the hollow part.

After the initial surgery, the pet can see again, but he's left severely far-sighted. Instead of 20/50, he'll see 20/800; he'll see the squirrel across the field but not the kibble in his bowl. Artificial lenses implanted in the eyes, just as in humans, correct the focus. The dog's vision can be restored to as good or better than it was before he had the cataracts.

After surgery, the pet stays in the hospital one to two days to make sure that the inflammation remains under control. Dog eyes suffer much more inflammation than a person's eyes. Owners need to give the dog eye drops several times a day for at least two weeks and possibly up to six weeks. Therefore, dogs who object to being medicated, or owners unwilling to faithfully give drops, may not be good candidates for the procedure.

Cushing's Disease

Cushing's disease (hyperadrenocorticism) was named for Dr. Cushing, who first described this syndrome in people. Dogs typically are middle-aged or older at the time of diagnosis. It is a common metabolic disorder of dogs, in which the adrenal glands produce too many steroid hormones, especially cortisol. The adrenal glands are located next to the kidney, one on each side, and are little, tiny kidney-bean shaped organs about 1 inch (2.5 cm) in length.

Cortisol affects the metabolism of carbohydrates, proteins, and fats and suppresses the body's inflammatory and immunological responses. Excess amounts reduce the dog's resistance to bacteria and viruses and promote infection. About 20 percent of cases are caused by a tumor of the adrenal glands, which can be benign or malignant. The majority result from a tiny and otherwise benign tumor that affects the pituitary gland in the brain. But Cushing's disease can also develop if cortisone-type medications (often used to control itchy skin conditions) are overused. The condition can affect any dog but is most typically seen in dogs who are six years old or older. The disease is a progressive one that is slow and insidious.

Dogs suffering from Cushing's disease act hungry and thirsty; eat, drink, and urinate more; and are lethargic. Dogs also can suffer a symmetrical hair loss on their body and often develop a progressive pot-bellied appearance, with wasting and weakening of the leg muscle. Color changes in the fur and/or the skin are typical, along with skin diseases that include

Training Tidbit

If you adopt a senior APBT, spend some time going over basic training. It will help you bond and let your new family member know the house rules.

Cushing's disease typically affects middle-aged or older dogs.

...inning and loss of elasticity, flaky scales, ...umpy irregularities, blackhead pimples ...particularly surrounding the nipples and ...enitals), and bleeding. When caused by a ...umor in the brain, neurological signs may ...nclude pacing, circling, a drunken walk, head ...ressing, or seizures.

...reatment

...nly a veterinarian can diagnose Cushing's ...isease using a battery of laboratory tests. ...ood screening tests evaluate the adrenal ...and function by measuring the amounts ...f circulating hormones when the dog is ...rest and in response to adrenal-gland ...imulating and suppressing drugs. Treatment ...epends on the location of the tumor.

Tumors of the adrenal gland can be surgically removed. But most times, medication controls the symptoms by destroying controlled amounts of the cortisol-secreting cells. The drug must be continued for the rest of the dog's life but typically reverses many of the symptoms.

If the tumor has progressed to causing neurological signs, radiation therapy may help. A drug called Anipryl (used also in canine cognitive dysfunction) may control symptoms but won't cure the disease. Dogs diagnosed at an earlier age and successfully treated often live for another five to ten years. After treatment, food consumption, as well as urination, returns to normal within days, physical activity and muscle strength return

Whatever the illness, ask your vet about the best treatment options for your senior APBT.

decrease in the muscle tone that provides bladder control. Dogs leave a puddle where they sleep, or dribble when very tired. Damage from urine not only is inconvenient and unhygienic, it's expensive to clean. There are a number of steps you can take to effectively manage the problem and preserve the loving bond you share with your pet.

Treatment

Your veterinarian can prescribe medicine to improve the strength of the bladder sphincter so that the dog regains control. Estrogen replacement therapy—diethylstilbestrol (DES)—helps some dogs. It must be given in tiny doses calculated by the veterinarian for you individual dog's needs. But the most effective and commonly prescribed drug to improve bladder sphincter control and treat incontinence is phenylpropanolamine (PPA). Compounding pharmacies can also adjust the dose into the tiny amounts necessary for drugs like DES or PPA. Compounding also puts the daily medication into a tasty form the dog relishes, such as liver- or chicken-flavored treats.

You can also help with management techniques. The fuller the bladder, the more th leakage. Accidents most often happen when a dog drinks too much before bedtime and can't "hold it" until the morning bathroom break. Pick up the water two hours before bedtime. Make sure that the pet has a chance to urinate before you go to bed.

in weeks, and substantial hair regrows within the first three months. Ask your veterinarian about the best treatment options for your pet.

Urinary Incontinence

Urinary incontinence most often develops when a pet loses the ability to control the bladder. Any dog can develop the problem at any age as a result of a spinal injury, for example. Urinary incontinence, however, most commonly affects aging spayed female dogs.

The amount of the hormone estrogen declines as the dog ages, and that causes a

Want to Know More?

For a refresher on how to teach basic obedience commands, see Chapter 4: Training Your American Pit Bull Terrier Puppy.

Save frustration and aggravation by confining the incontinent pet at night to easily cleaned areas, such as a laundry room that has linoleum. Protect carpet or furniture by putting down sheets of plastic. Spread absorbable housetraining pads on top of the plastic, or use disposable diapers to catch the urine. Remove covers on pet beds or sofa cushions, place the cushions inside plastic garbage bags, and then put the covers back on. That way, only the washable outside becomes soiled and can be easily removed and washed. Some pet product stores carry diaper-like products that are made for dogs and that come in a range of sizes.

TRAINING

Training a senior requires the same dedication and techniques as training a younger dog. Consistency and a fair but firm hand will achieve success. You'll also need to practice patience and look for unique motivators. An older dog may not have the same attention span as a younger dog. When taste or scent sense wanes, treat rewards may not get the same eager response as they did in your dog's youth.

Puzzles and Training Games

Puzzles, training games, and making the dog think improve cognitive function. Working the brain sharpens the memory. There's no reason that you can't teach dogs new words or a new cue—to shut a door or fetch the paper. With dogs and with people and with your body and your brain—if you don't use it, you lose it.

Obedience Commands

In addition, senior dogs with hearing or vision challenges may not be able to learn commands in the same way. You'll need to come up with creative ways to make the most of their abilities and adjust your expectations to what your senior dog can do well.

For instance, use visual signals when deaf dogs can no longer hear your voice. Many dogs take naturally to hand signals, so you can transition them from the spoken sit command to a "closed fist means sit" direction. Teach your senior that the porch light turned on and off means "dinnertime," so that he'll come to the door. His tummy will do half the work if you time this correctly, flash the lights to get his attention, and then show him the bowl.

Professional Sports

Dogs who have been active in their prime in obedience or other competition sports may become depressed when no longer able to participate. Adjust the challenges so that they can still be involved and succeed. If arthritis prevents high leaps, lower the bar so that your dog can still have feelings of accomplishment when going through an agility routine.

CHAPTER 14

END-OF-LIFE ISSUES

Dogs rarely outlive their owners. That's the deal we make when we welcome a special pet into our lives. Even though they live shorter lives, though, dogs pack many decades worth of joy into their short time on this planet. And while we know that our time with them may be limited, it makes the time we share with our dogs even more cherished.

WHEN IS IT TIME?

There is no cut-and-dried answer to this question. Every dog and owner experience unique relationships, and when to say goodbye varies between individual circumstances. But a combination of facts point to this final decision. When you love your dog and know him well, even the subtle changes in behavior can be a signal that your old friend's time has come. A loss of appetite and refusal to eat is one clear signal. You know your dog best. What lights up his eyes? Is there an activity that he loves more than any other? When playing with the ball no longer proves irresistible, that may be another clue. You want him to be happy, and when he stops enjoying life, ask yourself these difficult questions.

How many more days will you get that are better than today? When injury or disease keeps your dog struggling with pain and little hope of recovery; when your dog gives up and longs for release; when a longer life is not a better life—these measures are ones only you, as your dog's best friend, can make. Listen to your heart, and your dog will tell you when he's ready to say goodbye.

HOSPICE AND EUTHANASIA

The best time to plan for pet loss is before you lose your dog. Senior citizen canines may live with debilitating chronic illness for months or even years. Nursing your dog and maintaining quality of life can be a wonderful gift to you both and also give you time to come to terms with the eventual loss.

Want to Know More?

If and when you're ready to add a new dog to your home, see Chapter 2: Finding and Prepping for Your American Pit Bull Terrier Puppy or Chapter 5: Finding Your American Pit Bull Terrier Adult for some pointers.

By the Numbers

Old dogs who have been well cared for throughout their lives may never get sick at all. Rather than a slow decline, these dogs tend to stay engaged in life, vital, and active their entire life. They die suddenly, often with little warning, which can be shocking to owners but perhaps a blessing as well.

Sometimes you may wish to end your dog's life while he's still feeling good, rather than have him decline slowly or risk a traumatic, painful death as in the case of some cancers. When your dog lives with a terminal illness, any time can be the right time for euthanasia. Please know that the choices you make, although they may be different from what others might choose, are correct for you and your dog. Any choice you make with love in your heart cannot be wrong.

You can choose where and when to end your friend's life. Many owners want to stay with their pet until the end, but others may prefer not to be present, so that they can remember the dog during happy times. Veterinarians may agree to come to your home so that the dog isn't further stressed during these important last moments together.

When at the hospital, generally a separate room allows you to have private time alone with your dog before, during, and after the euthanasia. A catheter may be placed in the vein to make it easier to administer the euthanasia solution when the time comes. Chronically ill dogs may already have an IV catheter in place. Occasionally, the dog will

be sedated first, which makes him very sleepy. Then a slow IV injection of the euthanasia solution, a barbiturate anesthetic-type drug, is administered. It can be very quick acting; usually within a minute or two the dog will be gone.

GRIEF

When you love a dog and lose him, it is natural to grieve. People go through the same emotions losing a pet as they do when losing any loved one: denial, anger, bargaining, depression, and finally, acceptance.

You are not alone. It's normal to feel awful. It hurts terribly, but you are not crazy. Aren't other things, such as work or people, supposed to be more important? No. Your pet and grief are no less important, just important in a different way. He had a unique impact on your life, or you wouldn't miss him the way you do. There is no guilt or shame in being a caring person. Do not let anyone make you feel wrong for honoring your pet with tears.

Pet bereavement has unique qualities because we share very different parts of our lives with pets. We look on our pets as dependent children. Even more, an old pet may represent milestones in your own life—the dog was a childhood chum, accompanied you to college and was there for your wedding. Losing him feels like losing a part of yourself. Pet bereavement probably won't receive the same sympathy as the loss of a human loved one. People who have never experienced a close relationship with a pet have the most difficult time understanding our pain, and that can make the loss even more difficult to bear.

Sometimes there may be a delay of grief. At first, you feel no emotion—again, there is no right or wrong to the process. Delayed grief may come days, weeks, or even months later, when you find the dog's missing

Dogs raised together may experience "grief" at the death of a canine friend.

toy buried in the Christmas ornaments, and you have an emotional meltdown. Each person experiences grief in different ways. The process can be short or long, and the stages of grief are not necessarily sequential—you may feel depression, then denial and anger, for example. Guilt is common, even when you made all the right choices with your veterinarian's help. Have faith in yourself that you made the best decisions for your dog at that moment in time. Your dog couldn't have a better testimony to your love.

Seek out people who've been through pet loss themselves. Talk about your feelings. Remember your dog by sharing stories with other pet lovers. Eventually, honor your pet's memory by bringing another animal companion into your home and heart.

Explaining Pet Loss to Children

The death of a special dog will often be a child's first experience with loss of a loved one. Although a painful experience, this can teach them that death is a natural and essential conclusion to life.

Children take their cue from the way their parents react. When they see that an adult fears death, they become frightened too. Certainly allow children to know that you feel bad, and that's okay. And explain that all things must die. Even though pets live shorter lives, we become better people because of the wonderful love we share with them. The younger the child, the easier it will be for her to accept that death is a normal process and that her pet has gone to doggy heaven.

In trying to mute the pain of the loss, parents may use euphemisms that actually terrify the child. Avoid terms like "put to sleep," which can give children nightmares about falling asleep and never waking up. Statements that "God loved him so much He needed your dog in heaven" can leave children fearful that God will love them or

When your best friend has enjoyed practicing obedience commands all his life, he'll still understand the words even when unable to perform. This can be a measure of when to end his life. Is he still able or willing to "speak" on command, for example? Sometimes actions, or the lack thereof, speak volumes.

their parents and take them too. Instead, explain that even though the dog isn't physically with us, his memory lives on in our hearts to make us better people.

Being present during the euthanasia can be a gift to older children when the euthanasia can be painless, calm, and loving. It allows the relationship you and your children shared to be honored and respected. And it recognizes the spiritual side of the relationship between you and your dog.

Older children take less at face value. When the child is old enough to really comprehend, bring the child into the decision-making process. The parent will have the ultimate decision, of course. But such a loving decision should be made with input of the whole family group rather than the adults simply announcing what will happen without consulting the children. Teenagers, especially, should be involved and given the chance to say goodbye. Should your teenagers strenuously object, delay the decision for a few days to give them time to come to terms with the loss.

Helping Pets Deal With Loss

Although many American Pit Bull Terriers don't do well in multi-dog households, those who do may leave behind pet friends who mourn their loss. Dogs also seem to experience grief and can act depressed for days or weeks following the death of a canine friend.

It sometimes helps them to see the body after the animal has passed away. That way, the surviving pet understands that he's gone and won't spend time searching and crying for their lost buddy. But be prepared for any reaction from the surviving pets. Some animals become extremely upset and howl and cry, while others don't even sniff the body. After life has fled, the surviving pet may recognize that it's not the same dog anymore.

Simply give your remaining pets more of your time. Be sympathetic, but try not to reward depressed behavior, or they'll continue to mope. While they won't understand the words, the emotion will come through clearly when you say to them, "I'm sad, but it's not your fault, and I miss him too. And I love you and we'll get through this together."

Multi-Dog Tip

Not all dogs seem affected by the death of a canine friend. When they do, though, the surviving pet may seem restless, search for the missing dog, and cry or lose his appetite. Allowing surviving pets to actually see the body of the deceased can sometimes help ease the survivor's feelings.

You'll know if and when it's time to bring another companion into your home and heart.

50 FUN FACTS EVERY APBT OWNER SHOULD KNOW

1. Dogs arose from wolves and have been domesticated for at least 31,000 years.

2. The American Pit Bull Terrier, American Staffordshire Terrier, and Staffordshire Bull Terrier at one time were the same breed.

3. The APBT originated as a utility dog with a multitude of jobs.

4. Dog aggression is common in the breed.

5. Unlike other terriers that "go to ground" after prey, the APBT is a "catch dog" who grips and holds.

6. The first dog registered by the United Kennel Club (UKC) in 1884 was a Pit Bull.

7. Bad breath can be a sign of disease as well as dental problems.

8. The APBT breed standard accepts natural (uncropped) ears.

9. Chocolate contains theobromine, which can speed up the heart; a puppy can get sick from licking the frosting off of a cake.

10. No other breed can out-perform an APBT at weight-pull competitions.

11. A normal adult dog's total body water is about 60 percent of his body weight, and he'll suffer dehydration if he loses as little as five percent.

12. Puppies require twice as many calories as adult dogs.

13. APBTs are shown as puppies until 12 months old.

14. Aggression toward humans is rare in the APBT.

15. A parting stick humanely releases the bite of an APBT when he won't let go.

16. Breed-specific legislation may forbid you from owning "pit bull type" dogs in some places.

17. The APBT standard has no height or weight restrictions.

18. The APBT comes in any coat color except merle.

19. Puppies younger than four weeks of age have trouble regulating body temperature and shouldn't be bathed until older.

20. Puppies require a series of "core" vaccinations that include distemper, parvovirus, CAV-2, and rabies.

21. The APBT may be prone to hip and elbow dysplasia, skin disorders, and congenital heart or eye defects.

22. Harsh punishment-based training makes aggression worse.

23. The APBT's eyes can be any color as long as they match and are not blue.

24. A spring pole offers the APBT a legal, fun way to bite and play tug.

25. Puppies can safely be neutered as early as eight weeks old.

26. More than 250 kinds of fleas are found in the United States, but the most common type that afflicts dogs is *Ctenocephalides felis*—the cat flea.

27. Eighty percent of pets develop periodontal disease by age three.

28. Some insurance companies won't cover owners of APBTs.

29. Dogs live up to two years longer if kept lean throughout their lives.

30. Immunity develops in puppies several weeks after birth. Prior to that, the mother dog's first milk (colostrum) provides a transient protection.

31. Dogs are not carnivores (which means "animal eater"); they are omnivores like humans.

32. Jumping up is the dog's way of saying "howdy!"

33. Marking behavior includes leg lifting, which places urine at nose height.

34. Neutering reduces roaming and aggressive behavior as well as certain kinds of cancer.

35. Older dogs and those adopted from shelters can be prone to separation anxiety.

36. Dogs with floppy ears are more prone to ear infection than erect-eared dogs, due to poorer air circulation.

37. Prime puppy socialization lasts from six to eight weeks, and continues through 12 weeks.

38. Panting is the dog's way of air-conditioning his body.

39. Rolling on the back to expose the throat or tummy is the ultimate submissive posture.

40. Sudden cataracts can be a sign of diabetes.

41. Longer periods of light, not temperature increase, prompts seasonal shedding.

42. A two-month-old pup needs to eliminate every two hours.

43. Ticks, a common skin parasite of dogs, transmit diseases, including Lyme disease.

44. Up to 50 percent of dogs older than five years are obese.

45. Vomiting can be caused by more than 30 different conditions.

46. Whiskers are found in four places on each side of the head and in two places on the lower jaw and act like antennae to protect the eyes and keep the chin from scraping the ground.

47. Tapeworms look like grains of rice and are transmitted by fleas.

48. X-rays, technically called radiographs, are a diagnostic tool used to see inside the dog's body.

49. Avoid using retractable leashes, because they teach dogs to pull.

50. Warming food improves a reluctant dog's appetite.

RESOURCES

ASSOCIATIONS AND ORGANIZATIONS

Breed Clubs

All American Dog Registry (AADR)
P.O. Box 415
Winnabow, NC 28479
Telephone: (910) 253-4095
www.aadrdogs.com

American Dog Breeders Association (ADBA)
PO Box 1771
Salt Lake City, UT 84110
Telephone: (801) 936-7513
www.adbadog.com

American Kennel Club (AKC)
5580 Centerview Drive
Raleigh, NC 27606
Telephone: (919) 233-9767
Fax: (919) 233-3627
E-Mail: info@akc.org
www.akc.org

American Rare Breed Association (ARBA)
921 Frank Tippett Road
Cheltenham, MD 20623
ww.arba.com

Canadian Kennel Club (CKC)
89 Skyway Avenue, Suite 100
Etobicoke, Ontario M9W 6R4
Telephone: (416) 675-5511
Fax: (416) 675-6506
E-Mail: information@ckc.ca
www.ckc.ca

International All Breed Canine Association (IABCA)
4742 Liberty Rd S #159
Salem, Oregon 97302
Telephone: (503) 316-9860
www.iabca.com

National American Pit Bull Terrier Association
www.napbta.com

United Kennel Club (UKC)
100 E. Kilgore Road
Kalamazoo, MI 49002-5584
Telephone: (269) 343-9020
Fax: (269) 343-7037
E-Mail: pbickell@ukcdogs.com
www.ukcdogs.com

Pet Sitters

National Association of Professional Pet Sitters
15000 Commerce Parkway, Suite C
Mt. Laurel, New Jersey 08054
Telephone: (856) 439-0324
Fax: (856) 439-0525
E-Mail: napps@ahint.com
www.petsitters.org

**Pet Sitters International
201 East King Street**
King, NC 27021-9161
Telephone: (336) 983-9222
Fax: (336) 983-5266
E-Mail: info@petsit.com
www.petsit.com

Rescue Organizations and Animal Welfare Groups

American Humane Association (AHA)
63 Inverness Drive East
Englewood, CO 80112
Telephone: (303) 792-9900
Fax: 792-5333
www.americanhumane.org

American Society for the Prevention of Cruelty to Animals (ASPCA)
424 E. 92nd Street
New York, NY 10128-6804
Telephone: (212) 876-7700
www.aspca.org

The Humane Society of the United States (HSUS)
2100 L Street, NW
Washington DC 20037
Telephone: (202) 452-1100
www.hsus.org

Royal Society for the Prevention of Cruelty to Animals (RSPCA)
RSPCA Enquiries Service
Wilberforce Way, Southwater,
Horsham, West Sussex
RH13 RS
United Kingdom
Telephone: 0870 3335 999
Fax: 0870 7530 284
www.rspca.org.uk

Sports

International Agility Link (IAL)
Global Administrator: Steve Drinkwater
E-Mail: yunde@powerup.au
www.agilityclick.com/~ial

International Weight Pull Association
www.iwpa.com

The United National Weight Pull Association (UNWPA)
www.unitednationalweight
pullassociation.com

The World Canine Freestyle Organization, Inc.
P.O. Box 350122
Brooklyn, NY 11235
Telephone: (718) 332-8336
Fax: (718) 646-2686
E-Mail: WCFODOGS@aol.com
www.worldcaninefreestyle.org

Therapy

Delta Society
875 124th Ave, NE, Suite 101
Bellevue, WA 98005
Telephone: (425) 679-5500
Fax: (425) 679-5539
E-Mail: info@DeltaSociety.org
www.deltasociety.org

Therapy Dogs Inc.
P.O. Box 20227
Cheyenne WY 82003
Telephone: (877) 843-7364
Fax: (307) 638-2079
E-Mail: therapydogsinc@
qwestoffice.net
www.therapydogs.com

**Therapy Dogs International
(TDI)**
88 Bartley Road
Flanders, NJ 07836
Telephone: (973) 252-9800
Fax: (973) 252-7171
E-Mail: tdi@gti.net
www.tdi-dog.org

Training

**Association of Pet Dog Trainers
(APDT)**
150 Executive Center Drive
Box 35
Greenville, SC 29615
Telephone: (800) PET-DOGS
Fax: (864) 331-0767
E-Mail: information@apdt.com
www.apdt.com

**International Association of
Animal Behavior Consultants
(IAABC)**
565 Callery Road
Cranberry Township, PA 16066
E-Mail: info@iaabc.org
www.iaabc.org

**National Association of Dog
Obedience Instructors (NADOI)**
PMB 369
729 Grapevine Hwy.
Hurst, TX 76054-2085
www.nadoi.org

Veterinary and Health Resources

**Academy of Veterinary
Homeopathy (AVH)**
P.O. Box 9280
Wilmington, DE 19809
Telephone: (866) 652-1590
Fax: (866) 652-1590
www.theavh.org

**American Academy of
Veterinary Acupuncture (AAVA)**
P.O. Box 1058
Glastonbury, CT 06033
Telephone: (860) 632-9911
Fax: (860) 659-8772
www.aava.org

**American Animal Hospital
Association (AAHA)**
12575 W. Bayaud Ave.
Lakewood, CO 80228
Telephone: (303) 986-2800
Fax: (303) 986-1700
E-Mail: info@aahanet.org
www.aahanet.org/index.cfm

**American College of Veterinary
Internal Medicine (ACVIM)**
1997 Wadsworth Blvd., Suite A
Lakewood, CO 80214-5293
Telephone: (800) 245-9081
Fax: (303) 231-0880
Email: ACVIM@ACVIM.org
www.acvim.org

**American College of Veterinary
Ophthalmologists (ACVO)**
P.O. Box 1311
Meridian, ID 83860
Telephone: (208) 466-7624
Fax: (208) 466-7693
E-Mail: office09@acvo.com
www.acvo.com

**American Holistic Veterinary
Medical Association (AHVMA)**
2218 Old Emmorton Road
Bel Air, MD 21015
Telephone: (410) 569-0795
Fax: (410) 569-2346
E-Mail: office@ahvma.org
www.ahvma.org

**American Veterinary Medical
Association (AVMA)**
1931 North Meacham Road,
Suite 100
Schaumburg, IL 60173-4360
Telephone: (847) 925-8070
Fax: (847) 925-1329
E-Mail: avmainfo@avma.org
www.avma.org

**ASPCA Animal Poison Control
Center**
Telephone: (888) 426-4435
www.aspca.org

**British Veterinary Association
(BVA)**
7 Mansfield Street
London
W1G 9NQ
Telephone: 0207 636 6541
Fax: 0207 908 6349
E-Mail: bvahq@bva.co.uk
www.bva.co.uk

**Canine Eye Registration
Foundation (CERF)**
VMDB/CERF
1717 Philo Rd
P O Box 3007
Urbana, IL 61803-3007
Telephone: (217) 693-4800
Fax: (217) 693-4801
E-Mail: CERF@vmbd.org
www.vmdb.org

**Orthopedic Foundation for
Animals (OFA)**
2300 NE Nifong Blvd
Columbus, Missouri 65201-3856
Telephone: (573) 442-0418
Fax: (573) 875-5073
Email: ofa@offa.org
www.offa.org

**US Food and Drug
Administration Center for
Veterinary Medicine (CVM)**
7519 Standish Place
HFV-12
Rockville, MD 20855-0001
Telephone: (240) 276-9300 or
(888) INFO-FDA
http://www.fda.gov/cvm

WEBSITES
Nylabone
www.nylabone.com

TFH Publications, Inc.
www.tfh.com

INDEX

parasites in, 123, 124, **124**, 125, 126
preparing home for, 36–37
retained testicles in, 66
schedule for, 41–42
sociability of, **24**, 24–25, 26, 92, 167
spaying or neutering, 63–66
supplies for, 37–41
teething in, 162, 163
trainability of, 29, 145
training, 29, 33, 69–87
vaccinations for, 50–63
puppy kindergarten, 76
puppy mills, 36
puppy-proofing, 36–37
purebred puppy, 31–32, 35–36
puzzles, 200, 205

Q

quick of nail, 104–105
"quiet" command, 160–161

R

rabies, 51, 55–57, 122
rabies tag, 39
raisins, 141
rally, 173
ratting, 11
raw diet, 116
recall, 84, 150
registration documents, 35
release command, 149
rescue breathing, 138
rescue organizations, 93, 95–97, 214
resources, 214–216
retired couples and senior dogs, 188
retractable leashes, 40, 165
rewards, training, 41, 79, 148
ringworm, 126, 128–129
Roman Empire, 10, 11
room etiquette, 181
roundworms, 124

S

safety, 178, 191
sand box, 164
sarcoptic mange (canine scabies), 126, 128
schedules, 41–42
feeding, 46, **47**, 118, 197
vaccination, 51, 58
seat belts, 178
sebum, 99
semi-moist food, 114
senility, 200
senior dogs, 187, 193
aging signs in, 193–195, **194**
benefits of, 187–188, **188**
cancer in, 134–135

disadvantages of, 188–191
dog tolerance in, 205
end-of-life issues for, 207–210, **211**
feeding, 195–197
grooming, 197–198
health care for, 198
illnesses in, 189–190, 193, 198–205
pet sitters for, 183
separation anxiety in, 189, 191, 199
training, 191, 200, **200**, 202, 205, 210
senses, aging of, 191, **191**, 194–195
separation anxiety, 189, 191, 199
"shake" command, 123
shampoo, 38, 48, 101–102
benzoyl peroxide, 128, 130
dry, 197
flea, 126
shedding, 99–100
shelters
adopting from, 93–95, 189
ethical practices of, 96–97
evacuation to, 142
temperament testing by, 95
shock, 138
show dogs, retired, 92, **93**, 96–97. See also conformation (showing)
sight, loss of, 191, **191**, 194
singles and senior dogs, 188
"sit" command, **82**, 84–86, 117, 150
"sit-stay" command, 149–151
skin disorders, 28
contagious, 126, 127–129
puppy-specific, 64
skunk odor, 105
sleeping arrangements, 38, 42, 43
slimming down, 119
slip (choke) chains, 165–166
smelling sense, aging of, 194, 195
"snub-nosed dogs," 180, **180**
sociability
with children, **24**, 24–25
with other dogs and pets, 25–28
with strangers, 25, 75
"social dog," 25–26
socialization, 73–76, **74**, **75**, 167
soft foods, 196–197
spaying or neutering, 63–66
of adult, 96–97
aggression and, 158
benefits of, 63–64

obesity and, 119
procedures for, 64–66
special diets, 116–117
splint, fracture, 140–141
sports and activities, 169–183. See also exercise
agility, 172–173
bicycling, 169
camping, 169–170
canine freestyle, 173
Canine Good Citizen test, 25, 170–172, 177
Canine Partners program for, 173
conformation, 173–174, **174**
obedience, 175, **175**, 177
pet-quality dogs in, 32
resources for, 214
senior, 200, 205
therapy work, 176–177
trainability for, 29
travel, 177–182, **178**, **180**, **181**
walking/jogging, 170, **171**
weight pull, 14, 175–176, **176**, 177
spring poles, 41
Staffordshire Terrier and Staffordshire Bull Terrier, 14
"stand" command, 153, **153**
status-related aggression, 158
"stay" command, 148–149, **149**
"down" and, **151**, 151–153
mealtime training of, 117
"sit" and, 149–151
stool samples, 50, 122
strangers, sociability with, 25, 75
"Stubby," 15
stuffed toys, 40
suitability of APBT, 22–29
supplements, vitamin and mineral, 116, 117
supplies, 37–41
evacuation kit, 143
grooming, 38, 48

T

table scraps, 42, 117–118
tags, ID, 39, 143
tail, 21
tapeworm, 124–125, 126
taste sense, aging of, 194, 195
tattoos, 38–39
tear stains, 103
teeth. See also dental care
brushing, 106
problems with, 105, 195
teething, 162, 163
Tellington-Jones, Linda, 137
temperament, 34, 96

temperament testing, 25, 34–35, 95
temperature, rectal, 50, 122, 141
terriers, 12–13, 14
territorial aggression, 157, 158
testicles
removal of, 63, 64–65
retained, 66
testimonials, 33
therapeutic diets, 116–117, 196
for cognitive disorder, 200
dental, 105–106
for heart failure, 201
weight-loss, 119, 189, 199
Therapy Dogs International (TDI), 177
therapy work, 176–177, 215
ticks, 61, 122, 129
tone collars, 161
toothbrush and toothpaste, 48, 106
total hip replacement, 132
tourniquet, 140
towel, scenting, 43
toys, 40–41, **43**
chew, 162, 163
luring with, **80**, 81
rewarding with, 41, 148
tracheobronchitis, canine infectious, 51, 59–60, 122
trainability, 29, 145
trainers, 72–73, 76, 156
training, 69
adult, 145–153
for aggression, 167
attention span for, 80, 145
basic, 80–82
basic obedience, **82**, 82–87, **83**, **85**, **87**
by breeder, 33
Canine Good Citizen program for, 177
for car travel, 179
cat-proofing, 27–28
"chaining" behaviors in, 152
by children, 25
clicker, 81–82, 83, 85–87, 153
crate, **76**, 77
finding trainer for, 72–73
for grooming, 47–48, **49**, 50, 101, 104
housetraining, 77–80, **78**, 79
importance of, 70
intermediate obedience, 145–153, **146**, **149**,

VETERINARY ADVISOR

Wayne Hunthausen, D.V.M., consulting veterinary editor and pet behavior consultant, is the director of Animal Behavior Consultations in the Kansas City area and currently serves on the Practitioner Board for *Veterinary Medicine* and the Behavior Advisory Board for *Veterinary Forum*.

BREEDER ADVISOR

Kimberly Allison and her husband Ron, of Ro-Ki Reds APBT's, have been breeding, training, and showing the APBT for over 15 years. Kimberly is the current Vice President of the National APBT Association, as well as the Vice President of the Cascade APBT Club located in Washington State. She is an All Breed Judge in Conformation and both she and Ron are licensed Judges for Weight Pulling events held by the United Kennel Club. They have bred and co-own a record setting Weight Pulling dog, a National Champion, and many nationally ranked weight pulling year end winners. Visit them at www.rokireds.com

PHOTO CREDITS

Shutterstock:
rt_man, 3, 87; Chad Mahlum, 6; Chris Pole, 8; Naturablichter, 9; Lakatos Sandor, 10; Yuri Arcurs, 11; Henk entlage, 12; Martin Smith, 13; iofoto, 14; Casey K. Bishop 16 (top), 79, 88 (top), 194; Lars Chri stensen, 23; Tuller, 38; Jonathan Brizedine, 55; Katrina Brown, 63; mariait, 63 (bottom left); Shutterstock, 63 (bottom ght); Chad Mahlum, 90; magmarcz, 94; colour, 100; Denise Campione, 104; South 12th Photography, 112; Margarito Luevanos, 118; nilovsergei, 136; Quicksnap Photo 137; Alex Galea, 139; Vikacita, 154; Jan de Wild, 83; Brad Remy, 203, 206; iofoto, 211

over and all other photos courtesy of Isabelle Francais and TFH archives

ACKNOWLEDGMENTS

Many individuals and organizations made this book a reality by sharing their expertise, help, and encouragement. My husband Mahmoud who put up with all-nighters, my parents who properly "socialized" me during my formative years, colleagues from IAABC (and especially the Dallas gang!), and pet writers of all persuasion endlessly inspired me. My editors Heather Russell-Revesz and Stephanie Fornino and publisher Christopher T. Reggio, thank you for the surprise assignment of a lifetime. And of course, my "furry muse" who reminds me daily what's really important.

Special thanks to the generous folks at National American Pit Bull Terrier Association especially Michael Snyder, Kimberly Allison, and Carrianna M. Glenn who lent their time, shared their love of APBTs, and offered an inside look into this wonderful breed. Melissa of www.Muttsandstuff.com, and Michele Crouse of www.super-k9.com also provided important insights into rescue and rehab.

DEDICATION

This book is for all the "bully lovers" out there--those who breed responsibly, adopt intelligently, train rigorously, and rescue/rehome ethically. But above all it's for the dogs. May we be the heroes our dogs believe us to be.

ABOUT THE AUTHOR

Amy D. Shojai, CABC, a nationally known authority on pet care and behavior, is a certified animal behavior consultant, a spokesperson for the pet products industry, and the author of 23 nonfiction pet books and more than 1,000 articles. She hosts a twice-monthly TV "Pet Talk" segment at KXII-CBS, and the weekly "Pet Peeves" at PetLifeRadio.com. She currently appears as an expert on Animal Planet's DOGS 101 and CATS 101 and has been featured in many leading newspapers and magazines. Amy is a member of the International Association of Animal Behavior Consultants (IAABC), founder of the Cat Writers' Association (CWA), a member of the Dog Writers Association of America (DWAA), and past president of the Oklahoma Writers Federation, Inc. She frequently speaks at conferences on pet and writing issues. She and her husband live with Seren(dipity) the Siamese wannabe and Magic the German Shepherd in north Texas. Learn more at www.shojai.com